Anti-Muslim Prejudice

This collection makes a unique contribution to the study of anti-Muslim prejudice by placing the issue in both its past and present context. The essays cover historical and contemporary subjects from the eleventh century to the present day. They examine the forms that anti-Muslim prejudice takes, the historical influences on these forms, and how they relate to other forms of prejudice such as racism, antisemitism or sexism, and indeed how anti-Muslim prejudice becomes institutionalized.

This volume looks at anti-Muslim prejudice from a wide range of disciplinary perspectives, including politics, sociology, philosophy, history, international relations, law, cultural studies and comparative literature. The essays contribute to our understanding of the different levels at which anti-Muslim prejudice emerges and operates – the local, the national and the transnational – by also including case studies from a range of contexts including Britain, Europe and the US.

This book contributes to a deeper understanding of contemporary political problems and controversial topics, such as issues that focus on Muslim women: the 'headscarf' debates, honour killings and forced marriages. There is also analysis of media bias in the representation of Muslims and Islam, and other urgent social and political issues such as the social exclusion of European Muslims and the political mobilisation against Islam by far-right parties.

Maleiha Malik is Reader in Law at the School of Law, King's College, University of London.

Anti-Muslim Prejudice

Past and Present

Edited by Maleiha Malik

LONDON AND NEW YORK

First published 2010 by Routledge
2 Park Square, Milton Park, Abingdon, Oxon, OX14 4RN

Simultaneously published in the USA and Canada
by Routledge
270 Madison Avenue, New York, NY 10016

Routledge is an imprint of the Taylor & Francis Group, an informa business

© 2010 Taylor & Francis

Typeset in Palatino by Value Chain, India

British Library Cataloguing in Publication Data
A catalogue record for this book is available from the British Library

ISBN10: 0-415-54987-6
ISBN13: 978-0-415-54987-5

Contents

Notes on Contributors

Britons and Muslims in the early modern period: from prejudice to (a theory of) toleration

Nabil Matar is Professor of English at the University of Minnesota.

Anti-Turkish obsession and the exodus of Balkan Muslims

Slobodan Drakulic is Assistant Professor of Sociology at Ryerson University, Toronto. His most recent publication is 'Premodern Croatian Nationalism?', published in *Nationalism and Ethnic Politics* (vol. 14, no. 4, 2008). The research for this paper was supported by a Ryerson grant.

Can the walls hear?

Gil Anidjar teaches in the Department of Middle East and Asian Languages and Cultures and in the Department of Religion at Columbia University. His most recent book is *Semites: Race, Religion, Literature* (Stanford University Press 2008).

The crusade over the bodies of women

Sonya Fernandez is a lecturer in law at Canterbury Christ Church University. Her recent publications include entries on the Other, multiculturalism, multicultural integration, polygamy, forced marriages and honour killings in the *Oxford Companion to Law*. She is currently preparing an article on female genital cutting, and an exploration of constructions of consent in rape and forced marriages.

Muslim headscarves in France and army uniforms in Israel: a comparative study of citizenship as mask

Leora Bilsky is Assistant Professor in the Faculty of Law at Tel Aviv University. She is the editor of the journal *Teoria ve-Bikoret* (Theory and Criticism), and the author of *Transformative Justice: Israeli Identity on Trial* (University of Michigan Press 2004). She has written extensively on law, politics and feminist theory, and is currently preparing a book on 'Citizens, Impostors and Collaborators'.

Revisiting Lepanto: the political mobilization against Islam in contemporary Western Europe

Hans-Georg Betz has written several books and numerous articles on rightwing populism in Western Europe. He currently lives in Switzerland.

Susi Meret is preparing a doctoral candidate at the Department of History, International and Social Studies at the University of Aalborg in Denmark. She is preparing a dissertation entitled 'The Danish People's Party, the Italian

Northern League and the Austrian Freedom Party in a Comparative Perspective: Party Ideology and Electoral Support'.

Refutations of racism in the 'Muslim question'

Nasar Meer is a lecturer in the School of Social and Political Sciences at the University of Southampton. His forthcoming publications include *Identity, Citizenship and the New Politics of Multiculturalism* (Palgrave Macmillan).

Tariq Modood is the founding director of the Bristol University Centre for the Study of *Ethnicity* and Citizenship, and a founding co-editor of the journal Ethnicities. His recent publications include *Secularism, Religion and Multicultural Citizenship*, co-edited with Geoffrey Brahm Levey, foreword by Charles Taylor (Cambridge University Press 2009) and *Multiculturalism: A Civic Idea* (Polity 2007).

'Get shot of the lot of them': election reporting of Muslims in British newspapers

John E. Richardson is Senior Lecturer in the Department of Social Sciences at Loughborough University. He is co-editor of the online journal *Studies in Language and Capitalism*, on the editorial board of the journals *Discourse and Society, Social Semiotics* and the *Journal of Language and Politics*, and Special Issues editor for *Critical Discourse Studies*. His research interests include structured social inequalities, British fascism, racism in journalism, and (critical) discourse analysis and argumentation. His recent publications include *Analysing Newspapers: An Approach from Critical Discourse Analysis* (Palgrave 2007), the co-authored book *Key Concepts in Journalism* (Sage 2005), special issues of the journals *Journalism Studies, Social Semiotics* and *Critical Discourse Studies*, and articles analysing the discourses of newspapers, readers' letters and political party leaflets.

Where do Muslims stand on ethno-racial hierarchies in Britain and France? Evidence from public opinion surveys, 1988–2008

Erik Bleich is Associate Professor of political science at Middlebury College, Vermont. He has published articles on issues of racism, immigrant integration and policymaking in journals such as *World Politics, Comparative Political Studies* and *Theory and Society*. His book *Race Politics in Britain and France: Ideas and Policymaking since the 1960s* was published by Cambridge University Press in 2003. He is also the editor of the March 2009 special issue of the *Journal of Ethnic and Migration Studies*, 'Muslims and the State in the Post-9/11 West', which is forthcoming as an edited volume by Routledge.

Confronting Islamophobia in the United States: framing civil rights activism among Middle Eastern Americans

Erik Love is a Ph.D. candidate in sociology at the University of California, Santa Barbara.

Anti-Muslim prejudice in the West, past and present: an introduction

Academic research, since 9/11, has had to quickly 'catch up' with contemporary and popular interest in Muslims and Islam. Moreover, increased migration of Muslims into western liberal democracies in Europe and North America has meant that the analysis has had to move beyond the assumption of a sharp dichotomy between Muslims and Islam and 'the West'. There is an increased need to study Muslims and Islam 'in the West', as well as the response of non-Muslims to this changing demographic pattern.

It is impossible to analyse Muslims in the West today without a better understanding of how they were treated in the past. Quentin Skinner has noted that history can help us to understand how 'new' religious forms such as Islam can be accommodated into British society. He concludes that a study of history can 'show us how little we ever had to fear from the simultaneous flourishing in our society of different and powerful forms of the religious life. It is worth remembering, not denying, how readily these can be accommodated.'[1] The topic of anti-Muslim prejudice in the West, therefore, has to be placed in its historical context by considering the extent to which the mediaeval period is a forerunner to contemporary forms of prejudice, as well as questions about whether the term 'British' can accommodate religious minorities such as Muslims. Nabil Matar's essay on Britons and Muslim in the early modern period—which examines representations of Muslims and Islam in literature, diplomacy, theatre, painting and material culture—covers exactly this ground. It allows us to understand the early roots of prejudice against Muslims as well as pointing to further lines of enquiry about whether, and how, Muslims can ever truly be 'British'.

A historical perspective is also essential to understand the attempt to eradicate Balkan Muslims during the 1990s, including the Srebrenica massacre in 1995. Slobodan Drakulic's essay traces the socio-historical roots of Christian Slav prejudices against their Muslim ethno-linguistic kin in the Balkans. Drakulic concludes that the association of Balkan Muslims with Ottoman theocracy meant that they were perceived as a 'fifth column'. This is a recurring trope in contemporary far-right anti-Muslim discourse that presents British, Danish, Swiss or Italian Muslims as a 'fifth column' incapable of loyalty to liberal democratic states, elaborated here in the essays by John E. Richardson, and Hans-Georg Betz and Susi Meret. Drakulic also notes: 'The ethno-religious coalescence within, as well as the antagonism

---

1 Quentin Skinner, 'The place of history in public life', History and Policy Paper 35, November 2005, available on the History and Policy website at www.historyandpolicy.org/archive/policy-paper-35.html (viewed 2 July 2009).

between, religious communities survived the processes of secularization associated with modernity and provided fertile ground for the ethno-religious conflicts of the nineteenth and twentieth centuries.' His insight that secularization and modernity cannot provide a remedy against anti-Muslim prejudice casts doubt on contemporary political strategies that a solution to this problem lies in a stronger dose of traditional secularism.

Gil Andijar's essay 'Can the Walls Hear' provides us with an 'anthropology' of the Christian West that exposes its tendencies, historical and structural, to create prejudice. 'Christendom', he argues, is a specific construction that generates both external and internal divisions: walls, conceptual and political, between Self and Other, and between Good Other and Bad Other. 'It is in relation to such divided projection that this peculiar collective self, western Christendom, endures.' He goes on, in a 'techno-political' account, to elaborate how such divisions are part of a well-established strategy to facilitate colonial rule, and pave the way for

> the civilizing mission of Christian Europe upon 'colored people'. Law and education, Christian missionaries and the production of local elites, all the benevolent (that is, less bloody) techniques summarized under the old principle of 'divide and rule', that is to say exploiting, ruling and often, if not always, eradicating or exterminating communities and ways of life.

For Anidjar, this tendency in 'the West' to eliminate 'different' ways of life has not ended with colonialism or the Holocaust. Yet, like Quentin Skinner, he is not fatalistic about the exclusion of the Other from the West's history, power and politics.

> But it has followed what was by no means an inevitable trajectory (nor is it now inevitable), nor a tradition at all until it made itself so (by marginalizing or excluding, destroying, if not without remainder, that which was said to be Other in it, that which *remains* as Other in it) . . .

This insight, like Anidjar's title—'Can the Walls Hear?'—reverses the focus of the analysis. Rather than problematizing Muslims or Islam, this approach redirects critical attention towards 'Christendom' and its most cherished beliefs.

The essays by Sonya Fernandez and Leora Bilsky confirm that there are some 'who can hear' despite the walls that our societies erect against the Other. They both turn their attention on their own societies, thereby interrogating key 'western' concepts such as gender equality, liberalism and secularism. Fernandez, through a close analysis of the discourse on honour killings and forced marriages, problematizes the concept of gender equality by uncovering the way in which anti-Muslim prejudice is often subsumed and hidden within concern for the well-being of Muslim women. She argues that these stereotypes are not only damaging for Muslims, but they also prevent a constructive critique of practices that are harmful to all women in western societies. In this way, criticism of Muslim patriarchy may—paradoxically—act as an alibi that leaves non-Muslim patriarchy unchallenged. This misuse of gender equality as a pretext for anti-Muslim prejudice is a useful illustration of the 'hypocrisy' that Leora Bilsky identifies in her case study of the ban against Muslim headscarves in France and the prohibition of army uniforms by a Palestinian professor in Israel. Bilsky's comparison of these two seemingly different examples uncovers a similarity. In both cases, liberal principles of neutrality and equality become distorted. This entails a strategy of hypocrisy that turns the victims of anti-Muslim prejudice into perpetrators: French Muslim schoolgirls are transformed into a threat to republican values; the professor who bans Israeli army uniforms in his classroom becomes a nationalist who is 'passing himself off' as a humanist.

Hans-Georg Betz and Susie Meret's essay also identifies appeals to liberalism as part of the problem rather than the solution. In their study of radical right-wing political parties in Europe, Betz and Meret uncover the centrality of a 'defence of liberal culture' in forms of contemporary European nativism and far-right ideologies. They note that the representation of Islam as a threat to the 'spiritual foundations of the West' (values such as freedom, democracy, the rights of women) has been a prominent feature of virtually all anti-Muslim far-right parties. They conclude that appeals to the defence of liberal values is a key part of the far right's strategy towards Muslims:

> At the same time, these parties have started to put themselves forward as defenders of liberal values and principles with respect to gender equality and women's rights among ethnic minorities. As such, they advocate freedom of expression, open-mindedness, tolerance, solidarity and diligence as central values to be respected, accepted and adopted by ethnic minorities wishing to become part of European societies. On behalf of these values, the nativist right seeks to establish barriers preventing ethnic—particularly Muslim—minorities from gaining full access to some civic and social rights.

Betz and Meret also note that

> the nativist right has advanced numerous ideas, demands and policy proposals that would impede and ultimately reverse the integration of Muslims in Western European society. The intermediate goal of these initiatives has been to render Muslims—and Islam itself—invisible.

In the British context, these two aspects—rendering Muslim identity invisible and reversing Muslim integration—have been important because of the political and legal struggle over whether Muslims are an 'ethnic' or 'racial' group. Nasar Meer and Tariq Modood's essay considers the factors that have encouraged the 'refutation of racism in the "Muslim question"'. In the British context, as Meer and Modood note, liberal political elites have preferred a 'narrow view of racism', and they have not supported Muslim demands for recognition as a 'racial group' on the same terms as Jews and Sikhs. This has denied Muslims full coverage under race relations legislation that would encourage their integration by protecting them against exclusion and discrimination. Consequently, in the British context, it is not only the far right, but also liberals, who have deployed legal and political strategies that are more likely to render Muslims invisible, as well as impeding their integration into mainstream British society. Meer and Modood's analysis facilitates comparisons of anti-Muslim prejudice across historical contexts and between different countries. They identify anti-Muslim tropes that are also discussed in other essays: like Drakulic, they note the use of the idea that Muslims are a 'disloyal fifth column'; echoing Betz and Meret, they note that British liberals refer to freedom of expression (or the ridiculing of Muslims) as a sign of the health of intellectual debate in liberal democracies. Meer and Modood conclude that one salient, discursive trope takes Muslim minorities to task for the adoption of a 'victim mentality': 'Indeed, it would be no exaggeration to suggest that, instead of highlighting and alleviating anti-Muslim discrimination, the complaint of anti-Muslim racism and Islamophobia has, conversely and frequently, invited criticism of Muslims themselves.' Significantly, this dovetails with Bilsky's insight into the hypocrisy that turns the victims of anti-Muslim prejudice into perpetrators.

John E. Richardson's analysis of election reporting in British newspapers tells a similar story. One journalist wrote: 'Young Muslims ... are encouraged to put loyalty to their faith above personal responsibility to the country of their birth.' News reporting singled out Muslims as a group likely to vote according to their religious or ethnic affiliations rather than political or ethical principles. Richardson concludes:

> Such journalistic discourse should be viewed pragmatically, as serving the important function of removing British Muslims from empowered positions in and affecting the public sphere by demanding either their cultural and political assimilation or expulsion. It should be viewed as an example of a 'discourse of spatial management', founded on the 'white fantasy' of journalists and readers, according to which they have the right and ability to regulate the ethnic and religious parameters of British society.

The last two articles are case studies of Britain, France and the United States. Erik Bleich's essay assesses levels of anti-Muslim prejudice in Britain and France through a close study of public opinion polls between 1988 and 2008, and brings the analysis of anti-Muslim prejudice into the present. Bleich concludes that 'there is a compelling argument for worrying most about a group if it is sinking fast on a national [ethno-racial] hierarchy. Some measures imply that Muslims are slipping quickly both in Britain and France.' This suggests the need for states and civil societies to mobilize and act to combat anti-Muslim prejudice. The monitoring work of the European Union Agency for Fundamental Rights (FRA), formerly the European Monitoring Centre on Racism and Xenophobia, highlights the way in which non-legal interventions in the public sphere in the form of representations of minorities, as well as targeted social exclusion programmes, can be a useful tool in preventing the formation of prejudice and stereotype before they become entrenched and manifest themselves as harmful conduct.[2]

Erik Love's essay discusses anti-Muslim prejudice in the United States. He identifies the roots of the problem in American popular culture: the presentation of Middle Eastern 'terrorist' caricatures in films such as *True Lies* and *The Siege*. He also traces the factors that led to the transformation of anti-Arab sentiment into anti-Muslim prejudice, such as the events of 9/11, the use of racialized language by political leaders that focuses on Muslims and Islam, and the racialized origins of Straussian and neo-conservative policies that shifted the focus of attack from Arab nationalism to Islamism. Love's essay develops comparisons between the struggle against Islamophobia and other historical and sociological models of civil rights advocacy. This confirms that solutions to anti-Muslim prejudice need to take into account local conditions and possibilities. Yet, at the same time, Love notes that 'the Department of Homeland Security has a civil rights division, as does the FBI and the Department of Justice. Does the work of these offices amount to co-opting resistance, or do they effectively safeguard civil rights?' Despite the importance of local solutions, then, the events of 9/11 and the subsequent 'war on terror' are likely to mean that the international context and global conditions will remain important factors for understanding contemporary anti-Muslim prejudice.

The essays in this collection cover a wide range of humanities and social science disciplines, as well as theory and data. Nevertheless, there are a number of recurring themes that point us in the direction of a coherent research agenda for understanding anti-Muslim prejudice in the West. The study of anti-Muslim prejudice—as well as the lives of Muslims in the West—requires a complex approach across a wide range of academic disciplines: including politics, sociology, philosophy, history, international relations, law, cultural studies and comparative literature. Moreover, as well as theoretical analysis, research needs to consider the different spheres (politics, education and the media) as well as the different levels (the local, the national and the transnational) in which anti-Muslim prejudice emerges and operates.

Of course, social science methods are essential for understanding these contemporary developments. Yet, understanding Muslims also requires paying attention to their relationship to literature, culture and the arts. Developments in science and technology are also relevant. For example,

---

2 *The Impact of 7 July 2005 London Bomb Attacks on Muslim Communities in the EU* (Vienna: European Monitoring Centre on Racism and Xenophobia 2005).

advances in early modern printing (discussed by Nabil Matar) and the contemporary use of interactive media blogs/texts (analysed by John Richardson) have had an important impact on the form and content of anti-Muslim prejudice. These changes may allow prejudice to proliferate more rapidly. On the other hand—as Meer and Modood's example of the *Guardian*'s 'Blogging the Quran' project suggests—technological changes may also be an opportunity to develop imaginative strategies to counter anti-Muslim prejudice.

The main focus of this collection is on the 'negative' problems of anti-Muslim prejudice. However, the topic has to be perceived through a dual lens. Although it is important to look out for negative reactions and effects, it is also important to ensure that the positive contributions of Muslims and Islam in the West, in the past and present, are not ignored.

Maleiha Malik
Reader in Law, King's College London

Britons and Muslims in the early modern period: from prejudice to (a theory of) toleration

NABIL MATAR

ABSTRACT   Matar examines the representation of Muslims in English writings in the early modern period, roughly from the sixteenth to the eighteenth centuries. There were two views of Muslims: the first was generated by literary and theological writers whose depictions were predominantly negative and stereotypical. The second was generated by diplomats and traders who had interacted with Muslims, both in the Mediterranean and during ambassadorial visits in London. These latter writers furnished a less hostile image than the playwrights and preachers, and influenced John Locke who became the first European philosopher to argue for the toleration and the endenization of Muslims, *qua* Muslims, in Britain.

The civilization of Islam was the first non-Christian civilization that early modern Britons encountered as they ventured into their age of navigation and discovery. It was also the first civilization that inspired in them mixed emotions: fear, powerlessness and 'imperial envy'.[1] From 1511 on, British ships sailed the Mediterranean, from Beirut to Istanbul to Tangier, while travellers and traders crossed into Persia towards Hormuz and the Mughal empire, learning about the natural resources and manufactured products in the Islamic world. As they bought carpets and silks, raisins and spices, 'Barbary' horses and saltpeter, scimitars and coffee, Britons marvelled at the rich lands and the powerful military and religious cultures of the 'Mahometans'.

In this context of exploration and trade, prejudice against Turks, Moors, pagans and Saracens, Hagarians, Ishmaelites—the last two terms denigrated Muslims as descendants of Abraham's slave–concubine in the Judaic tradition[2]—and

---

1 The most comprehensive examination of this theme of imperial envy appears in Gerald MacLean, *The Rise of Oriental Travel: English Visitors to the Ottoman Empire, 1580–1720* (Basingstoke and New York: Palgrave Macmillan 2004).
2 Henry Teonge, a fleet chaplain, stated in 1675: Muhammad's 'Sectaries were the seed of Hagar (the handmaid of Sarah, Abraham's wife) and Ishmael, her son; and should have been called Hagarens or Ishmaelites; but, because they would not be thought to be born of a bond-woman, nor to descend from one that was thought to be a bastard, they called themselves Saracens': Henry Teonge, *The Diary of Henry Teonge*, ed. G. E. Manwaring (London: George Routledge and Sons 1927), 116.

Arabians began. Prejudice (*praejudicium*) is pre-judging, forming an opinion before and/or without possessing reliable data about the subject. Early modern Englishmen possessed little historical or documentary information about the Muslims they met in the various Mediterranean seaports and cities. As a result, they relied on literary tropes from the popular miracle and mystery plays, since their literature had not produced an equivalent to the Spanish, French, Portuguese and Italian national epics—*El Cid*, *La Chanson de Roland*, *Os Lusíadas* and *La Gerusalemme liberata*, respectively—that recalled Christian engagements and conflicts with Muslims. In mediaeval poetry, church plays and romances, English readers and audiences met with allusions that both misrepresented and demeaned Muslims: 'Mahound' was the god who sent Pharaoh after Moses across the Red Sea (York Plays); he was instrumental in the Massacre of the Innocents, since Herod was a 'Mahumetan' and dressed in Saracen clothes (Coventry Mystery Plays); and Muhammad took part in the crucifixion of Jesus, and both Caiaphas and Pilate were his followers (Coventry Mystery Plays).[3] On altar pieces and in paintings and tapestries, from Spain to Italy and Malta, travellers and visitors saw Muslims depicted as the crucifiers of Christ and the enemies of Christians.[4] Such images furnished the English public with its first pictorial representations of Islam.

The early modern period witnessed two parallel approaches to Muslims and Islam in Britain. First was the prejudice that was nurtured by a rich literary and theological imagination. Preachers, dramatists and poets, eager to gain attention for their works, invented images of the Muslims that nearly always had little or no relation to Islamic civilization and religion. What fuelled this imagination was the military danger of Muslims. With his accession to the Ottoman throne in 1520, Sultan Suleiman launched

3 See Dorothee Metlitzki, *The Matter of Araby in Medieval England* (New Haven and London: Yale University Press 1977); Katharine Scarfe Beckett, *Anglo-Saxon Perceptions of the Islamic World* (Cambridge and New York: Cambridge University Press 2003); and Iain Macleod Higgins, 'Shades of the East: Orientalism, religion, and nation in late medieval Scottish literature', *Journal of Medieval and Early Modern Studies*, vol. 38, no. 2, 2008, 197–228.

4 Muslims were shown to be complicit in the crucifixion of Jesus. *The Crucifixion* by the Umbrian painter Luca Signorelli (1445/50–1523), now in the National Gallery in Washington, D.C., shows soldiers surrounding the cross of Jesus with banners flying the Turkish symbol of the crescent; so too does *The Crucifixion* by the workshop of the German Hans Mielich (1516–73), also in the National Gallery, in which the soldier is wearing a Muslim turban. The magnificent *c.* 1535 altarpiece by an unknown Flemish artist now in the Philadelphia Museum of Art shows Turks and other turbanned horsemen at the foot of the cross, carrying spears and sponges. Because the victory of Lepanto took place on St Justina's day in 1571, processions were held, from 1572 on, to celebrate the saint while decrying the Turks whom she had defeated and, every year, the association between worship and anti-Islam was repeated. There were also sculptures and paintings to celebrate the victory of the saint: Paolo Veronese's *The Battle of Lepanto* (*c.* 1572) is perhaps the most important artwork in Justina's honour (now in the Gallerie dell'Accademia, Venice).

campaigns that reached Vienna in 1529 and led to the capture of vast regions of Europe. Numerous Englishmen travelled to the continent to fight against the Ottomans, whether in Crete (1522) or Algiers (1541), as Richard Hakluyt recorded in his *Navigations* (1589).[5] The military momentum declined in the last quarter of the sixteenth century as the Ottomans turned away from the Habsburgs to fight the Safavids but, in the mid-seventeenth century, the Ottoman fleet laid siege to Crete, the longest naval siege of a city in modern history (1645–69). In 1683 the Ottoman armies again attacked Vienna, where they met with a defeat that marked the beginning of their retreat from Western Europe. It was against the backdrop of this continuing destabilization of 'the common corps of Christendom' that Britons first came to learn about Islam and Muslims.[6] And it was a destabilization that the popular media transformed from a war of competing Ottoman–Habsburg empires into a cosmic conflict of Christianity against Islam, of the Christian cross versus the Muslim crescent. From the first decades of the sixteenth century until 1699, it was difficult for British writers—and their readers—to dissociate Islam and Muslims from the expansionist wars of the Ottoman empire.

But, as theologians declaimed against the 'Turk' and playwrights maligned the 'Moor',[7] Portsmouth seamen and Whitehall courtiers, along with employees of the East Levant and East India companies, were becoming familiar with the varieties of languages, ethnicities and histories among the Muslims.[8] This second approach towards Muslims was governed by national interests and a *Realpolitik* that could not afford ignorance or invention. Monarchs, from Elizabeth I on, wrote polite letters of co-operation to Muslim potentates, sometimes even emphasizing the propinquity between Islam and Protestantism and appealing to common ground. In the corridors of power and commerce, prejudice was counter-productive; precision, accuracy and proper data helped to reduce military danger and increase commercial profit. The diplomatic records kept by Britons who were active in the Islamic world and

5 Richard Hakluyt, *The Principall Nauigations, Voiages and Discoueries of the English Nation* (London: Printed by George Bishop and Ralph Newberie 1589).
6 Franklin L. Baumer, 'England, the Turk and the common corps of Christendom', *American Historical Review*, vol. 50, no. 1, 1944, 26–48.
7 For studies of the image of Muslims in English literature, see Samuel C. Chew, *The Crescent and the Rose: Islam and England during the Renaissance* [1937] (New York: Octagon 1974); Jack D'Amico, *The Moor in English Renaissance Drama* (Gainesville: University Press of Florida 1991); Jonathan Burton, *Traffic and Turning: Islam and English Drama, 1579–1624* (Newark: University of Delaware Press 2005); and Matthew Birchwood, *Staging Islam in England: Drama and Culture, 1640–1685* (Cambridge: D. S. Brewer 2007).
8 See Mordecai Epstein, *The Early History of the Levant Company* (London: George Routledge and Sons 1908), and Antony Wild, *The East India Company: Trade and Conquest from 1600* (London: HarperCollins 1999). For a survey of early Islamo-European interactions, see Jerry Brotton, *The Renaissance Bazaar: From the Silk Road to Michelangelo* (Oxford: Oxford University Press 2002).

that have survived in the British national archives and libraries reveal the vast amount of information that Britons amassed about Muslim societies, regions and histories.[9] Only through such detailed information could British merchants and diplomats, factors and residents oust their continental (French, Dutch, Venetian) rivals from the lucrative Mediterranean and Indian trades, and manufacture goods that would appeal to their religiously different clients. Openness towards Muslims was necessary, even if it went as far as permitting them to 'exercise theire religion ... in the kingdome of the King of Great Britaine'.[10]

By the end of the seventeenth century, John Locke called for the inclusion of Muslims (and other non-Anglicans and non-Christians) in the British body politic. Although voices had been raised earlier in the century for toleration of Muslims, it was Locke who, uniquely in early modern Europe, formulated a theory that moved the status of Muslims from the exclusion of prejudice to the inclusion of toleration. For centuries after Locke, his theory remained a theory and prejudice continued, but at least the English philosopher set in motion the long process of transforming the Muslim from an Other to a fellow subject of the crown.

The early modern period, therefore, witnessed the parallel development of two attitudes towards Muslims and Islam. A raging Turk or a lascivious Moor strutted on stage at the same time that a British ambassador in Istanbul or a consul in Algiers or Aghra conveyed information about diplomatic strategy and Arabian horses.[11] At the pulpit the preacher might demonize Muhammad and ridicule Islam, but letters would subsequently reach the Privy Council about the prospects for increased trade with the followers of Muhammad, about rich resources and distinct industrial needs in the lands of Islam. Still, prejudice remained dominant in the fertile world of the imagination: more so than in the corridors of power, where it was not absent but had to give way to financial, commercial and diplomatic priorities.

9   The material about North Africa and the Ottoman empire in British archives has not yet been edited. For the North African material in the National Archives, Kew, see my 'Resources for the study of British–North African relations in the early modern period', available online at www.hull.ac.uk/caravane/documents/sourcesmatar.pdf (viewed 2 April 2009). The material about India, now in the British Library, was catalogued by Sir William Foster, in *The English Factories in India, 1618–1669, a Calendar of Documents in the India Office, the British Museum and Public Record Office*, 13 vols (Oxford: Clarendon Press 1906–27).
10 Quoted from the treaty between Marrakesh and London, 22 September 1637, in Pierre de Cenival and Philipe de Cossé Brissac (eds), *Les Sources inédites de l'histoire du Maroc de 1530 à 1845 ... Archives et bibliothèques d'Angleterre*, vol. 3 (Paris: Geuthner 1936), 331.
11 For a study of the importance of Arabian horses in the eighteenth century, see Donna Landry, *Noble Brutes: How Eastern Horses Transformed English Culture* (Baltimore: Johns Hopkins University Press 2009).

Prejudice

One of the first publications on Islam in English, *Here Begynneth a Lytell Treatyse of the Turkes Lawe Called Alcaron* (1519?), included the woodcut of a Muslim preacher standing in front of the figure of a horned beast-like devil.[12] English parishioners also read translations of continental polemics against Islam, such as *Here after Foloweth a Lytell Treatyse agaynst Mahumet and His Cursed Secte* (c. 1530) and Paolo Giovio's *A Shorte Treatise vpon the Turkes Chronicles* (1546) with its rousing words on the title page: 'Wake up now, Christiens out of your Slumber. Of the Turkes to recouer your long lost glory.'[13] In the absence of a translation of the Qur'an or of documents from Arabic, Turkish or other Islamic civilizations, Britons saw Islam exclusively through the prism of Muslims attacking, enslaving, converting (as with the Janissaries especially) and killing Christians. The vast scientific, philosophical and artistic legacy of Islam was buried under the mantle of the Ottomans to the extent that surveys about the 'Mahometans' opened with a few pages devoted to the biography of the Prophet Muhammad (with his Jewish parents and Nestorian/heretical teacher) before shifting to the House of Osman and its dangerous legacy. Islam was the prelude to the Ottoman onslaught.[14]

English men and women became acutely aware of this Islam–war association in the mid-1560s. In 1565 they invoked God in 'common prayer every Wednesday and Friday' to assist the Christians of Malta 'to defend and deliver Christians professing his holy name, and in his Justice to repress the rage and violence of Infidels'.[15] In 1566 another 'common prayer' was used 'every Sunday, Wednesday, and Friday, through the whole Realm: To excite and stir all godly people to pray unto God for the preservation of those Christians and their Countries, that are now invaded by the Turk in Hungary, or elsewhere.'[16] The communal fear felt by English parishioners

---

12 *Here Begynneth a Lytell Treatyse of the Turkes Lawe Called Alcaron* (London: Printed by Wynkyn de Worde [1519?]). I am thankful to the anonymous reader who pointed out that this text is 'simply a reproduction of the section on Islam in Mandeville's *Travels*, which de Worde had printed in 1499, 1503 and 1510'.

13 *Here after Foloweth a Lytell Treatyse agaynst Mahumet and His Cursed Secte* ([London]: Printed by Peter Treuerys [c. 1530]); Paolo Giovio, *A Shorte Treatise vpon the Turkes Chronicles*, trans. into English by Peter Ashton (London: Edwarde Whitchurche 1536).

14 See, for example, Theodore Spandounes, *On the Origins of the Ottoman Emperors*, trans. from the Italian and ed. Donald M. Nicol (Cambridge and New York: Cambridge University Press 1997); Ǧorǧević Bartholemaeus, *The Ofspring of the House of Ottomanno*, trans. from the Latin by Hugh Goughe (London: Printed by Thomas Marshe [1570?]); and the account in John Foxe, *The Acts and Monuments of John Foxe* [1563], ed. George Townsend, 8 vols (London: Seeley, Burnside and Seeley 1843–9).

15 *Liturgical Services. Liturgies and Occasional Forms of Prayer Set Forth in the Reign of Queen Elizabeth*, ed. William Keatinge Clay (Cambridge: Cambridge University Press 1847), 519.

16 Ibid., 527.

at the Ottoman naval attack on the island where St Paul had been shipwrecked, as well as at the military campaigns in Central Europe, strengthened a collective national identity at the same time as it consolidated common prejudices. In this context, one book above all served in relentlessly reminding English parishioners of Muslim violence and their common cause with 'Christendom': the most popular sixteenth-century tome (after the Bible), John Foxe's *Acts and Monuments* (1563). The graphic description of Christian/Protestant martyrs nurtured the anti-Catholicism that under- pinned Elizabethan and, later, Puritan and non-conformist theology; with an elaborate section on 'The History of the Turks', Foxe joined the chorus of English and continental anti-Muslim detractors. Every republication (and expansion) of the book (1570, 1576, 1583) intensified the anti-Christian danger of the Muslims, especially as congregations repeated the 'Prayer against the Turks' that concluded that section:

> O lord God of hosts, grant to thy church strength and victory against the malicious fury of these Turks, Saracens, Tartarians, against Gog and Magog, and all the malignant rabble of Antichrist, enemies to thy Son Jesus, our Lord and Saviour. Prevent their devices, overthrow their power, and dissolve their kingdom.[17]

Such confused lumping together of all 'enemies' of Christ led to other confusions in which writers associated 'Turkes' with Protestant heretics or Catholic schismatics.[18] Antipathy to Muslims dominated every branch of theological exegesis and polemic, especially post-Reformation apocalyptic writing, the most influential form of Christian historiography at the time. From Thomas Brightman in London to Henry Meade in Cambridge, scholars and crazed 'prophets', sect leaders and 'mechanick' women (during the Civil Wars) used a range of fantasies that drew on the books of Daniel and Revelation to represent Muslims in the most bizarre, and daemonic, manner. Biblical allusions to animals were allegorically, anagogically or historically applied to the Muslim descendants of Hagar: scorpions, serpents, adders, locusts, dogs, wolves, donkeys, birds of prey and the ten-horned beast.[19] As English prejudice against Jews had led to their association with a special 'odour', so prejudice against Muslims led to their association with animals; and as Jews were stigmatized for 'crucifying' Christian children, so were Muslims stigmatized for circumcising Christians. From London to port cities

---

17 Foxe, *The Acts and Monuments*, IV, part 1, 122.
18 For a comprehensive study of this trope in the sixteenth century, see the first part of Matthew Dimmock, *'New Turkes': Dramatizing Islam and the Ottomans in Early Modern England* (Aldershot: Ashgate 2005).
19 See the chapter on 'Eschatology and the Saracens' in my *Islam in Britain, 1558–1685* (Cambridge and New York: Cambridge University Press 1998).

and the countryside, sailors and scholars and pedlars developed a fervent hostility to Islam, without having met, in most cases, a single Muslim.

Such ignorance/hostility underpinned the first account of Islam and the Ottoman empire by an English writer: Richard Knolles's *Generall Historie of the Turkes* (1603).[20] The chronicler-cum-historian presented a laborious survey, culled from various continental sources, of the 'present terror of the world', and showed how many communities of Christians had been at the mercy of the Turks since the beginning of the dynasty. At the same time, London theatre audiences, ranging from groundlings to royalty, saw complex, but fearsome, plays about Turks-as-Muslims in which the protagonists raged or lusted, killed their children or enslaved and brutalized Christians. They also saw 'Moors' (always black-skinned),[21] and the followers of the 'Sophie' in Persia. Shakespeare and Massinger (who borrowed from Cervantes), Greene and Heywood, Behn and Dryden disseminated images in the form of repeated narratives (the strangulation of Prince Mustapha by order of his father Suleyman and his stepmother Roxolana was grimly appealing),[22] costumes, religious phrases ('By sleepy Mahomet', 'O Haly', 'Your Alcoran'), and dramatic gestures that became indelible markers of Muslims. Also, from *The Fairie Queene* to *Paradise Lost*, the masterpieces of English epic imagination repeated the hostile image of the Muslim/Turk/pagan: Spenser's Sans Foi, Sans Joi and Sans Loi, along with Milton's association of the Grand Sultan with Satan in *Paradise Lost*.[23] So too did the English translations of continental epics, such as Tasso's *Jerusalem Delivered* (1600) or Camões's *Lusiads* (1655). These and other works were performed and studied, memorized and adapted, printed and reprinted, becoming the landmarks of national identity, religious certainty and ideological power. In the iconoclastic culture of Protestant Britain, printing was the means par excellence of repeating and diffusing stereotypes, thereby influencing child and adult, male and female. Increased literacy, availability

---

20 Richard Knolles, *The Generall Historie of the Turkes* (London: Printed by Adam Islip 1603).

21 For an exhaustive study of Blacks in England, some of whom were Muslims, see Imtiaz Habib, *Black Lives in the English Archives 1500–1677: Imprints of the Invisible* (Aldershot: Ashgate 2008). See also the last chapter in Gustav Ungerer, *The Mediterranean Apprenticeship of British Slavery* (Madrid: Editorial Verbum 2008).

22 For a survey of the Mustapha theme in English and continental literature, see the introduction by Galina Yermolenko in her edited volume, *Roxolana in History and Literature* (forthcoming from Ashgate).

23 For Spenser and Islam, see Benedict Scott Robinson, *Islam and Early Modern English Literature: The Politics of Romance from Spenser to Milton* (Basingstoke and New York: Palgrave Macmillan 2007). For a comprehensive study of Milton and Islamic references, see Eid Abdallah Dahiyat, *John Milton and the Arab-Islamic Culture* (Amman: Shukayr and Akasheh 1987); see also Gerald MacLean, 'Milton, Islam and the Ottomans', in Elizabeth Sauer and Sharon Achinstein (eds), *Milton and Toleration* (New York: Oxford University Press 2007), 284–99.

of paper and improvements in printing technology all led to the indus-
trialization of the book, which nurtured the culture of prejudice.

The impact of early modern print and other forms of mass media was
crucial in sustaining fear of the 'Turks', notwithstanding the deterioration in
Ottoman power at the beginning of the seventeenth century. Sir Thomas Roe,
living in Istanbul in the 1620s, repeatedly informed his correspondents in
London, from King James I to members of the Privy Council, that the
Ottoman empire was on the wane. The empire no longer evoked 'terror', he
wrote in January 1622, using the same word that had characterized Knolles's
account. The empire was like 'an old body, crazed through many vices', he
added in 1622.[24] But such information, conveyed in private correspondence,
could not counter the fear that was generated by Morocco's 'Moors' or the
Grand Sultan's Janissaries and spahis, or the earlier prostration of Sir
Thomas Roe at the feet of the Mughal emperor in Aghra,[25] or the Turkish
privateers who were seized on a vessel near London in 1617.[26] This
engrained fear of Muslims was paradoxically compounded by Islamic
openness to Euro-Christian emigration: many British sailors and traders
renounced their Christianity, converted to Islam and settled among the
'infidels'. The Turks were willing to co-opt Britons and integrate them into
their economy and religion; this precipitated social and financial exigencies
at home since the conversion of a sailor to Islam also meant desertion of wife
and children, all of whom would become a burden on parish charity. Like
thousands of continental Christians before and after them, Britons renounced king and country. Others did not have to renounce their religion
as they found Islamic society willing to accommodate disaffected Christians.
In 1610 English Catholics, fleeing from the post-Gunpowder Plot persecution, left their country in the hope of settling in Muslim North Africa;[27] and
soon after the financial collapse and civil turmoil in Britain in the late
Jacobean and Caroline periods, other Britons went to 'live in Turky' where
they could find security, livelihood and 'Liberty of Conscience'.[28]

The Islamic world attracted the unemployed to such an extent that well
before the beginning of the so-called 'great migration' to North America

---

24 Sir Thomas Roe, *The Negotiations of Sir Thomas Roe in His Embassy to the Ottoman Porte,
    from the Year 1621 to 1628*, ed. S. Richardson (London: London Society for the
    Encouragement of Learning 1740), 22, 36.
25 See the study of Roe by Richmond Barbour, *Before Orientalism: London's Theatre of the
    East, 1576–1626* (Cambridge and New York: Cambridge University Press 2003), ch. 5.
26 *Calendar of State Papers Domestic: James I, 1611–1618*, ed. Mary Anne Everett Green
    (London: Longman 1858), vol. 9, 427.
27 *Calendar of State Papers and Manuscripts Relating to English Affairs in the Archives
    and Collections of Venice, Vol. 12, 1610–1613*, ed. Horatio F. Brown (London: HMSO
    1905), 46.
28 Henry Robinson, *Liberty of Conscience, or the Sole Means to Obtaine Peace and Truth*
    (London 1643), 'Epistle Dedicatory', 10.

(*c.* 1629), there was the migration of Britons to North Africa and the Levant.[29] Sailors and traders and mercenaries went to Marrakesh with its gold-rich legacy of the Sa'dian dynasty (Thomas Heywood's *The Fair Maid of the West Part I* (*c.* 1600) ended with the English couple receiving a fabulous dowry from the generous Moroccan king); Algiers with its quaint white buildings, clean streets, thriving commerce and abundant fruit; and Tunis, where the English-turned-Turk John Ward lived in a palace of enviable opulence (as reported by the Scottish traveller William Lithgow).[30] And, of course, there was Istanbul with its fabulous wealth and, most importantly, its hard currency that paid for the warm English cloth that traders carried with them; and Isfahan whence turban-clad Robert Sherley set out to the court of King James I (and other European courts) in 1611 as ambassador of the Persian shah.[31] Christendom was losing out to the lands of Islam, and allegiance to monarch and God was giving way to Islamic employment (thus the British 'voluntaries' and soldiers serving in North Africa and the Levant), meritocracy and even marriages, as in Shakespeare's Claribel and the King of Tunis in *The Tempest* (1611).

The more success the Muslims had, the more Britons wondered: what was wrong with Christendom that Muslims were in the ascendant? Authors were puzzled and bewildered at God's inaction. There was such urgency for an explanation of Christendom's decline that, in 1663, Henry Marsh translated/ adapted (from a continental source) *A New Survey of the Turkish Empire* in which he assured his anxious readers that they had the better religion (than Islam) and that their God would defeat the enemy, as He had destroyed Sennacherib and Pharaoh. Christians, continued Marsh, possessed the better institutions and technologies, and enjoyed the higher 'abilities of bodies, capacities, and gifts of understanding'.[32] Still, he admitted, 'we are ... defeated' and 'get no victories'. 'Why', he asked, 'are our Ensigns adorn'd with Crucifixes, fearful formerly to Infidels and Devils, now trampled on and slighted?' The answer was unambiguous: 'I shall tell you in few words, and truth. We have a God most great, most good: but alienated from us so far.'[33]

To the question about what had gone wrong in Christendom—similar to the question Bernard Lewis has asked about contemporary Islam in *What Went Wrong?*[34]—Marsh turned to theology not history (as Muslims also do,

29 See my discussion in *Turks, Moors and Englishmen in the Age of Discovery* (New York: Columbia University Press 1999), ch. 3.
30 William Lithgow, *The Totall Discourse of the Rare Adventures & Painefull Peregrinations of Long Nineteene Yeares Travayles from Scotland to the Most Famous Kingdomes in Europe, Asia and Affrica* (Glasgow: J. MacLehose 1906), 317, 319.
31 D. W. Davies, *Elizabethans Errant* (Ithaca, NY: Cornell University Press 1967), ch. 11.
32 Henry Marsh, *A New Survey of the Turkish Empire and Government* (London 1663), 85. (There was another edition that same year; I am using the first, Wing M729A.)
33 Ibid., 85–6, 88.
34 Bernard Lewis, *What Went Wrong? The Clash between Islam and Modernity in the Middle East* (London: Weidenfeld and Nicolson 2002).

in Lewis's disingenuous argument). The reason for the success of the infidels and the defeat of the Christians was not that Christians had failed in their civilization but that they had failed in their religion, as the spread of heresies and schisms and 'hideous Sects' among them showed. After listing the failures of the nobility and the gentry, the soldiers and the rulers, in upholding their faith, Marsh concluded with the words of 'the Prophet, All have declin'd the ways of God, and are unprofitable; there's none that doth good, not even one'.[35] Marsh did not call on Europeans to improve their social infrastructures or re-evaluate their historiography. The failure of Christendom was religious and moral, not intellectual or technological: 'Turks leave their vices in their houses, from whence we carry ours. . . . What wonder then if they conquer who are preserved by sobriety, parsimony, diligence, fidelity and obedience?'[36] Only when Christian values and moral codes prevailed among the Christians would they be able to defeat the Turks and send them back 'to their old lurking holes, and caves and corners in Bythinia'; only then would the Holy Roman Emperor regain his seat in Constantinople, France acquire 'lesser Asia; England, part of Egypt; Spain, part of Africa; Italy, all Shores and Banks of the Mediterranean Seas; and last, the Pope, as a great Pastor of the Christian Church, will be extol'd and magnifi'd for such an union'.[37] It was imperative to recover Christian piety because only such a Christianity could bring about imperial conquest and wealth.

Marsh could not see the Euro-Christian failure before the Ottomans in any light other than a religious one. Despite the Catholic content of the book, with its praise for the pope, *The New Survey of the Turkish Empire* struck a chord with English Protestant readers and it was promptly republished that same year. Readers were convinced that the failure in the face of the Ottomans was a religious one; and it was a failure that was being repeatedly aggravated as Marsh and his compatriots watched with despair the growing allure and power of Islamic countries. There was also humiliation: from the end of the sixteenth century on, North African ships began to attack coastal English, Welsh and Irish harbour towns in a counter-offensive to what Molly Greene has called (contra Fernand Braudel) the 'Northern Invasion'.[38] During some of these piratical incursions, British women were taken captive, and large numbers of emigrants and indentured servants were seized while sailing to the North American colonies. Such seizures increased the national sense of powerlessness and anger, especially as the numbers of captives rose. Despite God being English, He was unable to protect His

35 Marsh, *A New Survey of the Turkish Empire and Government*, 89.
36 Ibid., 90–1.
37 Ibid., 96.
38 Molly Greene, 'Beyond the Northern Invasion: the Mediterranean in the seventeenth century', *Past and Present*, vol. 174, no. 1, 2002, 42–71.

English (and Cornish and Welsh and Scottish) people against the 'Mahometans'.[39]

The more failure Britons endured in confronting Islamic ascendancy, the more their prejudice exacerbated their hostility. Unable to fight back, they turned to denunciation, invective and invention. Prejudice created misinformation, which created further prejudice. English writers did not hold Muhammad in the same light as Muslims held Christ; and so they did not balk at denouncing both Islam's founder and Islam's followers interchangeably. Whatever was remiss and fearsome in Muslims, be they the Ottoman armies or the Barbary Corsairs, was traced back to the flaws of the founder and his buffoonishness, illiteracy, lust and warmongering. (Muslim writers never similarly traced Christian social ills back to 'Issa/Jesus, a prophet whom they venerated deeply.) That is why, throughout the period under study (and later, perhaps even into modern times), attacks on Muhammad and 'Mahometans', whether warranted or not, intruded themselves into the public media of poems, sermons, plays, broadsheets and masques. The Muslim became a timeless and universal anti-Christian and anti-English adversary, a trope that could safely be used to win readers and reassure them of the theological and intellectual validity of their ignorance. Richard Johnson's popular *The Seven Champions of Christendom* was first published in 1596–7 and was reprinted numerous times throughout the seventeenth century. In chapter fourteen, the author evoked the strangeness of the

> King of Moroco with hys tawnie Moores and coleblacke Negers: Likewise the Soldan of Persia: Ptolomie the Egiptian King: The Kinges of Arabia and Ierusalem euery one departed into their owne countries, cursing the time they attempted first so vaine an enterprise [of attacking Christendom].[40]

Inevitably, such vituperation in fiction against 'tawnie Moores' was translated into actions and reactions on the ground: when a Moroccan delegation wanted to sail back on board an English ship in October 1600, neither 'the marchants nor mariners' would agree to take them, thinking 'yt a matter odious and scandalous to the world to be too friendly or familiar with infidels'.[41] Pre-judgement produced judgement.

Just about that same time, William Percy wrote the first play in English to include the figure of Muhammad, showing the angel Gabriel holding 'him by the Bearde, or clawd him by the face'. Later the Prophet cleans the 'shooe'

---

39 For British women captives in North Africa, see my *Britain and Barbary, 1589–1689* (Gainesville: University Press of Florida 2005), ch. 3.

40 Robert Johnson, *The Seven Champions of Christendom (1596/7)*, ed. Jennifer Fellows (Aldershot: Ashgate 2003), 89.

41 John Chamberlain, *The Letters of John Chamberlain*, ed. Norman Egbert McClure, 2 vols (Philadelphia: American Philosophical Society 1939), i.108.

of the Arabian empress Epimede, before being asked to 'kiss [her] cul'.[42] Less than half a century later, in 1649, Alexander Ross published the Qur'an in English.[43] Undeterred that he did not know Arabic and was relying on a French translation, Ross assured his readers in his 'Caveat' that no one who read the text would be tempted to believe it. After all, the text was 'Newly Englished for the fascination of all that desire to look into the Turkish vanities'. The Qur'an was not serious but a piece of entertainment for those who were voyeuristically inclined: 'Who is so mad as to prefer the embracements of a filthy Baboon, to his beautiful Mistress, or the braying of an Ass to a Consort of Musick?'[44] Even a metaphysical poet like the Catholic Richard Crashaw could not avoid defaming Muslims for murderously seeking to apply their 'barbarous knife' to 'the Admirable Saint Teresa'.[45] The Anglican preacher Robert South, eager to vilify Cromwell, found none other than 'Mahomet' with whom to compare the dead despot: as Cromwell's rule had disintegrated, so would Islam, which has 'begun to totter, already; for Mahomet having promised to come and visit his followers, and translate them to Paradise after a thousand years, this being expired, many of the Persians began to doubt and smell the cheat'.[46] Every English man, woman and child, whether interested in Islam or not, could not avoid hearing it reviled and appropriated into current controversies: when coffee was introduced to English drinkers in the second half of the seventeenth century, the ale sellers, an interest group that was negatively affected by this new beverage, denounced the 'Mahometan Berry', accusing it of being Islam's secret weapon for the subversion of pious English customers.[47]

Prejudice against Islam and Muslims did not remain confined to verbal and cultural hostility. Unchallenged, it degenerated into threats of violence and 'holy war'. There was such support for war that every Christian—and

---

42 William Percy, *William Percy's* Mahomet and His Heaven: *A Critical Edition*, ed. Matthew Dimmock (Aldershot: Ashgate 2006), I.i.41, v.iii.31, v.iv.7.

43 Although Ross's name does not appear as the translator, George Sale, who prepared the superior 1734 translation, explicitly mentioned him in his preliminary 'To the Reader', in *The Koran, Commonly Called the Alcoran of Mohammed*, trans. from the Arabic (London: Printed by C. Ackers for J. Wilcox 1734). Ross was hauled before Parliament (or what was left of it) for translating the Qur'an: there is no evidence in the documents in the National Archives concerning his seizure that anyone else was suspected of the translation.

44 Alexander Ross, 'Caveat', in *The Alcoran of Mahomet translated out of Arabique into French* (London 1649).

45 Richard Crashaw, 'A hymn to the name and honour of the admirable Saint Teresa', line 70.

46 Robert South, *Ecclesiastical Policy the Best Policy: or, Religion the Best Reason of State* [1660], in Alan Rudrum, Joseph Black and Holly Faith Nelson (eds), *The Broadview Anthology of Seventeenth-century Verse & Prose* (Peterborough, Ontario: Broadview Press 2004), 1061.

47 See the discussion of this topic in my *Islam in Britain*, ch. 3.

not just English—military or naval victory over the Muslims, both on the continent and on the high seas, became part of the holy 'collision of the Eastern and Western Princes'.[48] Christianity was Western, and Islam was Eastern, and between the two there could only be war. As Muslim jurists (chiefly Hanbali) had argued for a House of Peace (*silm*) and a House of War (*harb*), so Christian writers also thought in polarized terms. After the defeat of the Ottoman armies at the gates of Vienna in 1683, Thomas Mills published *The History of the Holy War*, in which he reminded his readers of the Crusaders' mantra, 'God willeth it, God willeth it', and brought the history of holy war up to 'the Present War, managed by the Emperour, King of Poland, and several other Princes against the Turks'. He also emphasized that holy war was part of the legacy of all Englishmen, who gave 'a Testimony of their Courage, and Bravery against those Infidels',[49] a courage that had started half a millennium earlier and had not abated. Conflict with Muslims was timeless. Or timely: astrologers weighed in to assure their readers that the Bible had already fixed the date of the total destruction of Islam and the conversion of all Muslims to Christianity, namely 1701.[50]

A theory of toleration

At the same time that prejudice was consolidating, and being consolidated by, ignorance, numerous forms of social, commercial and diplomatic interactions between Britons, on the one hand, and North African, Levantine and Central Asiatic Muslims, on the other, were taking place. Queen Elizabeth co-ordinated her anti-Spanish strategies with both the Ottoman sultan and the Moroccan ruler,[51] at the same time that friendships developed between her subjects and 'Moors'.[52] Towards the end of her reign, a 'License'

48 'To the reader', in Marsh, *A New Survey of the Turkish Empire and Government*, also ch. 15 ('The interest of all the princes in Christendom upon the accompt of policy and religion in a war with the Turk').

49 Thomas Mills, *The History of the Holy War, Began Anno 1095, by the Christian Princes of Europe against the Turks* (London: Printed for Thomas Malthus 1685), 16, title page, A3.

50 See [John Shirley?], *The History of the Turks. Describing the Rise and Ruin of their first Empire in Persia; the Original of their Second* (London: Printed by Ralph Holt and John Richardson for Thomas Passinger, William Thackeray and Thomas Sawbridge 1683), 395; and John Holwell, *An Appendix to Holwel's Catastrophe Mundi, Being an Astrological Discourse of the Rise, Growth and Continuation of the Othoman Family* (London: Printed by J. G. for F. Smith 1683), 30.

51 Jonathan Burton, 'Anglo-Ottoman relations and the image of the Turk in *Tamburlaine*', *Journal of Medieval and Early Modern Studies*, vol. 30, no. 1, 2000, 125–56; Nabil Matar, 'Queen Elizabeth I through Moroccan eyes', *Journal of Early Modern History*, vol. 12, no. 1, 2008, 55–76.

52 See the interesting case described in Joan Taylor, *The Englishman, the Moor and the Holy City: The True Adventures of an Elizabethan Traveller* (Stroud, Gloucestershire: Tempus 2006).

was granted to a Turk from the 'vize Roye of argeir' allowing the 'bearer Bullocke Bazia to goe and passe for England to shewe your highenes such playe and pastime as he and his Company are able to shewe in token of good will'.[53] Muslim entertainers were to amuse the queen. When the Thirty Years War cut off English access to the continental markets, Lewes Roberts drew attention in his *The Marchants Mapp of Commerce* to 'Argier, and the trade thereof', where English entrepreneurs could buy 'Reisins, figgs, butter, honey, dates, oyle, soape … Almonds, cheese, cottons … Brasse, copper, waxe and drugs'.[54] Other commodities were available in Damascus and Aleppo, Tripoli, Alexandria and Istanbul. There were opportunities for trade with Muslim lands, as there were for establishing collaborative relations that might prove militarily beneficial. In 1666 the *London Gazette* reported: 'Two Turks Men of War lye in this Channel, which we finde contribute much to the security of those Seas at present.'[55] Unfortunately, the two Turkish ships soon left, which opened the way for the Dutch fleet to sail up the Thames and wreak havoc on Charles II's fleet. Muslim fleets protected the Anglo-Welsh coastline at the same time that Muslim seamen arrived in the port towns of England and Wales and mingled with the inhabitants.[56] A range of cross-cultural exchanges resulted from these interactions: in 1663 Paul Rycaut, the English consul in Smyrna, introduced an English printing press to Istanbul and used it to publish the capitulations with the Porte, making sure that he included the imprimatur of the emperor;[57] and, when Sir Dudley North, treasurer of the Levant Company in Istanbul from 1662 to 1680, wanted to discourage an Englishman from trying to convert the Great Turk in Istanbul, he resorted to having him 'drubbed upon the feet, after the Turkish manner'.[58] In 1681 William Crooke wrote that, in Tangier, 'The English and Moors seem'ed to differ in nothing but Religion';[59] a year later, Colonel Percy Kirke wrote to the Moroccan ruler, Mulay Ismail, how 'the Alcaids servants, and all other Moors that pleased, lived amongst us within the walls of this Town and were treated by us with all brotherly tenderness

53 License, n.d.: National Archives, Kew, FO 113/1/30–31.
54 Lewes Roberts, *The Marchants Mapp of Commerce* (London: Printed by R. O. for R. Mabb 1638), 70.
55 *London Gazette*, no. 57, 28–31 May 1666, 1.
56 In October 1655, North African sailors began docking at 'Falmouth for provisions', whereupon the Dutch grew worried about their trade in the Channel: *Calendar of State Papers Domestic: Interregnum, 1655*, ed. Mary Ann Everett Green (London: Longman 1881), 365.
57 Paul Rycaut, *The Capitvlations and Articles of Peace between the Majestie of the King of England … And the Sultan of the Ottoman Empire* (Constantinople: Abraham Gabai 1663).
58 Roger North, *The Lives of the Right Hon. Francis North, Baron Guilford … [and] the Hon. Sir Dudley North … and the Hon. and Rev. Dr John North*, 3 vols (London: Henry Colburn 1826), III.37.
59 [Lancelot Addison], *The Moores Baffled: Being a Discourse concerning Tanger* (London: Printed for William Crooke 1681), 18.

and affection'.[60] When rebellion was fomented in the early eighteenth century against Mulay Ismail by 'one of his Sons by an English woman', an English observer expressed pride in the fact that 'English Blood is averse to Slavery'.[61] English blood was running in Muslim veins.

In this context of growing familiarity with Islam, one aspect of Muslim theology attracted the attention of many English writers: how the Qur'an advanced the belief that all the prophets of monotheism—Moses, Jesus and Muhammad—offered equal avenues to God. William Biddulph, George Sandys, William Lithgow, Henry Blount and other English and Scottish travellers, and even captives like Joseph Pitts, confirmed that the Muslim empires, from Istanbul to Aghra, practised what the Qur'an preached (Qur'an 45:27). Englishmen were impressed by Muslim theological breadth: 'all men are to be saved by their own religion; so that neither Christian, Turk, nor Jew can curse either's faith, but, upon complaint to the magistrate, you may have them punished', confirmed one resident of Istanbul.[62] Equally impressive was that Christians and Jews were allowed to express their faith openly in the midst of Muslim lands. The Quakers praised the 'Turks' who never forcibly converted peoples they had conquered, unlike the Anglican establishment in England that was brutally persecuting them.[63] So sure were the Quakers of Islamic toleration that the Quaker Richard Holder 'set up an "Office for the Redemption of Captives" at Garoway's Coffee House in Sally, with hours from 1 to 3 each afternoon'.[64] And, while there is no record in the period under study of a Briton bringing back with him to England a Muslim wife, a Moroccan left London in 1683 after having married a local Englishwoman.[65] There was a place for the Christian in the Islamic polity—as a spouse as well as a visitor and a trader, from Galata in Istanbul to Khan al-Ifranj in Cairo to the Rue des consuls in Rabat—to live, work and raise a family.[66]

---

60 Letter from Col. Percy Kirke to Mulay Ismail, [August–December 1682]: National Archives, Kew, Colonial Office Records (Tangier), CO 279/30/380v.
61 'Journal of the mission kept by his [Charles Stewart] Midshipman [William?] Stewart al. Steward, 22 July 1720–8 August 1727': British Library, London, Leake Papers, Add. MS 47995, f. 45v.
62 North, *The Lives of the Right Hon. Francis North*, ii.345.
63 'G[eorge] F[ox,] a Quaker, to the Chief Magistrate, Rulers, Ministers, Justices and other Officers who profess Christ and Christianity', 28 January 1685, in *Calendar of State Papers Domestic: Charles II, May 1684–February 1685*, ed. F. H. Blackburne Daniell and Francis Bickley (London: HMSO 1938), 301.
64 Kenneth L. Carroll, 'Quaker captives in Morocco, 1685–1701', *Journal of the Friends' Historical Society*, vol. 55, 1985–6, 67–79 (70).
65 See the reference to her departure with her husband and other members of the Moroccan delegation on 18 January 1683, in *Calendar of State Papers Domestic: Charles II, January–June 1683*, ed. F. H. Blackburne Daniell (London: HMSO 1933), 19.
66 For the Christian presence in Istanbul, see Robert Mantran, 'Foreign merchants and the minorities in Istanbul during the sixteenth and seventeenth centuries', in Benjamin Braude and Bernard Lewis (eds), *Christians and Jews in the Ottoman Empire: The Functioning of a Plural Society*, 2 vols (New York: Holmes & Meier Publishers 1982), i.127–37.

It is not clear how much John Locke knew about the *samaha* (tolerance) of Islam. He had studied Arabic under Edward Pococke at Oxford and, in his library, he had a copy of Paul Rycaut's extensive description of the Ottoman empire, along with a manuscript of a dialogue between a Jew and a Muslim written in Arabic and translated by his friend John Greaves; he also had a copy of the French translation of the Qur'an by André du Ryer (1647).[67] It may well be that, by learning about the Muslim model, Locke came to believe that the Christian monarchy of Britain should grant not only toleration to non-Christians—like the toleration granted to Christians and Jews in the Ottoman empire—but also full 'civil rights' and endenization.[68] Despite fear of the Ottomans, which the rest of Europe shared, Locke still urged that ' . . . neither pagan nor Mahometan nor Jew ought to be excluded from the civil rights of the commonwealth because of his religion'.[69] Locke sought accommodation for Muslims because he knew how the co-operation of North African regions would be crucial to British navies and ground forces fighting against France (in the Nine Years War and the War of the Spanish Succession). Morocco, Algeria, Tunisia and Libya furnished Britain (and France) with wheat, corn, horses, leather and other necessities at the same time that they provided ports where British merchant ships on their way to the Levant could take on food and refit, as well as seek shelter from French and other (Christian) pirates.[70] Although Locke retained the seventeenth-century prejudice against Islam as a religion, he drew a line between theology and believers in order to mark the crucial divide between persecution and toleration. Since Muslims provided shelter and opportunity for Christian Britons in their lands, so should Britons provide legal status and shelter for Muslims in Britain. For Locke, religion could not and should not serve as an obstacle to full integration in the body politic. Citizenship was instrumental in overcoming prejudice against Muslims, as well as in sustaining co-operative military and commercial relations with them.

67 For a discussion of Arabic influences on Locke, see G. A. Russell, 'The impact of the *Philosophus autodidactus*: Pocockes, John Locke and the Society of Friends', in G. A. Russell (ed.), *The 'Arabick' Interest of the Natural Philosophers in Seventeenth-century England* (Leiden and New York: E. J. Brill 1994), 224–66.

68 For a full discussion of Locke and the endenization of Muslims, see my 'John Locke and the "turbanned nations"', *Journal of Islamic Studies*, vol. 2, no. 1, 1991, 67–77. See also the chapter on the toleration of Muslims and Jews in John Marshall, *John Locke, Toleration and Early Enlightenment Culture: Religious Intolerance and Arguments for Religious Toleration in Early Modern and 'Early Enlightenment' Europe* (Cambridge and New York: Cambridge University Press 2006).

69 John Locke, *Epistola de Tolerantia: A Letter on Toleration*, ed. Raymond Klibansky, trans. from the Latin by J. W. Gough (Oxford: Clarendon Press 1968), 145.

70 See my 'Islam in Britain, 1689–1750', *Journal of British Studies*, vol. 47, no. 2, 2008, 284–301.

Gordon W. Allport has stated: 'Prejudgments become prejudices only if they are not reversible when exposed to new knowledge.'[71] By the time John Locke died in 1704, writings about Islam and the Muslim empires had become widely available to English readers. Travellers, Orientalists, chroniclers, comparative theologians, captives, playwrights and diplomats (both consuls and ambassadors) produced an extensive range of information that was transcribed, printed and reprinted, and reached all sectors of literate British society. At the same time, Turks and Moors were arriving in England to trade, petition and negotiate, to the point in 1714 when Simon Ockley could meet in London 'the Moors themselves' and ask them the exact meaning of a word he was trying to translate.[72] By 1725 John Windus declared that 'we have been pretty well accustomed to see its [North Africa] Natives in our streets'.[73]

Notwithstanding these changes, Britons continued to view Muslims and their world through perspectives of difference and exclusion. In the royally designated Anglican church as well as the non-conformist conventicle, in the pages of the censored press as well as on the populist stage, the British public continued to meet vilifying portraits of the Prophet Muhammad, as in Humphrey Prideaux's *The True Nature of Imposture Fully Display'ed in the Life of Mahomet* (1697),[74] or accounts of the Muslim destruction of Eastern Christianity, as in Thomas Smith's *Remarks upon the Manners, Religion and Government of the Turks together with a Survey of the Seven Churches of Asia, as They Now Lye in Their Ruines* (1678).[75] The alternative to this hostility was the near unanimous adoption of the 'exotic': the publication of the Grub Street version of the *Arabian Nights* in the first decades of the eighteen century transformed Muslims and their worlds into entertaining images that 'orientalized' Islam for centuries.[76] The description of the harem, as Alain Grosrichard has stated, became 'the obligatory topos of all the accounts of travel [by Europeans] in the Orient',[77] accounts by men who claimed to have seen its interior but, more often, by men who admitted not to have seen it but

71 Gordon W. Allport, *The Nature of Prejudice* (Cambridge, MA: Addison-Wesley 1954), 9.

72 Letter from Simon Ockley, 8 June 1714: National Archives, Kew, Records of the State Papers Office, SP 102/2/178.

73 John Windus, 'Preface', in his *A Journey to Mequinez* (Dublin 1725). See also my 'The last Moors: Maghariba in early eighteenth-century Britain', *Journal of Islamic Studies*, vol. 14, no. 1, 2003, 37–58.

74 Humphrey Prideaux, *The True Nature of Imposture Fully Display'ed in the Life of Mahomet* (London: Printed for Willliam Rogers 1697). The 8th edition of this text was published in 1723.

75 Thomas Smith, *Remarks upon the Manners, Religion and Government of the Turks, together with a Survey of the Seven Churches of Asia, as They Now Lye in Their Ruines* (London: Moses Pitt 1678).

76 See the detailed discussion in Ros Ballaster, *Fabulous Orients: Fictions of the East in England 1662–1785* (Oxford: Oxford University Press 2005).

77 Alain Grosrichard, *The Sultan's Court: European Fantasies of the East*, trans. from the French by Liz Heron (London and New York: Verso 1998), 125.

still wrote authoritatively about the languid concubines.[78] Such images were used in the various forms of media that streamlined the consciousness of early modern Europeans: repetition, inter-appropriation and reprinting served to confirm prejudices and anxieties so that, wherever a Briton turned, a grim image of the 'Mahometan' appeared to him or her, on the page and on the stage, in the homily and in public art (the statue of Charles II stamping over the Turk),[79] in his native language as well as in Italian, Spanish or French.

By the beginning of the eighteenth century, 'British' became firmly identified with Anglicanism and with Britannia ruling waves and colonies. The new power of empire intensified prejudice, and difference from other peoples began to encompass not only religion, but also ethnic origin and skin colour. Even if the Muslim were to renounce Islam, there were still barriers of fierce exclusion. Towards the end of the century, a Turk from Istanbul fled to England after which he dictated his autobiography, the first by a Muslim in English.[80] 'Ishmael Bashaw' converted to (Anglican) Christianity, married an English woman and sought integration in British society. But, despite his total willingness to anglicize, he remained an object of unwavering prejudice. While an African slave in North America could liberate himself and become a man of property and possessions (his autobiography appearing in print one year after Ishmael's),[81] the 'Turk' remained poor and ostracized. Although there were people who sympathized with him, others remained abusive and threatening: 'When I returned to London I met with much abuse from the common people, carters, porters, & c. some of whom pulled me by my whiskers, and others threw me down; which circumstances, with the recollection of my former robbery, terrified me.'[82] The images that had been constructed in Britain about Muslims over the

---

78 Paul Rycaut, the English consul in Smyrna in the 1660s and 1670s, could not but add a description of the harem to his account of the Turkish empire, despite his admission that he had never set foot inside one. Well into the modern period, the veil and the harem provided Europeans with 'a fantasy and dangled the promise of exotic and erotic experiences', as Mabro stated in her introduction to Judy Mabro (ed.), *Veiled Half-Truths: Western Travellers' Perceptions of Middle Eastern Women* (London: I. B. Taurus 1996), 2.

79 See the reproduction in George de F. Lord (ed.), *Poems on Affairs of State: Augustan Satirical Verse, 1660–1714, Vol. 1, 1660–78* (New Haven and London: Yale University Press 1963), 269.

80 Ishmael Bashaw, *The Turkish Refugee: Being a Narrative of the Life, Sufferings, Deliverances, and Conversion of Ishmael Bashaw, a Mahometan Merchant, from Constantinople, Who Was Taken Prisoner by the Spaniards, and Made a Wonderful Escape to England* (London: Printed for I. Bashaw 1797).

81 Venture Smith, *A Narrative of the Life and Adventures of Venture, a Native of Africa but Resident above Sixty Years in the United States of America* (New London, CT 1798).

82 Bashaw, *The Turkish Refugee*, 16.

centuries still dictated both the perception and the treatment of the 'Mahometan'. The 'systems of representation' and prejudice, as Roxanne L. Euben has incisively stated, seem always to remain 'impervious to mechanisms of verification and argumentation'.[83]

---

83 Roxanne L. Euben, *Journeys to the Other Shore: Muslim and Western Travelers in Search of Knowledge* (Princeton, NJ: Princeton University Press 2006), 193.

Anti-Turkish obsession and the exodus of Balkan Muslims

SLOBODAN DRAKULIC

ABSTRACT   Drakulic examines the socio-historical grounding of Christian Slavs' prejudices against their Muslim ethno-linguistic kin in the Balkans, manifested in attempts at the latter's eradication in the region. His focus is on former Yugoslav republics, and his main argument is that Slav Muslims were ostracized due to a coalescence of ethnic and religious identities that transformed them from indigenous Slavs to quasi-Turks, repugnant to their Christian neighbours, and to political reversals that demoted them from ethno-religious majority to a regional minority. Their association with the Ottoman theocracy—perceived as oppressive, discriminatory and intolerable by the Balkan Christians—thus made them appear as ethno-religious quislings, to be eradicated in the struggle for liberation from Turkish rule.

A three-way ethno-religious war of secession and expulsion broke out between the Catholic Croats, Muslim Bosniaks and Eastern Orthodox Serbs of Bosnia and Herzegovina in 1992,[1] ostensibly confirming Samuel Huntington's hypothesis that peoples of different civilizations—defined primarily by their religion—are bound to clash.[2] This claim echoes an old conviction, widespread among the Christians of the Levant, the Iberian peninsula and the Balkans, that peaceful coexistence with Muslims is virtually impossible, because of their quasi-ontological otherness.

Christians have long held that 'Muhammed's religion was heretical because it rejected the redemptive power of Christ, denied the Trinity, and altered the true Word of God as contained in the Bible', and that Muhammad himself was a lecherous upstart 'attempting to supplant Christ'.[3] Moreover,

---

1 Vjekoslav Perica, *Balkan Idols: Religion and Nationalism in Yugoslav States* (Oxford and New York: Oxford University Press 2002), 166.
2 Samuel P. Huntington, 'The clash of civilizations?', *Foreign Affairs*, vol. 72, no. 3, 1993, 22–49; Samuel P. Huntington, *The Clash of Civilizations and the Remaking of World Order* (New York: Simon and Schuster 1996); Ayaan Hirsi Ali, 'Prada Islam' and Samuel P. Huntington, 'The clash of civilizations revisted', *New Perspectives Quarterly*, vol. 24, no. 1, 2007, 47–52 and 53–9, respectively.
3 Norman L. Jones, 'The adaptation of tradition: the image of the Turk in Protestant England', *East European Quarterly*, vol. 12, no. 2, 1978, 161–75 (161).

Muslims took over the Holy Land, invaded Christendom in the Iberian peninsula and Italy, virtually eradicated Christianity across North Africa, the Levant and Asia Minor, and encroached upon Europe through the Balkans. This fanned fears and hatreds that led to a crusade against Islam and the expulsion of Muslims from Spain, southern Italy and the Balkans. Unless redeemed by conversion, they were to be banished or, indeed, exterminated.[4] Such attitudes recently resurfaced in the Christian–Muslim wars in Lebanon, the Armenian–Azeri conflict in the Caucasus, and the Croat–Muslim and Serb–Muslim wars in Bosnia and Herzegovina.

The Christian rejection of Muslims may appear to have been logical at a time when religion underpinned social consciousness, and a proper model of human existence hinged upon a particular image of divinity and its relation to humanity, rendering other available images loutish, suspect or odious. A time when it likewise was praiseworthy to keep infidels out of the lands of true believers, and expel them when they penetrated them. Those heeding Pope Urban II's exhortation at Clermont in 1095, to take up the cross in the First Crusade, remembered him saying that the Holy Land and much of Byzantium had been taken by 'the Turks', an 'accursed race', a 'slave of the demons'. He urged his coreligionists 'to exterminate this vile race from the lands of our brethren', promising the 'remission of . . . sins' and 'the imperishable glory and kingdom of heaven' to participants.[5]

However, when secular consciousness is hegemonic, and presumably not interested in the question of the divinity of Moses, Jesus or Muhammad, or indeed in the relationship of divinity to humanity, such exclusionary attitudes should have become incomprehensible. If they have not, it might be because theocentrism outlasted its original cultural milieux and coalesced with ethnocentrism to become conducive to ethno-religious conflicts. This paper outlines the circumstances leading to such a coalescence of religious and ethnic identities in the Balkans, the effect of that process on interactions between people of different religious and linguistic backgrounds, and the way those interactions engendered ethno-religious groups or parties engaged in struggles within 'the sphere of power'.[6] It focuses on the conditions that were propitious for the fragmentation of western Balkan Slavs into separate ethno-religious categories, on the mutual antagonisms between them, and on

4 Tomaž Mastnak, *Crusading Peace: Christendom, the Muslim World, and Western Political Order* (Berkeley and Los Angeles: University of California Press 2002), 168–83.

5 Dana Carleton Munro (ed.), 'Urban and the crusaders', in *Translations and Reprints from the Original Sources of European History*, vol. 1 (Philadelphia: Department of History of the University of Pennsylvania 1897), 4–7.

6 Max Weber, *Economy and Society: An Outline of Interpretive Sociology*, ed. Guenther Ross and Claus Wittich, trans. from the German by Ephraim Fischoff *et al.*, 2 vols (Berkeley: University of California Press 1978), 938.

the ways in which those antagonisms contributed to the emergence of self-conscious nationalisms.[7]

The homogenization of ethno-religious categories and their transformation into self-conscious and more or less mobilized groups are often facilitated by the presence of suitable foes, because 'the common adversary brings otherwise mutual enemies together',[8] compelling the oppressed within to join their oppressors against an inimical Other. Christians thus united against pagans, Jews, Muslims or faithless Christians; Catholics against Protestants, Orthodox Christians, Jews, Muslims or faithless Catholics; and Muslims against the polytheists, Christians, Jews or faithless Muslims. Thus, due to changes in or between societies, or in their collective perceptions, Huntington's clash-of-civilizations hypothesis may find empirical support in one historical period, only to be left without justification one historical moment later. French Catholic royalty often closed ranks with the Porte or diverse Protestant powers against their German coreligionists; Orthodox Christians and Protestants were often allied, if not friendly, with Islamic powers, including the Ottomans. Yet, loyalties across religious divides were generally inspired by opportunity rather than fellow feeling. Therefore, while a common adversary *can* bring two erstwhile enemies together, this is more likely if they are not exceedingly dissimilar. A pair of bitter antagonists requires a more formidable common foe in order to form an alliance than a less embittered pair, and the transmutation from foe to friend requires exceptionally propitious socio-historical circumstances. Christian Slavic alliances were consolidated by the 'antagonistic religious tolerance' of the Ottoman *millet* system,[9] which nullified ethno-linguistic affinity between the Muslim and Christian Slavs and enhanced religious affinity on both sides. This constellation of factors and circumstances facilitated the rise of an 'anti-Turkish obsession',[10] directed against all Muslims alike—Turks, Albanians, Greeks, Slavs or Romanians—demanding their expulsion to Asia, where Islam and Muslims ostensibly belonged.

The ethno-religious coalescence within, as well as the antagonism between religious communities, survived the processes of secularization associated with modernity and provided fertile ground for the ethno-religious conflicts of the nineteenth and twentieth centuries. These conflicts triggered a Muslim exodus from the predominantly Christian regions of the Balkans, and a Christian exodus from areas where Muslims held sway, most recently in Bosnia and Herzegovina, Kosovo, Macedonia and Bulgaria, which witnessed

7   Georg Simmel, *Conflict and The Web of Group-Affiliations*, trans. from the German by Kurt H. Wolff andReinhard Bendix *et al.*, respectively (New York: The Free Press of Glencoe 1964), 98–9.
8   Ibid., 103.
9   Robert M. Hayden, 'Antagonistic tolerance: competitive sharing of religious sites in south Asia and the Balkans', *Current Anthropology*, vol. 43, no. 2, 2002, 205–31.
10 Slobodan Prosperov Novak, *Zlatno doba: Marulić—Držić—Gundulić* (Zagreb: Hrvatska sveučilišna naklada 2002), 35. All translations, unless other stated, are by the author.

massive displacements of populations. This paper attempts to deepen our understanding of the making of such events, in the elusive hope that we might be able to control that which we comprehend.

The Ottomans in Europe

Anti-Muslim prejudices among the Balkan Slavs emerged after the Otto-man arrival in the area in the fourteenth century, as mercenaries of the Byzantine factions that were immersed in dynastic strife, and as a shield against the rising power of Serbia under its king and emperor Stefan Dušan (1308–55). Their inconspicuous entrance into the region caused little concern among the local rulers until their expansion into Thrace. An alliance of headstrong heirs of Dušan's decaying empire confidently set out to expel the intruders in 1371, only to be crushed in the battle of Maritsa, near Adrianople. Another Serbian alliance, supported by a contingent sent by the Bosnian king Tvrtko and other forces, did not fare much better in the battle of Kosovo (1389). A crusader army sent to reverse the Ottoman successes in 1396 suffered defeat in the battle of Nicopolis, which led to the fall of Bulgaria.

Further Ottoman advances in the region were halted by their rout in the battle of Angora in 1402 by the forces of Timur.[11] As they turned eastward, the Ottomans resumed their Balkan conquests, aided by numerous *gazi* warriors, eager to expand Dār al-Islām, and acquire the spoils of war. Having crushed two crusader attempts to overcome Byzantium in the battles of Varna (1444) and Kosovo (1448), the Ottomans took Constantinople in 1453, followed by Serbia, Bosnia, Albania, Herzegovina and Montenegro before the century's end. While their armies ravaged Croatia, Dalmatia, Slovenia and Italy, the Ottomans took Belgrade in 1521, and most of Pannonia after the Hungarian rout at Mohács (1526), although Vienna withstood an assault in 1529.[12]

The anti-Turkish obsession

Such Ottoman triumphs and Christian defeats appeared to be catastrophic to Balkan Christian minds, causing the Dalmatian humanist lawyer and cleric Juraj Šižgorić (*c.* 1420–1509) to rage against 'the barbarians' menacing his

11 Leften Stavros Stavrianos, *The Balkans since 1453* (New York: Holt, Rinehart and Winston 1966), 42–9.
12 Géza Perjés, 'Game theory and the rationality of war: the battle of Mohács and the disintegration of medieval Hungary', *East European Quarterly*, vol. 15, no. 2, 1981, 153–62; Jason Goodwin, *Lords of the Horizons: A History of the Ottoman Empire* (New York: Henry Holt 1999), 79–89.

'sacred faith and sweet fatherland'.[13] Marko Marulić (1450–1524), acclaimed as the father of Croatian literature, similarly likened the Turks to 'pagan beasts'.[14] In Wallachia, Vlad III Dracula (*c.* 1430–76)—locally dubbed Tepeş or the Impaler and tragicomically immortalized by Bram Stoker—called the Turks 'the most cruel enemies of the Cross of Christ', vowed to resist 'their savagery' and perished fighting them.[15] The anti-Turkish sentiments of the Balkan literati and potentates joined the chorus of anonymous composers of folk epics and tales bemoaning the Muslim triumphs and glorifying Christian victories. Emerging during the Ottoman conquests and dedicated to 'what was most hateful' to the local Christians—'the oppressive rule of the Turks'[16]—this folklore contributed significantly to the emergence of the anti-Turkish obsession and Muslim expulsions from Europe.

For these same attitudes spread to western and northern Europe, perturbed by the approaching Ottoman menace. Luther's initially conciliatory stance towards Islam dissipated after the fall of Belgrade, the rout at Mohács and the siege of Vienna. With Ottomans near his gates the 'great reformer' cast tolerance aside and determined that 'the Turk was the scourge of God', no less loathsome than the Antichrist of Rome and to be treated accordingly. Such views spread all the way to the British Isles,[17] underpinning sentiments evocative of the early crusades. But their fiercest manifestation was seen in the Iberian and Balkan peninsulas, both conquered by Muslims and subsequently retaken.[18]

The Arabs conquered most of the Iberian peninsula between 711 and 759, and the Christian powers destroyed the last Islamic Iberian state of Granada in 1492,[19] soon after converting or expelling the local Muslims alongside the Jews.[20] This pattern of conquest and forced conversion or expulsion was widely celebrated as liberation, and seen as logical and necessary throughout Christendom. Indigenous converts to Islam were perceived as native aliens who should disappear with the foreign regimes with which they had associated. Thus justified, their forcible removal only awaited propitious circumstances.

13 Ante Kadić, 'Croatian renaissance', *Studies in the Renaissance*, vol. 6, 1959, 28–35 (33); Ante Kadić, 'The Croatian renaissance', *Slavic Review*, vol. 21, no. 1, 1962, 65–88 (70).
14 Novak, *Zlatno doba*, 33–4.
15 Kurt W. Treptow (ed.), *Dracula: Essays on the Life and Times of Vlad Tepeş* ([Boulder, CO]: East European Monographs 1991), 315–16, 317.
16 Dragutin Subotić, *Yugoslav Popular Ballads: Their Origin and Development* (Cambridge: Cambridge University Press 1932), 16.
17 Jones, 'The adaptation of tradition', 163.
18 Subotić, *Yugoslav Popular Ballads*, xiv–xv; Ira M. Lapidus, *A History of Islamic Societies*, 2nd edn (Cambridge: Cambridge University Press 2002), 198.
19 Albert Hourani, *A History of the Arab Peoples* (Cambridge, MA: The Belknap Press of Harvard University Press 1991), 84–6.
20 Lapidus, *A History of Islamic Societies*, 315–19.

In the Balkans, those expulsions were realized during the (re)conquests spearheaded by Austria and Venice in the late seventeenth century, which occasioned the kind of religious intolerance rampant in the Iberian region two centuries earlier. The failure to uproot the Balkan Muslims as thoroughly as their Iberian confrères, however, was due less to the Austrian, Venetian or local Balkan liberators' tolerance than to the resilience of the sizeable Muslim populations of Bosnia, Herzegovina, Albania, Kosovo, Macedonia, Dobruja,[21] and the Rhodope mountains.[22]

From anti-Turkish to anti-Muslim obsession

Most Balkan Muslims are descendants of converts whose ethnic links to Ottoman or other Turks are negligible. Christian nobles converted to retain their social status, and burghers to avoid becoming *rayah*, a member of the lower class of Ottoman society. Peasant families might appoint one member to convert who would thereby pass into the ruling Muslim order and protect his unconverted kin. But opportunism was not the only motive behind conversions: 'In most cases worldly and spiritual motives for conversion blended together.'[23]

There is an ongoing debate about which local Christian denomination provided the most converts to Islam. In the eastern and southern regions of the Balkans the converts were more likely to be Orthodox. In the northern and western areas, they could have been Catholic, Orthodox, Protestant or Bogomil.[24] The Balkan Bogomils can be likened to the Cathars of Languedoc, who were quashed by the northern French Catholics in a thirteenth century crusade.[25] Bogomilism, called *haeresia Bulgarorum*, the 'Bulgarian heresy', spread from Bulgaria to Bosnia, and was severely persecuted by the local potentates. The code of 'the true believing Tsar Stephan [Dušan]' of 1349 punished them with facial branding and ostracism,[26] and Hungarian kings,

21 Jennifer Scarce, 'Muslim communities in Romania: presence and continuity', in Celia Hawkesworth, Muriel Heppel and Harry Norris (eds), *Religious Quest and National Identity in the Balkans* (London: Palgrave and School of Slavonic and East European Studies 2001), 158–67.

22 Nadège Ragaru, 'Islam et coexistence intercommunautaire en Boulgarie post-communiste', in Xavier Bougarel and Nathalie Clayer (eds), *Le Nouvel Islam balkanique: les musulmans, acteurs du post-communisme 1990–2000* (Paris: Maisonneuve et Larose 2001), 241–88.

23 Lapidus, *A History of Islamic Societies*, 198.

24 Janko Lavrin, 'Bogomils and Bogomilism', *Slavonic and East European Review*, vol. 8, 1929–30, 269–83.

25 Frank Chalk and Kurt Jonassohn, *The History and Sociology of Genocide: Analyses and Case Studies* (New Haven: Yale University Press 1990), 114–34.

26 Malcolm Burr, 'The code of Stephan Dušan, tsar and autocrat of the Serbs and Greeks', *Slavonic and East European Review*, vol. 28, 1949–50, 198–217, 516–39 (200).

the papacy and Franciscans organized crusades to suppress them.[27] Whatever the converts' religious background, however, conversions were initially 'gradual and slow' and, towards the end of the fifteenth century, Muslims represented less than 14 per cent of the total population of Bosnia.[28] This rose above 46 per cent several decades later as Ottoman triumphs at Belgrade and Mohács encouraged conversions. On the other hand, reversals in the naval battle of Lepanto (1571) and at the Croatian town of Sisak (1593) 'slowed the rate of Islamicisation'.[29]

The Ottoman military successes abroad and conversions to Islam in the Balkans fanned the flames of the anti-Turkish obsession, which was sparked by a fear of extinction and an urge to put paid to any uncertainty as to which faith was truer to God's word. The indigenous converts to Islam were by the end of the sixteenth century identified with the Turks and rejected alongside them as ethno-religious traitors.[30] By converting, they 'turned Turk', and were to be banished at the time of the Christian liberation from Islam. The anti-Turkish obsession had become anti-Muslim.

Unlike the converts to Islam, however, Protestants were not perceived as ethnic renegades, but as apostates and heretics. The Croatian Reformation theologian Matija Vlačić Franković Ilirik (1520–75)—a protegé of Luther and Melanchton, and a prominent Protestant scholar in his own right[31]—did not become German by converting to Protestantism, merely a heretic. His compatriots might shun him, and the Venetian authorities (whose subject he was) might execute him—like his relative Baldo Lupetina (1502–62), condemned to death by the Inquisition—but as a religious and not as an ethnic traitor. Muslim apostates were seen as double traitors—religious *and* ethnic—and thus 'wholly Other', alongside the Turks.[32]

Conversions between Catholicism and Eastern Orthodoxy were a case in the middle. The Bishop of Rome viewed his Orthodox colleagues as schismatics, even heretics, yet redeemable by the church union. The Uniate churches emerged this way, with clerics who married and followed Eastern Orthodox rites but recognized the primacy of Rome. Moreover, Catholic and Orthodox Christians remained coreligionists and, as long as they faced the Ottoman menace on their doorstep, they were allied against it. As that menace subsided, Catholic Croats and Orthodox Serbs became less tolerant

27 Noel Malcolm, *Bosnia: A Short History* (London: Macmillan 1994), 27–42.
28 Alexander Lopasic, 'Islam in the Balkans: the Bosnian case', in Hawkesworth, Heppel and Norris (eds), *Religious Quest and National Identity in the Balkans*, 141–57 (143).
29 Ibid., 145, 150.
30 Milica Bakić-Hayden, 'Nesting orientalisms: the case of former Yugoslavia', *Slavic Review*, vol. 54, no. 4, 1995, 917–31 (927).
31 Mijo Mirković, *Matija Vlačić Ilirik* (Zagreb: Jugoslavenska akademija znanosti i umjetnosti 1960), 74–121.
32 Milica Bakić-Hayden, 'National memory as narrative memory: the case of Kosovo', in Maria Todorova (ed.), *Balkan Identities: Nation and Memory* (London: Hurst 2004), 25–40 (35).

of each others' religious 'idiosyncrasies' and more likely to come into conflict. Only then would they consider the Muslim Slavs as compatriots, and indeed as allies, either against each other or the foreign overlords that replaced the Porte, primarily the Austrians and Hungarians.

With the waning of the Ottoman empire, the outright rejection of indigenous Muslims gave way to pressure to adopt their Slavic kin's ethnicity and become Croat or Serb Muslims. Advancing secularism favoured such identifications, as collective identities were decoupled from religion and linked rather with language. However, the emergence of Balkan Muslim ethnic identities impeded these developments. Bosnian Muslims adopted the old Bosniak identity, and ethno-religious boundaries solidified into battle lines: this was not due to perennial religious schisms beyond human control, but to their revival by contemporary political actors. Yet, while the Porte remained supreme in the Balkans, neither the Christian–Muslim Slav reconciliation nor the Catholic–Orthodox antagonism could become firmly entrenched. That started changing in the seventeenth century.

Reconquests and the Muslim exodus from Hungary and Croatia

The turn of the geopolitical tide was due to the exhaustion of the military *élan* of the Ottomans and the growing might of the Christian powers confronting them, backed by Rome. The latter's military successes, emissaries and frontiersmen incited Christian uprisings inside the Ottoman realm that were not forceful enough to break its hold over the Balkans but sufficient to weaken its authority. The Porte was further disadvantaged by facing adversaries on two fronts: Austria, Venice, Poland, Russia, Spain and the papacy in Europe, and the Safavid Persian empire in Asia.[33]

Yet the Porte suffered no serious setbacks in Europe until an inferior Polish–Cossack force repulsed an Ottoman army under Sultan Osman II in the battle of Chocim (1621). Osman soon perished in a Janissary revolt;[34] the Ottoman empire was in disarray, and Christendom rejoiced. A writer from Dubrovnik, Gjivo (or Ivan) Gundulić (1589–1638)—filled with 'hatred for Islam',[35] and hopeful that the long-awaited ebbing of Ottoman power had arrived[36]—idealized the victory in his unfinished 1638 epic *Osman*.[37] Circulated in handwritten copies until its completion

33 Goodwin, *Lords of the Horizons*, 164; Lapidus, *A History of Islamic Societies*, 234–7.
34 Edward D. Goy, 'Gundulić and his *Osman*', in Ivan Gundulić, *Osman*, trans. from the Croatian by Edward D. Goy (Zagreb: Jugoslavenska akademija znanosti i umjetnosti 1991), vii–xlv (xii).
35 Goy, 'Gundulić and his *Osman*', xvi.
36 Novak, *Zlatno doba*, 173.
37 Gundulić, *Osman*.

and publication in the nineteenth century, *Osman* was an instant success.[38] The anti-Turkish obsession had reached modernity hale and hardy.[39]

A more serious challenge to Ottoman rule in Europe occurred during the Veneto–Ottoman war of 1645–69. The Porte took Crete, triggering more conversions to Islam than ever before in Greek lands,[40] but merely held its own against the Venetian-backed Christian rebels and borderland irregulars in Dalmatia, Herzegovina and Montenegro.[41] The war brought no territorial changes in the Balkans, but it caused a shift of consciousness among the Christians. They no longer felt themselves to be abject victims of an overwhelming alien power, but the avengers of injuries inflicted on them in the past. The feeling that the Turks could be driven out of Europe resurfaced and turned against all Muslims alike.

The sense that mere resistance was a thing of the past and the time for offensive action had arrived provoked a proliferation of calls for European alliances to form in support of Christian insurrections in the Balkans. One such plan was submitted to the Russian court by Juraj Križanić (1618–83), a Croatian Catholic priest committed to pan-Christian and pan-Slav unification. Križanić was banished to Siberia for unclear reasons, and his treatise written in 1663–6 and known as *Politika*, which called upon the tsar to modernize and strengthen his realm, and help liberate his Slavic kin from the Turks, was ignored.[42] The manuscript lay in the Russian archives until the nineteenth century,[43] when it was published and joined the growing body of pan-Slav and Yugoslav ideological works that continued to be anti-Turkish and anti-Islamic.

Another advocate of a combined Christian offensive against the Ottomans was the early modern Croatian historian Ivan Lučić (1604–79). In 1666 he called for the combined forces of 'all Slavs who wish to throw off the Turkish

38 *Osman* was finished in 1844 by Ivan Mažuranić (1814–90), politician, poet and viceroy of Croatia. Mažuranić was the author of another noteworthy epic of Christian–Muslim relations in the Balkans: Ivan Mažuranić, *Smail-aga Cengić's Death* [1840], trans. from the Croatian by Charles A. Ward (Zagreb: Association of Croatian Writers 1969).

39 Ibid., 137.

40 Molly Greene, *A Shared World: Christians and Muslims in the Early Modern Mediterranean* (Princeton, NJ: Princeton University Press 2000), 39–40.

41 Gligor Stanojević, *Jugoslovenske zemlje u mletačko–turskim ratovima XVI–XVIII veka* (Belgrade: Istorijski institut 1970), 198–300.

42 Juraj Križanić (i.e. Iurii Krizhanich), *Russian Statecraft: The* Politika *of Iurii Krizhanich*, ed. and trans. from the Croatian by John M. Letiche and Basil Dmytryshyn (Oxford and New York: Basil Blackwell 1985); Ivan Golub, *Križanić* (Zagreb: Kršćanska sadašnjost 1987), 30.

43 Angelo Tamborra, 'La scoperta di Juraj Križanić nella seconda metà del sec. XIX e il suo significato', in Ljubo Boban (ed.), *Znanstveni skup u povodu 300. obljetnice smrti Jurja Križanića (1683–1983)*, vol. 2 (Zagreb: Jugoslavenska akademija znanosti i umjetnosti 1986), 303–15.

yoke' to 'break down the Ottoman empire'.[44] A similar proposal arrived in Moscow with the Transylvanian Serbian Orthodox bishop Sava, the elder brother of Count Đorđe Branković (1645–1711), pretender to the throne of an Illyrian kingdom to be erected on the ashes of the Ottoman empire.[45] Christian irregulars in the Austrian or Venetian service, and insurgent highlanders of Herzegovina, Montenegro and Albania meanwhile threw off 'the Turkish yoke' by marauding, mostly against the Muslim Slavs. These actions further weakened ethno-linguistic affinity between the Slavic Christians and Muslims, and reduced the differences between Catholic Croats and Orthodox Serbs.

The first serious Ottoman defeat in Europe came suddenly and unexpectedly. A vast Ottoman force besieging Vienna in 1683 was routed by a relief German–Polish army. This was followed by the Austrian (re)conquest of much of Hungary and Croatia, while the Serenissima took most of Dalmatia. As the Austrian armies and Christian insurgents broke into Serbia and Macedonia, Muslims from those areas fled to the remaining Ottoman lands.

In 1690 the Porte counterattacked—relieved by the Habsburg redeployment of troops to Germany after it was invaded by Louis XIV—and forced the Austrians across the Danube with thousands of Serbian refugees in train, including the patriarch of the Serbian Orthodox Church, Arsenije III. Emperor Leopold I granted them ethno-religious autonomy, but would not consider extending any privileges to the Muslims. They therefore fled to Bosnia, Herzegovina, Serbia and further southeast, fanning anti-Christian sentiments among their coreligionists.[46] Antagonistic interactions were increasing the homogeneity of the two religious camps, and further weakening the ethno-linguistic ties between the Christian and Muslim Slavs.

While the Austro-Venetians and Ottomans effected 'exchanges of populations' through war, a purge of Muslims began in Montenegro. Preserved in local tradition as a single event—which was glorified as righteous and heroic by the Montenegrin bishop-prince-poet Petar Petrović Njegoš[47]—it was more likely a lengthy Muslim exodus from the areas beyond Ottoman control to safer ground. This purge is remembered as *istraga poturica*, the total eradication, leaving no trace (*trag*) of those who became 'Turks' by converting to Islam.[48] Since the Ottomans were the arch-enemies of the Balkan

44 Giovanni Lucio (i.e. Ivan Lučić), *O kraljevstvu Dalmacije i Hrvatske* [1666] (Zagreb: Latina et Graeca VPA 1986), 361.

45 Jovan Radonić, *Grof Đorđe Branković i njegovo vreme* (Belgrade: Srpska kraljevska akademija 1911), 137–8.

46 Branislav Đorđe, Bogo Grafenauer and Jorjo Tadić, 'Sazrijevanje uvjeta za početak nacionalnih pokreta i oslobodilačke borbe', in Branislav Đorđe, Bogo Grafenauer and Jorjo Tadić (eds), *Historija naroda Jugoslavije*, vol. 2 (Zagreb: Školska knjiga 1959), 1390–6 (1392).

47 Petar Petrović Njegoš, *Gorski vijenac* (Vienna: Mehitarista 1847).

48 Gligor Stanojević, *Crna Gora u doba vladike Danila* (Cetinje: Istoriski Institut Crne Gore 1955), 31–44.

Christians, becoming 'Turk' meant committing ethno-religious treason, logically punishable by death or ostracism.

Wars of independence and Balkan Muslims

The next Muslim exodus occurred in the aftermath of the Serbian and Greek liberation wars of 1804–15 and 1821–9, respectively, which inspired Balkan nationalisms,[49] as well as a desire to remove all Muslims from the region. While the Greek and Serbian Christians celebrated their autonomy from the Porte, their Muslim ethno-linguistic kin bemoaned it because the provisions of the treaties between the Ottomans and their seceding provinces forbade 'Turks' from living in the countryside, limited their settlement to specific towns or required their removal. In 1830 the Porte thus ordained that 'no Turk except those who garrison the fortresses shall be allowed to inhabit Serbia'—autonomous within the Ottoman empire —allowing civilians 'a year of grace in which to sell their various properties'.[50]

By the mid-nineteenth century a general sense prevailed that Muslims did not belong to the nascent Balkan nation–states but to Turkey, and Turkey to Asia. (This sense has not dissipated to the present day, lingering on in the European rejection of Turks as 'Asiatics', and in characterizations of Balkan peoples as quasi-Orientals.[51]) This prompted and justified forced migrations of Muslims from Greece, Montenegro, Serbia, Bosnia and Herzegovina, Bulgaria, Crete and Macedonia, to Thrace and beyond. In Crete, even the Bektashi Muslims, traditionally on good terms with Christians, fled in droves 'after the troubles of 1897', such that their numbers in Iráklion and Réthimnon fell from 5,000 and 3,000, to 500 and 1,000, respectively.[52]

These expulsions were legitimized by European politicians and scholars who recalled the old anti-Turkish obsession in their scornful censure of brutal 'Asiatic' Turkish rule over the Balkans. During the First Balkan War of 1912, Sir Arthur Evans hailed the Balkan alliance that had taken from 'Asiatic keeping' and 'reclaimed for European civilization ... a long roll of ancient sites and cities freed at last from the Turkish incubus',[53] the

49 Leften Stavros Stavrianos, *The Balkans 1815–1914* (New York: Holt, Rinehart and Winston 1966), 19–29.
50 T. W. Riker, 'Michael of Serbia and the Turkish occupation I', *Slavonic and East European Review*, vol. 12, 1933–4, 133–54 (135); Miladin Stevanović, *Drugi srpski ustanak* (Gornji Milanovac: Dečje novine 1990), 163.
51 Bakić-Hayden, 'Nesting orientalisms', 918.
52 Frederick William Hasluck, *Christianity and Islam under the Sultans* [1929], ed. Margaret M. Hasluck (Mansfield Centre, CT: Martino Publishing 2006), 534.
53 Arthur J. Evans, 'The drama of the Balkans and its closing scenes', *Contemporary Review*, vol. 102, 1912, 761–76 (761).

same incubus invoked by Leften Stavros Stavrianos half a century later.[54] The death of such a spectre was welcomed, not least because 'Turkey has been for many years passing through the last phase of a declining dynasty' and engaging in 'terrorism', like the 'massacres' in Bulgaria, Bosnia and Herzegovina,[55] largely committed by the 'feudal lords and their retainers' or 'irregular forces' of indigenous Muslims.[56] Such views underpinned the presumption that the Ottoman empire was inherently and exceptionally oppressive. But was that the case?

Contradictory claims regarding the Ottoman reign

Historians from the Balkans and beyond have long argued that Ottoman rule in Europe was a 500-year enslavement that deprived its Christians subjects of a dignified existence,[57] and 'half smothered' them 'under the heavy mantle of Orientalism'.[58] Others counter that this image of the Ottoman state is a myth 'fostered in the nineteenth century by the various Balkan peoples ... fired by their ... national consciousness',[59] and that the Porte was fairly tolerant of non-Muslim religions, both for fiscal reasons and because of sharia law, which requires toleration of scripturians, People of the Book.[60] Some stress that, in the Ottoman realm, 'the distinction between the rulers and the ruled was not the same as that between the Muslims and non-Muslims', because 'the ruling elites and the subject populations included both'.[61] And, while 'irregularities and abuses were fairly common in the Ottoman judicial system', the Porte, and 'especially Suleiman the Magnificent, issued special *kanuns* ... to curb corruption'.[62]

54 Leften Stavros Stavrianos, 'Antecedents to the Balkan revolutions of the nineteenth century', *Journal of Modern History*, vol. 29, no. 4, 1957, 335–48 (342).
55 Arthur J. Evans, 'W. Denton, *The Christians of Turkey: their Condition under Mussulman Rule*; Anonymous, *Slavs and Turks: the Border-Lands of Islam in Europe*' (review), *Academy*, vol. 238, New Series, 1876, 511–12 (512).
56 Evans, 'The drama of the Balkans and its closing scenes', 765, 766.
57 Oskar Halecki, *Borderlands of Western Civilization: A History of East Central Europe* (New York: Ronald Press 1952), 159; Alex N. Dragnich, 'The rise and fall of Yugoslavia: the omen of the upsurge of Serbian nationalism', *East European Quarterly*, vol. 23, no. 2, 1989, 183–98.
58 A. Angeloff, 'Why nationalism flames in the Balkans', *Current History*, vol. 28, no. 3, 1928, 435–41 (435).
59 Stavrianos, *The Balkans since 1453*, 96–7.
60 Justin McCarthy, *The Ottoman Turks: An Introductory History to 1923* (London: Longman 1999), 127.
61 Lapidus, *A History of Islamic Societies*, 264; see also Stanford J. Shaw, 'The aims and achievements of Ottoman rule in the Balkans', *Slavic Review*, vol. 21, no. 4, 1962, 617–22.
62 Wayne S. Vucinich, *The Ottoman Empire: Its Record and Legacy* (Princeton, NJ, Toronto and London: D. Van Nostrand 1965), 39.

The Ottoman state was merely antagonistically tolerant, and many conversions to Islam were forced, part of *devşirme*, a levy on children practised between the fourteenth or fifteenth and seventeenth centuries.[63] Countless young boys were taken away every few years, circumcised, converted to Islam, raised as Muslims and enrolled into the elite Ottoman infantry, the Janissaries.[64] Süleyman the Magnificent's Grand Vizier, Mehmed Paşa Sokollu, a native of Bosnia, was such a convert who rose through the military ranks to a level of authority second only to the sultan. Yet most conversions were voluntary, prompted by the desire for social promotion in the Islamic theocracy,[65] by a need to deflect the outbursts of Muslim 'anti-Christian fanaticism',[66] the *Doppelgänger* of Christian anti-Islamic obsession, by personal circumstances, such as marriage to a Muslim,[67] or because of a sincere conviction that there was no god but Allah and that Muhammad was indeed his prophet.

Devşirme was among the foremost Christian grievances against the Ottomans, reviled as oppressive and cruel. Yet, the Ottomans were not alone in vile practices. Their Christian foes in the Venetian or Austrian service—Uskoks, Morlachs and *hajduki*, often hailed as freedom fighters—routinely sold their Muslim (and sometimes Christian) captives into slavery, mostly in Italy, the cradle of humanism and the Renaissance. None would become potentates there. Slavery flourished in Süleyman the Magnificent's empire, as it did in the Portuguese, Spanish, English, French and other Christian realms. But while *devşirme* disappeared in the seventeenth century, the offspring of slaves in the United States 'had next to no guaranties against indiscriminate separation from their parents' two centuries later,[68] and their promotion to positions of power took another century. Being an Ottoman slave was bad. Being a British, French, Portuguese, Spanish or American slave might have been worse.

The Ottomans were theocratic; they privileged their religion and practised a premodern form of apartheid known as the *millet* system, which segregated ethno-religious groupings within the empire spatially, culturally, economically and politically.[69] And, while scripturians were free to practise their religion, they could not proselytize or build any new temples without permission, because the Porte was merely antagonistically tolerant. The Ottoman rulers and military were often brutal towards their Christian subjects or captives, and their rule *was* often arbitrary, corrupt and cruel.

63 Hasluck, *Christianity and Islam under the Sultans*, 487; Vucinich, *The Ottoman Empire*, 14; Stavrianos, *The Balkans since 1453*, 39.
64 Hasluck, *Christianity and Islam under the Sultans*, 485.
65 Ibid., 450.
66 Ibid., 471.
67 Ibid., 454.
68 Stanley M. Elkins, *Slavery: A Problem in American Institutional and Intellectual Life* (Chicago: University of Chicago Press 1959), 54.
69 McCarthy, *The Ottoman Turks*, 127–32.

Their troops raided, pillaged, killed, raped, razed and enslaved, and they were widely perceived as vicious torturers.[70]

Yet, on the Christian side, Huguenots were nearly annihilated in France by religious wars and massacres, such as the one on St Bartholomew's Night in 1572; Catholics were barely tolerated in Protestant Britain and oppressed in Ireland; Russia would not tolerate Catholics, Protestants or followers of the Old Creed; Jews were persecuted or banished from much of Europe until the late eighteenth century; and Muslims were eradicated or greatly reduced in numbers from Portugal and Spain to the Balkans, Ukraine and Russia. Europe was antagonistically *in*tolerant. Moreover, 'the pleasures of the torture chamber' were well appreciated by the holy fathers of Christendom,[71] and by most, if not all, civilizations.[72]

The Porte was exploitative, especially after its expansion faltered and the spoils of war or tributes from subjugated polities dwindled. Before that, Christian plebaeians often found Ottoman fiscal demands less onerous than those of the Christian lords. It seems that the lower classes in at least some parts of the Balkans did not feel that their lot under the Porte was overly oppressive. So, while the Ottomans were viewed with apprehension understandable in a conquered population, the anti-Turkish obsession emerged gradually, due to military reverses and the declining power of the Porte, no less than to its earlier ascendancy.

A mixture of loathing and admiration in late fifteenth-century accounts of the Ottomans gave way to belligerent spitefulness after the Porte reached Vienna under Süleyman the Magnificent.[73] The failure of any significant further conquests strained the Ottoman empire's finances, in turn making its administration at once more repressive and more resented.[74] The double pressure of Balkan Christian resistance backed by Austria, Russia or Venice compelled the Porte to abandon magnanimity and resort to punitive

---

70 See George Ryley Scott, *A History of Torture throughout the Ages* (London: Bracken Books 1994), 209, 216; Edward Peters, *Torture* (Oxford: Blackwell 1985), 94–5; Bonnie Millar-Heggie, 'Sanctity, savagery and Saracens in Capystranus: fifteenth century Christian–Ottoman relations', *Al-Masāq*, vol. 14, no. 2, 2002, 113–21.

71 John Swain, *The Pleasure of the Torture Chamber* (London: Noel Douglas 1931).

72 Scott, *A History of Torture throughout the Ages*; Georges Bataille, *Les Larmes d'Éros*, revd edn (Paris: Jean-Jacques Pauvert 1971).

73 Albrecht Classen, 'The world of the Turks described by an eye-witness: Georgius de Hungaria's dialectical discourse on the foreign world of the Ottoman empire', *Journal of Early Modern History*, vol. 7, no. 3–4, 2003, 257–79; Gunther E. Rothenberg, 'Aventius and the defense of the empire against the Turks', *Studies in the Renaissance*, vol. 10, 1963, 60–7; Nina Berman, 'Ottoman shock-and-awe and the rise of Protestantism: Luther's reactions to the Ottoman invasions of the early sixteenth century', *Seminar*, vol. 41, no. 3, 2005, 226–45.

74 Traian Stoianovich, 'Factors in the decline of Ottoman society in the Balkans', *Slavic Review*, vol. 21, no. 4, 1962, 623–32; Peter F. Sugar, 'Major changes in the life of the Slav peasantry under Ottoman rule', *International Journal of Middle East Studies*, vol. 9, no. 3, 1978, 297–305.

campaigns. These were immediately labelled, and long evoked, as 'the Turkish reign of terror', carried out by 'Asiatic barbarians' who therefore deserved banishment from Europe.[75] Whether it was deserved or not, the Turks entered the twentieth century as widely loathed and feared ethno-religious foes repugnant to Christendom. Such sentiments engendered the rejection of both Turkish and non-Turkish Muslims, slotting the latter for eradication as those who turned 'Turk' and betrayed Christendom, Europe and their own Balkan ethnic kin.

The fall of the Ottoman empire and after

At the opening of the twentieth century the Ottoman empire was nearing its end. Bosnia and Herzegovina, occupied by Austria–Hungary in 1878, were annexed by it in 1908. In the First Balkan War (1912), the alliance of Bulgaria, Greece, Montenegro and Serbia took from the Ottomans all but eastern Thrace with Istanbul. In the First World War the Porte collapsed and was replaced by a secular Turkish republic. Its European provinces became a topsy-turvy social world in which the Muslims were ruled by their former underlings everywhere but in Albania.[76] Moreover, they were demographically in decline.

In Bosnia and Herzegovina, the number of Muslims increased, but their share of the population declined from 38.7 to 32.3 per cent between 1878 and 1910.[77] In Bulgaria, their numbers declined absolutely and relatively, from 21.4 to 15 per cent, or to 676,215 out of *c*. 3.2 million in 1890.[78] In 1890 Croatia–Slavonia and Hungary registered no Muslims;[79] Greece recorded 13,163 out of *c*. 2.2 million people,[80] Serbia, 16,764 out of *c*. 2.1 million,[81] and Romania, 46,082 out of *c*. 5 million.[82]

75 Vladimir Dedijer, Ivan Božić, Sima Ćirković and Milorad Ekmečić, *History of Yugoslavia*, trans. from the Serbian by Kordija Kveder (New York: McGraw-Hill 1974), 192; Mark Mazower, *The Balkans* (London: Weidenfeld and Nicolson 2000), 10.
76 Alexandre Popovic, *L'Islam balkanique: les musulmans du sud-est européen dans la période post-ottomane* (Wiesbaden: Otto Harrassowitz 1986), 15; Ger Duijzings, *Religion and the Politics of Identity in Kosovo* (New York: Columbia University Press 2000), 158–65.
77 Popovic, *L'Islam balkanique*, 271.
78 Glavna Direktsiya na Statistikata—Direction Génerale de la Statistique, *Statisticheski Godishnik' na B'lgarskogo Tsarstvo, godina p'rva 1909—Annuaire Statistique du Royaume de Bulgarie, première année 1909* (Sofia: D'rzhavna pechatnitsa—Imprimerie de l'État 1910), 38; Jacques Bertillon, *Statistique internationale résultant des recensements de la population exécutés dans les divers pays de l'Europe pendant le XIXe siècle et les époques précédentes* (Paris: G. Masson 1899), 155.
79 Bertillon, *Statistique internationale*, 80, 83.
80 Ibid., 151.
81 Ibid., 159.
82 Ibid., 163.

After the First World War, Greece and Turkey fought a war and 'exchanged populations': Christians had to leave Turkey and Muslims Greece, regardless of ethno-linguistic background. Muslims were better off in Yugoslavia, where they often entered ruling coalitions. During the Second World War, some joined the Communist-led partisans fighting against the Nazi–Fascist occupation by Germany, Italy, Hungary, Bulgaria and Italian-dominated Albania, and against the local fascists and royalists. Others joined the Croatian Ustaše regime, allied to Germany and Italy—which recognized them as Croats—and some joined the Muslim 13th Division of the Nazi SS.[83]

After the war, the Communist Yugoslav government recognized Muslim Serbo–Croat speakers as an ethnic group and nation, and registered them as such in the 1971 census, ten years after President Tito pronounced the issue of a Slav Muslim nationality to be 'nonsense'.[84] Elsewhere in the Balkans, Communist regimes proclaimed religious tolerance *and* a secular state— a modern avatar of antagonistic tolerance—while Greece regarded Muslims as virtually extinct as did Turkey its Christians. The Christian–Muslim conflict seemed to have come to an end, one way or another.

But not for long. The failed annexation of Cyprus by Greece in 1974 revived the old anti-Islamic obsession that continues to keep the Turkish part of the island out of the European Union. The Communist regimes of Europe meanwhile embraced nationalism to shore up their diminishing legitimacy, only to reawaken the ethno-religious identities that would, in the first instance, help topple them and, then, turn them against each other. By the time the Yugoslav federation broke up, a century of Christian and secular dominance in the Balkans had engendered a sense both of ethno-religious affinity among the Balkan Muslims *and* Christians, and of mutual animosity that contributed to antagonistic interactions.

This stand-off is reinforced by the resurgence of ethno-religious atavisms in the Balkans and beyond.[85] Europeans of the 'old' and 'new' continents tend to harbour profound prejudices about Muslims and non-Europeans, regarding them as socio-culturally regressive *and* aggressive, bent on undermining the European social order and way of life. Muslims and non-Europeans perceive Christians and Europeans as politico-economically aggressive and repressive, bent on undermining societies and cultures unlike their own. The latter view appears in *The Islamic Declaration: A Programme for the Islamization of Muslims and the Muslim Peoples*, penned by the Muslim president of Bosnia and Herzegovina four decades ago.[86]

---

83 Enver Redžić, *Muslimansko autonomaštvo i 13. SS divizija: Autonomija Bosne i Hercegovine i Hitlerov Treći Rajh* (Sarajevo: Svjetlost 1987), 81–90.

84 Atif Purivatra, *Nacionalni i politički razvitak Muslimana: rasprave i članci* (Sarajevo: Svjetlost 1969), 13.

85 Tariq Ali, *The Clash of Fundamentalisms: Crusades, Jihads and Modernity* (London: Verso 2003).

86 Alija Izetbegović, *The Islamic Declaration: A Programme for the Islamization of Muslims and the Muslim Peoples* [1970] (Sarajevo 1990).

The post-1995 Bosnian Muslim educational system may not be taking this 'programme' to its extremes, but it does demonstrate a turn to Islamic authors and content in school textbooks. A struggle for the minds of believers is on, pitting the relatively liberal interpretations of Islam traditionally hegemonic in Bosnia against more fundamentalist imports.[87] The triumph of the latter—uncertain but imaginable—would likely hamper the secularization of society and aggravate Muslim–Christian relations, as it cannot fail to arouse its Christian twin.

On the Christian side, school curricula exhibit ethnocentrism and Eurocentrism, including a turn away from broader Balkan or Yugoslav themes to narrowly ethno-national (Albanian, Croatian, Romanian, Serbian or Slovenian) ones, with Macedonia being one possible exception.[88] This distancing of ethnic communities may be beneficial as a respite, allowing all sides to move beyond past conflicts, but it could also mark merely a lull in ongoing ethno-religious antagonisms.

The way beyond such an outcome does not attract many travellers, as it necessitates the transcendence of the presently ubiquitous twin influences of the cultural monism of religion and the political monism of ethnocracy on public life. This might be achievable by means of tolerant, yet vigorous secularism and cultural relativism in public life, and the relegation of ethnic and religious beliefs, histories and rituals to homes, temples, collective memories and myths. The entrenchment of theocratic and/or ethnocratic authoritarianism near the centres of political power increases the likelihood that the *danse macabre* of antagonistic ethno-religious interactions may resume in the future, and there appears to be neither the social consciousness nor the political will to head another way—in the Balkans and elsewhere.

87 Smail Balić, 'Islamic religious education in Bosnia', in Christina Koulouri (ed.), *Clio in the Balkans: The Politics of History Education* (Thessaloniki: Center for Democracy and Reconciliation in Southeast Europe 2002), 339–43.
88 Valentina Duka, 'Albania'; Snježana Koren, 'Croatia'; Mirela-Luminiţa Murgescu, 'Romania'; Dubravka Stojanovic, 'Yugoslavia'; Božo Repe, 'Slovenia'; and Emilija Simoska, 'FYR Macedonia', all in Koulouri (ed.), *Clio in the Balkans*, 475–8, 479–81, 497–500, 538, 501–2 and 495–6, respectively.

Can the walls hear?

GIL ANIDJAR

ABSTRACT   In order for walls to hear, they first need to be erected. Anidjar's essay is concerned with the walls and divisions that have long isolated the Christian West from its Others, while functioning to divide and separate these Others from themselves and from each other. These walls are also, first of all or finally, internal divisions (religion and politics, antisemitism and Islamophobia etc.) that constitute and structure *prejudice* as a singular mode of self-identification that is also a self-denial ('the West doesn't exist', 'secularity is not Christianity'). An anthropology of Christianity.

The time of the ear dooms it to obsolescence.
                    —Charles Hirschkind[1]

But the domestic circumstances are, in my view, more interesting.
                    —Talal Asad[2]

What Martin Harries describes as 'one of the more haunting of the spectral moments in the writings of Adam Smith' articulates something like a thought experiment, imagining something that appears all too obvious today, even necessary and unavoidable. Blissfully ignorant of what Euro-America would come to experience after 9/11, 'Smith imagines that we might sympathize with the dead'. Such exercise of the imagination seems awkward and anachronistic today for who would want to withhold or question sympathy? Whose imagination has failed by now to be learned in the experience of sympathy? That some, among the dead, appear more worthy of sympathy than others is not in doubt, it may even be inevitable, yet what Harries rightly points out as remarkable is that, for Smith, this

1 Charles Hirschkind, *The Ethical Soundscape: Cassette Sermons and Islamic Counterpublics* (New York: Columbia University Press 2006), 27.
2 Talal Asad, *Genealogies of Religion: Discipline and Reasons of Power in Christianity and Islam* (Baltimore and London: Johns Hopkins University Press 1993), 272.

sympathy itself has to be interrogated. In fact, as much as we have come to take it for granted, the sympathy of which Smith writes is unavoidably marked by failure, 'the inevitable failure and significant consequences of such sympathy'. Harries accounts for this failure by limpidly explaining that the motion of this emotion, though highly dynamic, never quite reaches its object. It is rather 'a road that travels from the self all the way to the projections that self has cast onto the condition of the dead'. It represents no more than a 'detour'. (One thinks of Freud's famous comment on life as a kind of detour taken by death as it turns and returns to itself.) This specific detour 'never reaches any "other" at all'. Nor does it reach back, in any precise sense, to a self to speak of. On this road, getting there is more than half the fun, most of it really, since the trajectory consists of the peripatetic articulation of a division *as* self. Steeped in imagination, and sympathy, our relation to the dead, or, more precisely, the sympathy with the dead that has become our lot, the obviousness of our relation to 'them', all of this has no more than a 'fictional status', for both self and Other. It is, in Harries's rendition, 'a mistaking of a fantasy of self for an other'. Still, we go on sympathizing, and everything is as if the dead were our proper addressees. And we theirs. We do carry on, on this road most travelled, imagining the dead and sympathizing with them. More than that, and crucially so, 'we imagine that their existence is like ours, only marked by a much greater dreariness'. This is where our imagination turns out to have 'real social consequences', and all the more so because it habitually deploys 'a powerful force founded on epistemological error'. What does this force do? According to Harries, it 'guards and protects society'. Our sympathy with the dead, in other words, erects walls around us.[3]

Like the selves they enclose or exclude, these walls may be figures, at times even fictions, yet they constitute extensions and effects of a peculiar and particular subject, the structure, habits and affects of which can be recognized in its relation to a wide set of fictions, with 'real social consequences', whereby the existence of Others is repeatedly imagined, more or less like ours, though 'marked by a much greater dreariness' (that is why we must help them, of course, and emancipate them—or at least their women—from their dreary existence, eradicate them if need be, for their own good). The emotions thereby aroused in this collective self are sometimes recognizable as the enactment of sympathy, but equally often as that of a kind of antipathy, even hatred. (Harries earlier evokes 'the desire to witness destruction', perhaps also for 'self-destruction' and the fact of a 'lethal politics'.[4]) Sympathy, Adam Smith knew, is therefore a complicated matter, since, more often than not, the peculiar and collective self here at work 'experiences'—in a manner that could not be reduced to the

3 Martin Harries, *Forgetting Lot's Wife: On Destructive Spectatorship* (New York: Fordham University Press 2007), 111–12.
4 Ibid., 98, 114.

psychological—at once attraction *and* revulsion. The fictional object of its attention is thereby also divided according to a familiar (perhaps even familial) script. It is a body that has been 'imagined as divided, fragmented, and distributed in new and ever-stranger ways'.[5] What remains more or less stable, I think, is that one element is deemed worthy of sympathy, the other deserving of hatred.[6]

We are more than closely acquainted with this phenomenon in the history of prejudice, and it is to some extent banal to recall it. There are, however, reasons to revisit the recurring and polymorphous revivals and reiterations this enduring phenomenon takes, along with its real social consequences. I am referring, of course, to the fictional status and division of 'woman' into the virgin and the whore, but also to the division of 'the Jew' in modern France into *juif* and *Israélite*, or, in pre-Nazi Germany, into 'Germans of the Mosaic confession' and *Ostjuden* (Oriental Jews). One may also think, and even more so today perhaps, of the deep connections between philo- and antisemitism. One thinks most readily of what Mahmood Mamdani has so aptly described under the title of 'good Muslim, bad Muslim'.[7] All of these are but a few instances intended to recall otherwise well-known iterations of the phenomenon Adam Smith asks us to imagine and interrogate under the figure of our emotional investments and affective dispositions, however benevolent. Again and again, a detour that 'never reaches any "other" at all' articulates itself around sympathy and even love (and antipathy and hatred), affirms the existence of Others *as we imagine them*, an existence construed to be more or less like ours, 'only marked by a much greater dreariness'.

What is important to note here, I think, is that these supple if also stable forms of 'affective, kinesthetic, and gestural modalities of bodily experience within processes of ethical learning' have had, and indeed continue to have profound social and political consequences.[8] Their emotional significance—even if we assume that emotions are psychological before they are political—is secondary at the very least. It certainly pales in

---

5 Ibid., 94.
6 Talal Asad discusses 'empathy' in proximate terms when he argues that 'the European wish to make the world in its own image is not necessarily to be disparaged as ungenerous. If one believes oneself to be the source of salvation, the wish to make others reflect oneself is not unbenign, however terrible the practices by which this desire is put into effect' (Asad, *Genealogies of Religion*, 12).
7 Mahmood Mamdani, *Good Muslim, Bad Muslim: America, the Cold War, and the Roots of Terror* (New York: Pantheon 2004).
8 Hirschkind, *The Ethical Soundscape*, 83. I borrow from Hirschkind's gripping 'anthropology of sensual reason', its subtle descriptions of affective potentialities and modalities, and his elaboration of 'listening as performance', for the powerful supplement, and counterpoint, it provides to what Harries argues is the twentieth century's 'particular investment in a formal logic that placed the spectator in a spot where that spectator had to contemplate her own destruction' (Harries, *Forgetting Lot's Wife*, 9). My title is meant to gesture, however, inadequately, towards the kind of auditory ethics Hirschkind describes so eloquently.

comparison with the force of its historical and institutional endurance. It has long constituted a privileged and rapidly mutating means whereby our society is guarded and protected. At a time when this guard and protection—call it 'the war on terror'—takes the increasingly concrete form of concrete walls, which incidentally make perfectly visible the contours of the peculiar self I have begun to describe, it may also be time to ask about the 'we' that speaks it, that speaks and enacts its simultaneous unity and division. It may be time broadly to acknowledge that, 'although the West contains many faces at home, it presents a single face abroad'.[9] It is time—but perhaps it is already too late—to ask not whether the subaltern can speak, but whether the walls can hear.

Good Semite, bad Semite

Following Edward Said's claim that, retrieving the history of Orientalism (and that aspect of which we might call today anti-Muslim prejudice, indeed, Islamophobia), he found himself, 'by an almost inescapable logic . . . writing the history of a strange, secret sharer of Western anti-Semitism',[10] I have tried to elaborate an argument that follows lines of thought akin to those with which I began the present essay. In Said's claim, as I understand it, it is western Christendom that constitutes and maintains itself trans-historically as a stable if elusive subject, projecting itself—with real social and political consequences—on to the condition of two enemies. Otherwise put, 'the Jew, the Arab' (Judaism and Islam, if you will) constitute the condition of religion and politics.[11] The two are more aptly thought of as one, however, along the difficult unity and separation of specifically Christian theologico-political faultlines. True to the famous division of the king's body, which Ernst Kantorowicz documented, they are 'the enemy's two bodies'.[12] It is in relation to such divided projection that this peculiar collective self, western Christendom, endures.[13] It does its work of identification, 'a mistaking of a fantasy of self for an other'. Surrounded and divided by walls, this self, this subject, is no essence, therefore. It is rather the evolving work of an

---

9   Talal Asad, *Formations of the Secular: Christianity, Islam, Modernity* (Stanford: Stanford University Press 2003), 13.

10 Edward W. Said, *Orientalism* (New York: Vintage 1979), 27.

11 Gil Anidjar, *The Jew, the Arab: A History of the Enemy* (Stanford: Stanford University Press 2003), xi.

12 Ernst Kantorowicz, *The King's Two Bodies: A Study in Mediaeval Political Theology* (Princeton: Princeton University Press 1997).

13 I have begun to elaborate on the historical—rather than essential—lines of continuity within Christianity (i.e. western Christendom) in my *The Jew, the Arab* and since. I take it that Harries articulates a proximate position when he argues against 'the persistence of the power of a figurative reading' at work in 'destructive spectatorship' (Harries, *Forgetting Lot's Wife*, 113).

imagination—and of a set of affects, like sympathy—that impersonates an otherwise changing and divided self, and enemy. As I will argue in the second part of this essay, it gives itself the political forms—and force—to cast its condition on to the enemy within and beyond the wall. Thus, following the logic of internal division that I have outlined, the enemy is never one. Nor is the Christian West (and its secular divisions). In this particular and peculiar context, there is never one undivided self and always more than one enemy. And so the Jew, the Arab, in my argument, testify primarily and precisely to the self-divided *endurance* of Christianity, in so far as it has spent much time on a popular route, on that 'road that travels from the self all the way to the projections that self has cast', this detour that 'never reaches any "other" at all' but may well be deadly to those identified with it. In the end, Martin Harries aptly writes, 'we may learn as much about how we imagine subjects from how we imagine their destruction as from how we imagine the ways in which they are made'.[14] The Jew, the Arab: good Semite, bad Semite.

11 September 2001 brought no fundamental change (the walls—with or without ears—had been planned and even erected long beforehand), although it may have constituted an intensification of the divided, and divisive, dialectic of sympathy and antipathy that defines western Christendom and its history. We speak from within it (from within walls), from within 'a universe of forms of identification', forms that 'tend to incorporate—and, by incorporating, to annihilate—the other'.[15] It speaks in and through us, whether it presents itself as the 'Judaeo-Christian tradition' or as the agent of the seemingly universal, if contested, values of freedom, democracy and the American dream. There is no question that it speaks, nor that it has the ability to erect walls to define its boundaries: south of the American border, the Schengen borders around the European Union and, most particularly, on the North African coast, in Israel/Palestine, the West continues its 'mistaking of a fantasy of self for an other', guarding and protecting society. More than any conceptual argument, the walls erected to guard and protect our societies participate in defining an elusive subject, no doubt, but a collective self nonetheless, one that carries efficacious, if also changing, names. Beyond the unavoidable work of paleonymy (why *this* name rather than *that* name), there are the enduring operations of sympathy—and antipathy. Divide and rule. And so, once again, the Jew, the Arab. Or good Muslim, bad Muslim. I mean: good Semite, bad Semite.[16]

In what follows, I want to pursue an examination of sorts into some of the enduring walls and divisions cast on to the world, divisions that effectively prevent still something like a *reflexive* history of the enemy: a domestic and inward-looking history, or anthropology, of a collective subject, western Christendom, as a peculiar prejudice, as a mode of governance and as the

---

14 Harries, *Forgetting Lot's Wife*, 15.
15 Ibid., 114, 113.
16 See my *Semites: Race, Religion, Literature* (Stanford: Stanford University Press 2008).

networks of power that constitute and sustain it, guarding and protecting it. Who or what is the subject of this history? What is its substance, if any, and attributes? How does it operate in the world? This is not an enquiry into the putative addressee of prejudice, but an internal, indeed, *domestic* interrogation, for, as Talal Asad succinctly puts it, it is the 'domestic circumstances' that are 'more interesting'.[17]

Before I go on, though, I want to clarify this attempt at self-reflexivity (a hopefully thoughtful engagement with, among others, motives—motions and emotions), a contribution, as it were, to 'the anthropology of Christianity'.[18] Such an anthropology would correspond, as Asad explains, to a reading of texts and contexts focused on the hither side of things, on the road that travels 'from the self all the way to the projections that self has cast'. Consider therefore the significance of the 'we' that Asad upholds and interrogates in the following call for a self-reflexive and critical endeavour to come.

> In all the recent concerns with writing ethnographies, we have tended to pay insufficient attention to the problem of reading and using them, to the motives we bring to bear in our readings, and to the seductions of text and context we all experience. In reading ... we inevitably reproduce aspects of ourselves, although this is not simply a matter of arbitrary preference or prejudice. We are all already-constituted subjects, placed in networks of power, and in reproducing ourselves it is also the latter we reproduce. To do otherwise is to risk confronting the powers that give us the sense of who we are, and to embark on a dangerous task of reconstructing ourselves along unfamiliar lines. It is, understandably, easier to use our readings to confirm those powers.[19]

Our projections, our readings—the motives we bring to bear, and the seductions of texts and contexts—can, and do, deploy and reinscribe the 'networks of power' within which we find ourselves. They build and rebuild the walls that guard and protect society, and partake of its reproduction; they tread the well-travelled roads upon which we are constituted. On these roads, on these projective readings, we produce and reproduce ourselves and reaffirm the enabling condition of our social and political existence. It is, however, one thing to enjoy the privilege of blissful ignorance (or ever more brilliant knowledge). It is another to justify and legitimize it. No doubt, to behave otherwise, to read otherwise, involves turning ourselves inside out,

17 Asad, *Genealogies of Religion*, 270, 272.
18 Elsewhere, I try to follow Talal Asad and his considerations on 'The idea of an anthropology of Islam' in order to argue for a different asymmetric endeavour, an anthropology of Christianity, which I find operative, although not unproblematically, throughout Asad's work. I am hardly alone in this enterprise, of course, as a volume by that title also follows Asad's lead: Fenella Cannell (ed.), *The Anthropology of Christianity* (Durham, NC: Duke University Press 2006).
19 Asad, *Genealogies of Religion*, 270.

turning internal divisions ('aspects of ourselves', 'networks of power') into domestic sites of confrontations. It is at any rate no wonder that such turns on to less travelled roads, if at all possible (can the walls hear?), tend to appear as part of a confrontation, the adoption of denunciatory endeavour, or worse. Sometimes, and this may be unavoidable, it bears all the attributes and semblance of an accusatory saying.

Were it possible, an anthropology of Christianity would by definition appear to take this kind of confrontational and accusatory pose, for it would have to consist in an *exposure* of western Christendom, albeit from within. At the very least, it would have to unfold the trajectory of forms of identification that resist, precisely, identification. That is why exposure must be understood less as the effect of a determined Other located in a position of exteriority than as the consequence of internal folds and pre-emptive divisions, such as those we have begun to consider, indeed, to uncover. From within 'domestic circumstances', then, there emerges a subject that speaks and reads (or projects, as Harries describes) and is *thereby* exposed. What Emmanuel Levinas refers to, in a proximate context, as a 'saying' is or gives rise to this exposure, which must be thought of as reflexive and self-critical, rather than as a pronunciation (or denunciation) that would come from some presumed outside. From within, then, there resonates a saying that 'uncovers the one that speaks, not as an object disclosed by theory, but in the sense that one discloses *oneself* by neglecting one's defenses, leaving a shelter'.[20] Through it, the walls come down that have been erected, as this saying also casts and projects—in the name of Europe, of the United States of America, of modernity or of western civilization, of progress and enlightenment, of democracy and human rights—all otherwise unproblematic assertions of a subject quite convinced of its existence, and unified in its purpose, over against undeniable divisions. Intentionality may remain an aspiration to be filled, but 'the centripetal movement of a consciousness that coincides with itself, recovers, and rediscovers itself ... rests in self-certainty, confirms itself, doubles itself up, consolidates itself, thickens into a substance'.[21] Its walls must therefore be at once acknowledged (as intended and unintended effects and consequences) and brought down in order for it to turn itself inside out (the subject's 'bending back upon itself is a turning inside out'), in order for the subject to be described as a self.[22] Understood in this way, an anthropology of Christianity would have to *correspond* to a certain passivity, the domestic account or experience of an exposure. This co-respondence—if one can spell the word in this awkward fashion—is already a *response*, however. Levinas writes: 'The passivity of the exposure *responds* to an assignation that identifies me as the unique one,

20 Emmanuel Levinas, *Otherwise Than Being, or, Beyond Essence*, trans. from the French by Alphonso Lingis (Pittsburgh: Duquesne University Press 1999), 49, emphasis added.
21 Ibid., 48.
22 Ibid., 49.

not by reducing me to myself, but by stripping me of every identical quiddity, and thus of all form, all investiture, which would still slip into the assignation.'[23] And, although Levinas speaks here of a singular self, he enables a recovery of the structures whereby the collective self that interests us here always already experiences its description as assignation, as a self under accusation. To add to it, while unavoidable, only compounds the problem. It may even heighten the walls. In Levinas's concise formulation, at any rate: 'The subject is described as a self, from the first in the accusative form (or under accusation!).'[24]

Whether intended or not, then, this accusation—or its semblance—is constitutive of an anthropology of Christianity. It is the effect of an affirmation of a self, called upon to answer regardless of its place, hereby situated in 'the null-site [*non-lieu*] of subjectivity, where the privilege of the question "Where" no longer holds'.[25] The accusative—an identification of forms of identification as the constitution of a self—'derives from no nominative; it is the very fact of finding oneself while losing oneself'.[26] Ultimately, 'it is someone who, in the absence of anyone is called upon to be someone, and cannot slip away from this call. The subject is inseparable from this appeal or this election which cannot be declined.'[27] But can the walls hear? It is at any rate this walled-in subject 'called upon to be someone' that I seek to describe in what follows under the name of Christianity and under the heading of 'an anthropology of Christianity', and here specifically perhaps a techno-political anthropology.

Divide and rule: take two

The history of the Christian West traces a tradition (a diversity of traditions) of social movements and gestures that deploys, for overdetermined reasons, specific historical and political, as well as religious, figures.[28] As I have already indicated, these are figures marked by divisions (conceptual walls, if you will), none of which are marginal: the king's two bodies correspond to the enemy's two bodies, the good Semite and the bad Semite. At work here is also a tradition of governance, ways of ruling, managing or treating groups of people, masses of them, on a local and international stage: a series of projections a self has cast on to the condition of others. And politics is also war, of course, by other and not so other means.

23 Ibid., emphasis added.
24 Ibid., 53.
25 Ibid., 10.
26 Ibid., 11.
27 Ibid., 53.
28 The following pages are a revised extract from my 'When killers become victims: anti-Semitism and its critics', *Cosmopolis: A Review of Cosmopolitics*, no. 3, 2007.

According to legal scholar Karl-Heinz Ziegler, it was Abu Hanifa, a Muslim thinker and founder of one of the major Islamic schools of juridical interpretation, 'who first forbade the killing of women, children, the elderly, the sick, monks and other non-combatants. He also condemned rape and the killing of captives.'[29] Commenting on the effects of these recommendations on the history of law and, more importantly, on the history of war conducted by western powers, Sven Lindqvist points out that the attempt has yet to succeed 'to make war more humane by setting forth rules that were not accepted in Europe until several centuries later'.[30] Indeed, it seems fair to say that, to this day, such rules are 'still not accepted, or in any case not practiced, when colored people [are] involved'.[31] It is as if the struggle for the rights of the oppressed had an extended tradition but one that was, if not absent, surely ineffective. Like any other struggle, it had to contend with, and adapt itself to, evolving modes of rules, management of populations and technologies of power, many of which rendered possible, and not always ungenerously, as Talal Asad insists, the most atrocious acts of war and genocide in human history, culminating with the Holocaust. This is why I want to turn to the government and management of populations—the erection of walls—as a description of domestic, namely western Christian, affective modalities and projections.

Until the Second World War, the bomb served as a major instrument in these technologies of rule and management. The bomb has served as one of the main tools in the legal and practical division and differentiation between white Christian Europeans (and Euro-Americans) and the rest of the 'colored people' of the world. More specifically, as Lindqvist painstakingly documents, it was not just any bomb but its evolved, modern version, the bomb that dropped from airplanes. 'Airplanes and bombs were examples of progress in military technology. And technology was civilization ... Bombs were a means of civilization.'[32] What David Noble called 'the religion of technology' deployed ever newer means whereby those whose lives were imagined as 'marked by a much greater dreariness' than ours would soon be deserving of sympathy, burning to ensure their own salvation.[33] The first bomb—the first 'civilizing' bomb—ever dropped from an airplane exploded on 1 November 1911. It came from an Italian machine flying over North Africa. Its geographical target was an oasis near Tripoli. Its human targets were Arabs. By 1924, by the time of the bombing of the town of Chechaouen, 'bombing natives was considered quite natural. The Italians did it in Libya,

---

29 Quoted in Sven Lindqvist, *A History of Bombing*, trans. from the Swedish by Linda Haverty Rugg (New York: New Press 2001), 9.
30 Ibid.
31 Ibid.
32 Ibid., 34.
33 David F. Noble, *The Religion of Technology: The Divinity of Man and the Spirit of Invention* (New York: Penguin 1999).

the French did it in Morocco, and the British did it throughout the Middle East, in India, and East Africa, while the South Africans did it in Southwest Africa.'[34] By 1939 Hitler had embraced and enhanced this tradition, deciding that

> Poland shall be treated as a colony. . . . In short: the ruthless expansionist policies carried out by Italy in Ethiopia and Libya, Spain in Morocco, the United States in the Philippines, and the Western European democracies of Belgium, Holland, France and England throughout Asia and Africa for more than 100 years were now brought home to Europe by Hitler and applied in an even more brutal form to the Poles.[35]

Such colonial policies and practices, along with improved technological and legal means, the accumulation of decades of 'race science' and eugenics, made the Nazi genocide of Jews, Sinti and Roma possible, along with the massive incarcerating and killing of communists and homosexuals, and the incendiary bombing of almost every major city in Europe (if not only there) by both German and Allied planes and rockets. The technology of the civilizing mission had come home to roost—'domestic circumstances', indeed. Aimé Césaire speaks of this movement as of 'a terrific boomerang effect' inflicted on the European bourgeoisie, indeed, on the European population at large.[36] It is about them that Césaire comments that, before they suffered from Nazism, 'before they were its victims, they were its accomplices . . . they tolerated that Nazism before it was inflicted on them . . . they absolved it, shut their eyes to it, legitimized it, because until then, it had been applied only to non-European peoples'. 'Yes', writes Césaire, 'it would be worthwhile to study clinically, in detail, the steps taken by Hitler and Hitlerism and to reveal to the very distinguished, very humanistic, very Christian bourgeois of the twentieth century that without his being aware of it, he has a Hitler inside him'. Equally important (and perhaps more so) is the fact that this collective subject cannot forgive Hitler for his crime, for the humiliation, for 'the fact that he applied to Europe colonialist procedures which until then had been reserved exclusively for the Arabs of Algeria, the "coolies" of India, and the "niggers" of Africa'.[37]

As I have already suggested, airplanes and bombs were only the most recent among the ruling and dividing instruments dispensed and deployed by the civilizing mission of Christian Europe upon 'colored people'. Law and education, Christian missionaries and the production of local elites, all the benevolent (that is, less bloody) techniques summarized under the old

34 Lindqvist, *A History of Bombing*, 74.
35 Ibid., 83.
36 Aimé Césaire, *Discourse on Colonialism*, trans. from the French by Joan Pinkham (New York: Monthly Review Press 2000), 36.
37 Ibid.

principle of 'divide and rule', had long been efficient means of transforming and civilizing, that is to say exploiting, ruling and often, if not always, eradicating or exterminating communities and ways of life. Writing of Algeria in the 1830s and 1840s, Alexis de Tocqueville is well aware of the fine nuances of political and military rules and their effects, and he unapologetically advocates a view from above that would later become the pilot's vantage point, although distinct from it as well. Tocqueville affirms the importance of erecting walls and of distinguishing between 'the two great races'—Arabs and Berbers (or Kabyles)—that inhabit the conquered land. 'It is obvious that we must tame these men through our arts and not through our weapons (*Il est évident que c'est par nos arts et non par nos armes qu'il s'agit de dompter de pareils hommes*).'[38] But the distinction he proposes goes further than the recognition of different races, and of different ruling techniques. It is more refined, more discriminating. It divides reality and redistributes knowledge along novel lines. 'With the Kabyles, one must address questions of civil and commercial equity; with the Arabs, questions of politics and religion.'[39] It is not just that there is a difference between Kabyle and Arab, then, but also that the very epistemological realm to which each 'group' or 'community' belongs or is allocated is, in fact, different. Further on, Tocqueville will calibrate his concerns further, zooming in on the distinction between religion and politics. It is imperative, he says, to downplay the religious hostility that opposes the Muslims to the French, the latter being clearly perceived, and perceiving themselves, as Christians. Instead, Muslims must be made to feel that their religion is not under threat, that colonialism is not a war of religion. The goal of this pacification (an infamous euphemism, if there ever was one) is nonetheless clear. 'Thus, religious passions will finally die down and we shall have only political enemies in Africa.'[40] Tocqueville understands that the distinction between religion and politics is quite tenuous and difficult to maintain in Algeria and elsewhere. Still, in defining the political enemy as distinct from the religious enemy, he is forcefully deploying the divisions (of knowledge or of emotions) that we have already encountered (if precisely inverted), here one most characteristic of Orientalist and imperial practices, and that in turn enable the division of populations along distinct lines of belonging and classification. Hence, Muslims must not be made to feel that their religion is in danger, but that is because the goal is to have—to recognize—only *political* enemies. War is thus negotiated first by determining the battlefield as political and, subsequently

38 Alexis de Tocqueville, *Sur l'Algérie*, ed. Seloua Luste Boulbina (Paris: Flammarion 2003), 52; on the 'Kabyle myth' and its use in French colonial policy, see Charles Robert Ageron, *Politiques coloniales au Maghreb* (Paris: Presses Universitaires de France 1972) and Patricia M. E. Lorcin, *Imperial Identities: Stereotyping, Prejudice and Race in Colonial Algeria* (London and New York: I. B. Tauris 1995). Unless otherwise stated, all translations are by the author.
39 Tocqueville, *Sur l'Algérie*, 52.
40 Ibid., 59.

(or simultaneously), by restricting, then denying, its religious dimension. Indeed, what must be prevented is precisely the awareness that what opposes France to Algeria is religious difference. It is as if this particular wall had to remain invisible; as if what had to be prevented was the religious association that could transcend local divisions, precisely, or disable organized resistance against the French conquerors.

> The only common idea that can link and relate all the tribes that surround us is religion. The only common feeling upon which one could rely in order to subjugate them [and therefore lead them], is hatred against the foreigner and the infidel who came to invade their land.[41]

Religion and politics therefore appear as *strategic* divisions, fighting words and fighting walls, as it were, that not only distinguish *between* communities but also *within* them for military and ruling purposes. Kabyles and Arabs are thus not only distinguished and separated on the basis of race, they are also said to belong to different realms (commerce on the one hand, religion and politics on the other). And the separation of realms, the distinction between religion and politics, further divides communities from themselves. It disables the possibility of collective action, the ability to recognize, and fight, the true enemy. Still, whatever its success, it is revealed as a technology of rule and governance.

The technological sophistication of colonial walls and divisions harks back to ancient and well-tried principles (such as *divide et impera*, of course), but, like the bomb and the airplane, they combine earlier techniques with new scientific advances. Commerce and politics, race and religion—spheres of modernity in its benevolent and fighting faces—such as they were deployed in the colonies of Christian Europe came to function as divisions of knowledge whereby old alliances, different conceptions of community and of sociability, older forms of identity, were renamed, reshaped, abolished and, indeed, destroyed. Contemporaneous with Tocqueville's visits in Algeria, Jesuit missionaries were deploying the same means of distributing knowledge, the same divisive understanding, aimed to create 'pure Christian spaces' in Mount Lebanon.[42] They expressed 'revulsion at the intermingling of Muslim and Christian, at the Christian's practice of adopting Muslim names, and at their habitual invocation of the prophet Muhammad'.

> We are sorry, these Jesuits wrote, that there was a sort of coexistence (*fusion*) between the Christians and the Muslims of Sayda. They visited each other frequently, which resulted in intimate relations between them and which introduced, bit by bit, a community of ideas and habits all of which was at the expense of the Christians. These latter joined in the important Muslim feasts, and

---

41 Ibid., 103.
42 Ussama Makdisi, *The Culture of Sectarianism: Community, History, and Violence in Nineteenth-century Ottoman Lebanon* (Berkeley: University of California Press 2000), 91.

the Muslims [in turn] joined in the Christian feasts; this kind of activity passed for good manners, sociability, while in truth it resulted in nothing more than the weakening of religious sentiments.[43]

The 'danger' of coexistence was to be prevented not only by separating communities, but by dividing them from themselves, from their own habits and practices, by fostering a different division of reality. The erection of walls, the modern separation of spheres described by Max Weber, and by Karl Marx before him, found its origins and terrain of application in particular technologies of governing, embodied technologies that divided populations, but also divided colonial labour: the missionary is neither settler nor diplomat, the governor is neither priest nor general. They do not serve the same function. In the colonies, this complex political, religious, military and economic apparatus, this novel technology, divided Druze from Maronite, Arab from Berber, Hindu from Muslim, and Hutu from Tutsi—and, still, Semite from Semite. It marks a rupture and a beginning, a very modern beginning of communalism, of sectarianism. In Mount Lebanon, it marks 'the birth of a new culture that singled out religious affiliation as the defining public and political characteristic of a modern subject and citizen'.[44] In India, it puts into place the essential (even if not inevitable) premises of partition. Moreover, and in a way that remains more difficult to recognize but to which Tocqueville alerts us, the new or renewed technologies of colonial divisions were at their most efficient in the realm of knowledge. These forms of 'colonialist knowledge' were about restructuring knowledge and functioned so as to separate religion from politics, politics from commerce, and commerce from religion and politics.[45] And each of these separations, each of these walls, was enacted, incarnated in the restructuring, the management of communities and that soon-to-be-invented object of demography, 'populations'.[46] The point was less to eradicate enmity, as Tocqueville makes clear, than to manage enemies, to rule and discipline them by refusing to grant them political identities or preventing their unification on the basis of religion. Colonial rule and knowledge was about preventing religion from becoming politics, hiding that conquest and commerce were a Christian enterprise, in which Christian powers competed but also collaborated. Not just divide and rule, then, but divide knowledge and rule, calling one group a race, another a religion, a third a polity. Calling this religion, and calling that race; calling this commerce, and calling that

43 Ibid., 92.
44 Ibid., 174.
45 Gyanendra Pandey, *The Construction of Communalism in Colonial North India* (Delhi and New York: Oxford University Press 1990), 6.
46 See Kamel Kateb, *Européens, 'indigènes' et juifs en Algérie (1830–1962): représentations et réalités des populations* (Paris: Institut national d'études démographiques 2001); and Hervé Le Bras (ed.), *L'Invention des populations: biologie, idéologie et politique* (Paris: Odile Jacob 2000).

science. The very remoteness and distinction between quite precisely similar phenomena (effects of policies emerging from the same centres) named tribalism, communalism, sectarianism and, more recently, *communautarisme*, testify to the efficacy of these divisions.[47]

Like the bomb and the airplane, which were exported and imported in and out of Europe, colonial rule, along with its theologico-political divisions, along with race science and legal devices to claim territories or redistribute land, was practised outside of Europe and inside it as well. The balancing movement between Europe and the 'coloured' world is, however, a complicated one. It is said, for example, that Columbus took an Arabic-speaking Jewish translator with him for he thought he would thus be able to communicate with the natives of India, whom he expected to encounter. In the conclusion of this essay, I want to turn briefly to another domestic site in the anthropology of Christianity—its role in the reproduction and the enforcement of the division between Jews and Arabs—in order to describe some of the ways in which the dividing walls that continue to separate these 'groups' have been constructed by means of technologies of rule and governance such as I have been describing so far.

Jews and Arabs

In-dissociable in the theological and political imagination of western Christendom, as well as in the rich history of their social and cultural contacts, Jews and Arabs continue to function as paradigmatic markers of distance and antagonism rather than proximity and affinity. This is increasingly the case in France, the United States and, of course, Israel/Palestine, and beyond a geographical logic that seems to maintain an East/West division. More and more visibly (or so one hopes, and fears) the antagonism between Jews and Arabs operates, like the colonial technologies I was just describing, on a number of levels and dimensions: historical (Holocaust versus colonialism), sociological (sexual difference, antisemitism versus Islamophobia), political (the hegemony of liberal, secular democracies and the so-called 'war on terror') and religious (the 'Judaeo-Christian tradition'). Following Edward Said, I have argued that these dimensions partake of two histories that have been kept separated for strategic reasons, two histories divided by not so virtual walls and that come under the headings of 'Islam and the West' and 'Europe and the Jews'. I conclude, therefore, with the (only seemingly paradoxical) claim that these two histories are, in fact, one: the singular management of Jew *and* Arab in western Christendom through its

47 Laurent Lévy explains how, in a strikingly similar way, the lexicon of *communautarisme* in France has managed to raise the threatening spectre of one community in particular, namely, Maghrebian Muslims: Laurent Lévy, *Le Spectre du communautarisme* (Paris: Éditions Amsterdam 2005).

transformations (Roman Catholicism, Reformation, colonialism, secularism). I argue, in other words, that the divided figure of the Semitic enemy testifies to the divided unity of western Christendom.

Let me move towards this goal by quoting again from the description by Jesuits of the coexistence that existed between Christians and Muslims on Mount Lebanon.

> They visited each other frequently, which resulted in intimate relations between them and which introduced, bit by bit, a community of ideas and habits all of which was at the expense of the Christians. These latter joined in the important Muslim feasts, and the Muslims [in turn] joined in the Christian feasts; this kind of activity passed for good manners, sociability, while in truth it resulted in nothing more than the weakening of religious sentiments.[48]

There is no question that this kind of coexistence is predicated on vastly different understandings of political rule and legal regime, social relations and collective identity, a distinct distribution of resources as well as a different way of negotiating violence and conflict. For better or for worse, it is the kind of coexistence (what Marc Abélès has called 'convivance'[49]) that was brought to an end with modernity. In the specific case of the Jews, the transformation entailed a reflected division, a logic of separation that was meant to increase the political and conceptual distance between Jews and Arabs, Jews and Muslims. A well-known and determining example was the Crémieux decree of 1870 (which was operating alongside the 1865 legal formulations that, applicable to Muslims only, would constitute the basis for the Code de l'indigénat and its ensuing discriminations),[50] but equally important and no doubt more massive in terms of the numbers affected and the depth of its reach were the activities of the French-based network of schools of the Alliance Israélite Universelle. As one of the teachers of the Alliance wrote in Damascus in 1930: 'France has achieved the moral conquest of the Jews in the East.'[51] Working in a way that is uncannily

---

48 Makdisi, *The Culture of Sectarianism*, 92.

49 Marc Abélès, *Politique de la survie* (Paris: Flammarion 2006).

50 See, most recently, Sidi Mohammed Barkat, *Le Corps d'exception: les artifices du pouvoir colonial et la destruction de la vie* (Paris: Éditions Amsterdam 2005). In 1870 the Crémieux decree (named after the French Minister of Justice Adolphe Crémieux) granted French citizenship to the Algerian Jews under French colonial jurisdiction. Although it took much effort, and a few decades, for the decree to be implemented in practice, by the time of the independence struggles, most Jews had come to embrace their newfound legal and political identity. In contradistinction, and beginning in 1865, various incarnations of what would become the Code de l'indigénat began to articulate and enforce increasingly strict distinctions between colonizer and colonized, and, by extension, between Muslims and Jews.

51 Quoted in Aron Rodrigue, *Images of Sephardi and Eastern Jewries in Transition: The Teachers of the Alliance Israélite Universelle, 1860–1939* (Seattle: University of Washington Press 1993), 269.

similar to the missionaries of Mount Lebanon, the Alliance furthered the goals of the French civilizing mission and participated in making the Jews into aliens in their native environment. It pursued this goal as an explicit moral *conquest*, and it achieved it, claiming victory over a human territory. What is essential to remember, however, is that the attention lavished by the different empires with varying degrees of success on newly constructed 'minorities' (the Maronites, the Kabyles, the Jews) was part of a new management of populations, a larger restructuring of rule and knowledge, an extensive redefinition, the universalization of the separation of politics and religion, race and ethnicity, and so forth.

It is in this context that two crucial and related vectors become, I think, ever more significant. First is the general lack of attention to Edward Said's assertion that the history of Orientalism, the history of Islamophobia, is 'the history of a strange, secret sharer of Western anti-Semitism',[52] an assertion that, grounded in the sound knowledge of a still invisible history, sought to alert us anew to Aimé Césaire's insight into the relations that link colonialism and the Holocaust. Second is the lack of attention directed at the history of the category of 'Semites', its sources and its enduring effects. Particularly troubling is the complete ignorance of the way this category functioned, the way it was deployed (or not) by the Nazis in their racial doctrine and policy. Until 2002, no enquiry had been conducted—or at least published—regarding the presence or absence of Arab or Muslim detainees in Nazi concentration camps. Similar, and equally striking, is the fact I have already alluded to, namely, that there has been little reflection on the name given to the most haunting figures among Auschwitz inmates, those named *Muselmänner*, or Muslims.[53] That name, widely disseminated throughout the most canonical works of post-Holocaust writing and scholarship, remains massively ignored at the same time as it—the witness, the survivor, as well as the impossibility of both—has become the very paradigm, the very image of our collective lament. Any knowledge of the issues sedimented in these two illustrations would make it obvious that Holocaust denial is tantamount to colonial denial of the kind practised in and by the French state, among others. Clearly, the two events—the Holocaust and colonialism—are distinct and unique events (as all historical events must be, by definition), but they emerge from the same (if divided) culture; they partake of the same logic, the same movements, technologies and conceptions I have tried to describe in this essay. Moreover, the division between them, characteristic as well of the Holocaust industry described by Peter Novick and Norman Finkelstein,[54] and its strategic purposes are singularly illuminated when one

52 Said, *Orientalism*, 27.
53 I have elaborated on this point in my 'Muslims (Hegel, Freud, Auschwitz)', in Anidjar, *The Jew, the Arab*, 113–49; see also Anidjar, *Semites*, esp. ch. 1.
54 Peter Novick, *The Holocaust in American Life* (Boston: Houghton Mifflin 1999); Norman G. Finkelstein, *The Holocaust Industry: Reflections on the Exploitation of Jewish Suffering* (New York: Verso 2000).

considers the revisionist law promulgated by the French parliament on 23 February 2005, that is, one month minus one day after the much-publicized sixtieth anniversary of the liberation of Auschwitz. For it is clear that this law functioned precisely to maintain a distinction that has been foundational to colonial knowledge and practice.

At a time when the distinction between Jew and Arab—good Semite, bad Semite—is serving so many interests in Palestine/Israel (where 'Jew' and 'Arab' constitute distinct 'nationalities' that form that basis in the law for the discrimination and the separation—the apartheid logic—that constitute the dominant horizon of a 'solution' to the conflict), in France (where antisemitism is used to obscure the presence of other forms of racism, indeed, used to enforce old and new forms of racism and inequalities; where Arab Jews are turned against Arab Muslims), and in the United States (where the 'war on terror' is waged on Arabs and Muslims while laws condemning antisemitism are increasingly promulgated; while support for Israel grows ever more unconditional, ensuring American hegemony in many more, if less publicly discussed, ways), it is imperative to recognize that Jews and Arabs, Jews and Muslims, continue to constitute one of the main foci of modern technologies of rule and governance on an ever growing global scale, as well as a site of massive investment that operates concretely in mass movements (not to mention mass media). This, then, is the tradition within which we are still inscribed, the domestic circumstances that persist in defining us. For to uphold the division between Jew and Arab, between Jew and Muslim, is to reproduce the origins of racism and of antisemitism at once: the history of Christian prejudice. It is to maintain a singular political tradition, to uphold the division of sectarianism and nationalism, between religion and secularism, religion and politics: an affective division that serves a Christian-dominated hegemony, a Christian view of 'religion'—and of 'politics'. It is to maintain the division between Holocaust and colonialism, the spread of democracy and capitalism and missionary activity, and so forth. To uphold these divisions, even if it is to combat either Islamophobia or antisemitism (or to spread democracy), is therefore to engage in an old and familiar gesture that constitutes a 'ludicrous denunciation of a secret known to all and the divulging of which, far from having to overcome any obstacle, is encouraged by all the media of dominant opinion, the imaginary confrontation with power where it does not exist'.[55] To uphold these divisions is to serve the power and interests of those who, like Tocqueville, show selective concern for the enslaved and the oppressed; those who, like Tocqueville, seek to 'tame' populations by making them into convenient enemies, turning them against each other and, more dangerously, against their own selves.

55 Jacques Rancière, *Les Scènes du peuple: les révoltes logiques, 1975–1985* (Lyon: Éditions Horlieu 2003), 306.

I want to insist, in conclusion, that I do not conceive of the arguments presented here as proposing an essential and essentialist view of Christianity. Quite the contrary. At stake is rather a historical, highly divided and transformative understanding of Christianity as it has evolved and cast itself, and continues to do so, effectively in the world, out of one of its 'cradles', in and out of Western Europe. I seek therefore to insist on and highlight unacknowledged continuities (not prior or predestined intentions) such as those belonging to a cultural and political sphere that has been otherwise recognized—that has at times proudly recognized itself (as 'the Judeo-Christian tradition', for example)—as having a definite, if fragile and conflicted, contested, integrity. This integrity, which '*is*, rather than expresses a certain *will* or *intention*', has varied, more marked at some times than at others, more significant in some dimensions than in others, more hidden, and perhaps more powerful, in some sites than in others.[56] It has constructed and reconstructed walls that have reinforced, without a doubt, the theological and political, and again fragile, integrity of western Christendom. But it has followed what was by no means an inevitable trajectory (nor is it now inevitable), nor a tradition at all until it made itself so (by marginalizing or excluding, destroying, if not without remainder, that which was said to be Other in it, that which *remains* as Other in it), until it *named* itself so, repeatedly and more or less rightly, more or less correctly (but who would judge what 'true' or 'correct' Christianity might be?). It made itself so at each juncture it reiterated itself, with or without difference, every time it effectively reinscribed a certain, selective and selected past, doing so by way of practices of all kinds, signs and justifications of all sorts. To the extent that there are continuities, then, to the extent that they are inscribed in history and operative in the present, it testifes to the endurance of a profound mistake, 'a fantasy of self for an other', our continued march on 'a road that travels from the self all the way to the projections that self has cast onto the condition' of others, the powerful force that guards and protects our society. It testifies to ever higher, ever earless, walls.

56 Said, *Orientalism*, 12.

The crusade over the bodies of women

SONYA FERNANDEZ

ABSTRACT Anti-Muslim prejudice finds its roots in the history of the West. Since the time of the Crusades, Islam and its adherents have been cast as the strange and deviant Other, the polar opposite to the reasonable and civilized West. It is suggested, however, that it is only in recent times that we have seen such prejudice become a normalized part of the very *fabric* of society. 9/11, 7/7 and the 'war on terror' have propelled Muslims and their faith into the limelight, forcing them to become accountable *en masse* for the sins of the few. Rhetoric—both social and legal—focuses on the barbarity, brutality and oppressiveness that is Islam, and the bodies of women form the battlefield on which this verbal crusade is waged. Starting with this premise, Fernandez suggests that anti-Muslim prejudice is increasingly subsumed and hidden behind a concern for women. She explores the discourse around gender-based practices such as veiling, forced marriages and honour killings to reveal the ways in which expressions of Islamophobia have become normalized and neutralized through the articulation and juxtaposition of traditions of patriarchy and gender inequality within Islam and counter traditions of gender equality in the West. She argues that the effect of this is two-fold. First, it unquestioningly reinforces the idea that *Islam* is oppressive to women, homogenizing and generalizing such oppression as representative of the whole rather than as specific to the few. Second, it allows for the silencing of the voices of Muslim women while simultaneously proclaiming a desire to free them from such silencing. Fernandez suggests that it is this duality hidden behind a facade of concern for gender equality that facilitates the institutionalization of Islamophobic norms.

In many respects, the legacy of the Crusades infuses and characterizes the current relationship between Islam and the West as one of conflict, violence and *fundamentally* irreconcilable differences.[1] Following 9/11, 7/7 and the so-called 'war on terror', Muslims have been increasingly subject not only to acts of overt physical violence, but to subversive forms of epistemic

---

1 See 'Remarks by the President [Bush] upon arrival: the South Lawn', press release, 16 September 2001, available on the Yale Avalon Project website at http://avalon.law.yale.edu/sept11/president_015.asp (viewed 16 May 2009).

violence,[2] manifested through the racist appropriation of discourse and the positing of racist stereotypes as 'truth'. Islamophobia has become accepted and even *expected*,[3] and is now so commonplace that there is little awareness of and resistance to what can only be considered to be a form of racism.[4]

The language of good and evil deployed in popular socio-political discourse invokes images of a divine battle against the very forces of darkness: a battle between two civilizations or, rather, one civilization against an (un)civilization.[5] The universal goods of liberal democracy (freedom, equality, rights, liberties and tolerance) are hailed by the West in the fight for moral supremacy against the evils of Islam (barbarism, savagery, oppression and subordination). These polarized constructions are then mapped on to gender-based issues such as veiling, honour killings and forced marriages to evidence the West's promise of liberation and Islam's all-conquering brutality. 'Westernization' offers freedom; Islam offers coercion and compulsion. The problem with this epistemological deception is that it results in seemingly preordained parameters of analysis and interaction that allow for the dichotomous polarization of the world into us/them, Islam/West, savage/civilized, free/unfree. Muslim identity and belonging become dependent on a willingness to transcend these dualisms by picking a side.[6] The effect of this ultimatum is to facilitate and encourage the perpetuation of Islamophobic norms and stereotypes that in turn inform understandings of modern liberal legality.[7]

Muslim women find themselves situated at the heart of this matrix of conflicting morals, norms, values, religions, ideologies, politics and civilizations. The purpose of this article is neither to solve the problems of women nor to deny that, in certain instances, culture and religion can

2 Gayatri Chakravorty Spivak, 'Can the subaltern speak?', in Cary Nelson and Lawrence Grossberg (eds), *Marxism and the Interpretation of Culture* (London: Macmillan 1988), 271–316 (281).

3 Commission on British Muslims and Islamophobia, *Islamophobia: A Challenge for Us All* (London: Runnymede Trust 1997).

4 While some have sought to establish a distinction between racism and Islamophobia, this distinction is arguably misleading and pernicious. Fear (phobia) on grounds of religion and hatred on grounds of racial, ethnic or cultural differences have the same end consequence: 'unfounded hostility' towards a particular group on the basis of particular perceptions, misconceptions and stereotypes. Alleged differences are in many ways purely semantic. Victims of Islamophobia generally tend to experience abuse on grounds of their race; slurs such as 'raghead', 'Paki', the (mistaken) violence against Sikh men, do not occur because someone is (necessarily) visibly identifiable as 'a Muslim' but, rather, at first instance, because their skin colour is perceived as marking them out as potentially Muslim.

5 Samuel P. Huntington, *The Clash of Civilisations and the Remaking of World Order* (New York: Simon and Schuster 1998).

6 Gary Younge, 'The right to be British', *Guardian*, 12 November 2001; Gary Younge, 'We can choose our identity, but sometimes it chooses us', *Guardian*, 21 January 2005.

7 This phrase is used to connote law, 'legal instrumentalities, discourse, and legal consciousness': David Theo Goldberg, *The Racial State* (Oxford: Blackwell 2002), 139.

and do play a role in the oppression and subjection of women. It is undeniable that honour killings, forced marriages and forced veiling are unacceptable practices. However, while much attention has rightly been focused on strategies for preventing violence against women, these critiques sometimes arguably further entrench the problem by reinforcing, consciously or otherwise, particular (racist) stereotypes through the use of essentialist conceptions of culture, religion and gender roles that obscure the workings of patriarchy in majority as well as minority contexts. Thus the aim here is to engage in an analysis of these conceptions in order to offer a means of seeing more clearly effective strategies for tackling violence against women that co-operate with communities rather than demonizing and ostracizing them.

The crusade to save Muslim women from Muslim men obscures the racist binaries that inform polemics about the oppression of Muslim women, and instead plays on some inherent sense of equality and freedom that is perceived as the sole preserve of the West and the (sufficiently) westernized.[8] The focus on gender issues such as veiling, honour killing and forced marriage acts as the perfect prop for justifying the forceful imposition of western values on the cultural Other, by pointing to the oppression of women in Other cultures while simultaneously ignoring the oppression of women within the dominant culture. The construction of these particular practices as particularly *Islamic* has wrought a blend of mistrust, suspicion and hostility towards Muslims fundamentally rooted in racist thought. The effect is to disguise the imperialist motivations and generalizations that demarcate Other cultures as inherently *more* patriarchal, rather than *differently* so, behind a concern for gender equality. It is without question that practices such as honour killings and forced marriages must be eradicated. However, in order to do so, there is a need for a more honest critique of existing attitudes towards them.

Paternalistic interest in the bodies of Other women is as much a part of western liberal tradition as John Stuart Mill and Jeremy Bentham. Exploring the socio-political, legal and historical discourse surrounding gender-based issues such as veiling, honour killing and forced marriage exposes the assumptions and stereotypes that inform discussions and influence perceptions of the body of the female Other. This then enables us to see more clearly how these perceptions are played out in the context of certain gender-based 'Islamic' practices, and so reveal the (not so) latent Islamophobia that

8 See Laura Bush's comments in 'Report on the Taliban's war against women', 17 November 2001, available on the U.S. Department of State website at www.state.gov/g/drl/rls/c4804.htm (viewed 16 May 2009); see also 'Remarks by the President at signing ceremony for Afghan Women and Children Relief Act of 2001', press release, 12 December 2001, available on the Yale Avalon Project website at http://avalon.law.yale.edu/sept11/president_117.asp (viewed 16 May 2009); Ruth Gledhill, 'Cherie Blair speaks out against the veil', *The Times*, 31 October 2007.

embodies the savages-victims-saviours prism through which such cultural practices are viewed.[9] The aim is to draw attention to the constructed eternal victimhood of the agency-less Muslim woman against the eternal savagery of the Muslim man, which serves to demonize Islam as a religion without examining the socio-political and cultural contexts from which gender-based oppression arises.

Underpinning these narratives is a tendency towards colonial imaginings of the female Other's body. As part of their attempts to civilize the savage, colonial missionaries undertook to eradicate gender-based practices such as sati, polygamy, veiling, female genital cutting and child marriage, with little or no effort made to locate these within their socio-cultural context.[10] Instead, these practices were cited as examples of the controlling barbarism of the colonized male and the oppression of the colonized female, and so designating women's bodies as a key battle site of cultural imperialism, a designation that continues to inform modern western responses to the practices of the Other. Any engagement with, and deconstruction of, the 'racial and religious superiority'[11] that informs modern liberal legality and its encounters with the bodies of Muslim women necessitates an understanding of the racialized meaning that has been imputed on to the Other woman's body.

Veiling liberal racism

Nowhere is this importation of meaning and ignorance of context more apparent than in responses to the veil. Dismissal of the multifaceted motives for veiling derives from a framework that indulges the 'fantasy of a superior nation who must discipline and instruct culturally inferior peoples',[12] maintained and justified on presumptions of the gender inequality intrinsic in the veil. Interestingly, negative attitudes towards and perceptions of the veil as a symbol of inequality appear to transcend socio-cultural contexts, particularly within Europe. In upholding the federal court of Switzerland's

---

9   Makau Matua, 'Savages, victims, and saviours: the metaphor of human rights', *Harvard International Law Journal*, vol. 42, no. 1, 2001, 201–44.

10 Cynthia Fernandez-Romano, 'The banning of female circumcision: cultural imperialism or a triumph for women's rights?', *Temple International and Comparative Law Journal*, vol. 13, no. 1, 1999, 137–61 (145). For an insightful analysis of colonial attitudes towards the practice of sati, see Lata Mani, *Contentious Traditions: The Debate on Sati in Colonial India* (Berkeley: University of California Press 1998).

11 Ratna Kapur, 'Human rights in the 21st century: take a walk on the dark side', *Sydney Law Review*, vol. 28, no. 4, 2006, 665–87 (674).

12 Sherene H. Razack, 'Imperilled Muslim women, dangerous Muslim men and civilised Europeans: legal and social responses to forced marriages', *Feminist Legal Studies*, vol. 12, no. 2, 2004, 129–74 (132).

decision to prohibit a primary school teacher from veiling while at work, the European Court of Human Rights commented:

> The Court accepts that it is very difficult to assess the impact that a powerful external symbol such as the wearing of a headscarf may have on the freedom of conscience and religion of very young children ... In those circumstances, it cannot be denied outright that the wearing of a headscarf *might* have some kind of proselytising effect, seeing that it appears to be imposed on women by a precept which is laid down in the Koran and which ... is hard to square with the principle of gender equality. It therefore appears difficult to reconcile the wearing of an Islamic headscarf with the message of tolerance, respect for others and, above all, equality and non-discrimination that all teachers in a democratic society must convey to their pupils [emphasis added].[13]

This reasoning constructs a formal notion of equality as sameness, whereby veiled women are viewed as different and implicitly unequal. That veiling is seen as discriminatory is somewhat ironic since the practical effect of a prohibition is to discriminate against Muslim women on grounds of their sex, denying them the same freedom to exercise their legal agency as Muslim men. In concretizing the symbolism of the veil in this manner, the court simultaneously denies the voices of women while professing a desire for their voices to be heard. The implicit suggestion is that girls and women who choose to veil do so from within frameworks of coercive constraint. Indeed, one of the key concerns in the infamous Begum case was whether the applicant's decision to wear the jilbab was made entirely freely or whether she had been subject to familial pressure, in particular from her brother.[14] Such concerns appear to ignore the reality of a legal framework that promotes a permissive understanding of adolescent autonomy in the context of consent to medical treatment,[15] or to body piercing.[16] The underlying assumption of a coercive element works to deny the possibility

13 *Dahlab v. Switzerland*, no. 42393/98, ECHR, 15 January 2001, [13]. See also the comments of the court in *Leyla Şahin v. Turkey*, no. 44774/98, ECHR, 29 June 2004, esp. [115–16]. It is not my intention to offer an analysis of the legal issues and arguments but, rather, to highlight the language and rhetoric of the courts.

14 *R (on the application of Begum (by her litigation friend, Rahman)) (Respondent) v. Headteacher and Governors of Denbigh High School (Appellants)* [2006] UKHL 15; *R (on the application of SB) v. Governors of Denbigh High School* [2005] 2 All ER 396; *R (on the application of Begum) v. Headteacher and Governors of Denbigh High School* [2004] All ER (D) 108 (Jun).

15 *Gillick v. West Norfolk and Wisbech Area Health Authority* [1985] 3 All ER 402 (HL). Lord Scarman stated: 'As a matter of law the parental right to determine whether or not their minor child below the age of 16 will have medical treatment terminates if and when the child achieves sufficient understanding and intelligence to enable him to understand fully what is proposed.'

16 According to the Sexual Offences Act 2003, children aged thirteen and above are deemed capable of consenting to nipple and genital piercing. For further discussion

of free choice, so drawing a veil over parallel frameworks of oppression in western society.[17] While there is a very real need to protect women of all races and religions from coercion and oppression, beginning from an assumption that such coercion exists can only result in a framework of analysis and response that obstructs rather than aids in combatting violence against women. As Anne Phillips notes: 'To avoid the trap of treating certain groups of people, particularly women, and particularly women from non-Western or minority cultural backgrounds—as less capable of autonomous choice than others, we have to go primarily by what people say.'[18] In maligning the veil as a symbol of gender inequality, the courts issue judgements from within a framework of a constrained perception that defines the Muslim female in a manner that refuses to permit any degree of idiosyncrasy, and instead offers her up as the symbol of all that is oppressive about Islam. The gradual mutation of the veil from a symbol of religious identity to a contentious marker of difference paves the way for further contamination of the hijab as a sign of inequality, hostility to a democratic society, fundamentalism,[19] as well as the blurred line between Islam and terror, breathing life into the savages-victims-saviours construct.

The idea that there is 'something aggressive about the veil'[20] makes the hijab a tangible embodiment of violence,[21] and ignores the multiplicity of meanings attached to it: as a symbol of identity, personhood, religious and cultural beliefs, nationhood and national identity.[22] In giving life to the tensions surrounding the hijab, arguments based on tolerance, equality and

---

of minor consent to body modification, see Paul Lehane, 'Assault, consent and body art: a review of the law relating to assault and consent in the UK and the practice of body art', *Journal of Environmental Health Research*, vol. 4, no. 1, 2005.

17 Sheila Jeffreys, *Beauty and Misogyny: Harmful Cultural Practices in the West* (London and New York: Routledge 2005); Isabelle Gunning, 'Arrogant perception, world-travelling, and multicultural feminism: the case of female genital surgeries', *Columbia Human Rights Law Review*, vol. 23, 1992, 189–248; Kathryn Pauly Morgan, 'Women and the knife: cosmetic surgery and the colonization of women's bodies', *Hypatia*, vol. 6, no. 3, 1991, 25–53; Kathy Davis, 'Remaking the she-devil: a critical look at feminist approaches to beauty', *Hypatia*, vol. 6, no. 2, 1991, 21–43; Kathryn Abrams, 'Sex wars redux: agency and coercion in feminist legal theory', *Columbia Law Review*, vol. 95, no. 2, 1995, 304–76.

18 Anne Phillips, *Multiculturalism without Culture* (Princeton, NJ: Princeton University Press 2007), 177.

19 *R (on the application of Begum (by her litigation friend, Rahman)) (Respondent)* v. *Headteacher and Governors of Denbigh High School (Appellants)*; *Leyla Şahin* v. *Turkey*; *Karaduman* v. *Turkey*, no. 16278/90, ECHR 3 May 1993, 74 DR 93.

20 Jon Henley, 'Something aggressive about veils, says Chirac', *Guardian*, 6 December 2003.

21 See, for example, the outrage following the murder of WPC Sharon Beshenivsky and the allegation that the perpetrator escaped wearing a niqab: Paul Stokes, 'Murder suspect fled under Muslim veil', *Telegraph*, 21 December 2006.

22 For example, the protest against the French ban on religious and political symbols by French women using the tricolour flag as a headscarf asserting religious and national

the fear of fundamentalism are deployed to justify imposing (mis)conceptions about Islam and the veil on Muslim women, distinguishing those who continue to veil as coerced purveyors of terror. The paradoxical deployment of such notions thus acts to obscure the imperialism within the law, and disables any attempt to unpack the totalizing assumptions surrounding the hijab. Acts of assertion are then translated and interpreted as signs of coercion and brainwashing, subverting the 'defiant' into the 'victim'. The failure to acknowledge the possibility of the autonomy and agency of Muslim women reinforces imperialistic gender and cultural assumptions. It furthermore entrenches dangerous notions of a 'monolithic victim group who are all similarly oppressed',[23] and of an 'essentialised [Muslim] culture and [Muslim] woman',[24] that ensure the continued representation of Muslim women as voiceless victims.

Muslim women's identity is then never more than the experience of their oppression, and their (perceived eternal) victimhood acts as a double-edged sword with which to deny recognition of both sexes' agency and autonomy, so placing the (de)sexualized body centre stage. Within this prism, Muslim men are framed as forever denying Muslim women the freedom to explore and exercise their agency (read: sexuality) and, in so doing, are forever posited as the barbaric controlling Other. Three themes emerge as inextricably intertwined in this gendered construction of race: the equation of sexuality with agency, which, in turn, bolsters the savage construct with which Muslim men find themselves inescapably identified, and the consequent positing of Muslim women as unfree and in need of saving. Images of the acquiescent Muslim woman as victim permeate conceptions of racialized womanhood so that those who are free are those who conform to particular perceptions of (sexual) freedom: provocative dress, cosmetic surgery, ladette culture. Within this framework, those who do not conform to such measures of freedom, by *choosing*, for example, to veil, contract polygamous marriages or engage in female genital cutting, can only ever be seen as constrained in their exercise of free and reasoned choice. This 'constraint' then becomes the justification for the crusade against 'illiberal' Muslims.

Situating Muslim women within such a framework posits western liberal conceptions of freedom and agency, oppression and subordination as 'the primary referent in theory and praxis'.[25] Hence, when Muslim women assert their desire to veil as an expression of freedom, independence or religious identity, their articulations are read through a solipsistic prism that obstructs

---

identity: Samah Jabr, 'Hijab in the West: the railroad starts in Paris', *Washington Report on Middle Eastern Affairs*, April 2004, 36–7.

23 Ratna Kapur, 'The tragedy of victimisation rhetoric: resurrecting the "native" subject in international/post-colonial feminist legal politics', *Harvard Human Rights Journal*, vol. 15, 2002, 1–38 (27).

24 Ibid.

25 Saraswati Raju, 'We are different, but can we talk?', *Gender, Place and Culture*, vol. 9, no. 2, 2002, 173–7.

all *other* epistemological standpoints. This insistence on the victimhood of Muslim women demands their gratitude for the 'blessings' of western liberal legality,[26] which seeks to free them from the victimizing (sexual, physical and mental) violence of their religion, their culture and their men. The effect is two-fold. In the context of veiling and forced marriages, the victim-construct acts to deny the agency of Muslim women. Conversely, in discussions of honour killings, the victim status of Other women is used to legitimate, or at the very least ignore and so implicitly condone, violence against women in the culture of the West. The result is the normalization of the Muslim woman as victim and the legitimation of racist words, deeds and stereotypes, such as Cherie Blair's 'Batman' mime to illustrate the oppression of veiled Afghani women,[27] or Elisabeth Badinter's comment:

> The veil is a symbol of the oppression of a sex. Putting on torn jeans, wearing yellow, green or blue hair, this is an act of freedom with regards to the social conventions. Putting a veil on the head, this is an act of submission. It burdens a woman's whole life. Their fathers and their brothers choose their husbands, they are closed up in their own homes and confined to domestic tasks.[28]

Consequently, neither sexism nor racism comes fully into view. Sexism is thus regarded as a problem of uncivilized cultures and religions such as Islam, and of limited relevance to women in the West,[29] while 'concern' for Muslim women disguises the racism that colours the lens through which Other communities are too often viewed. One of the difficulties arising from such a distorted view is that western(ized) women too often remain blind to their own oppression; with their freedom posed as the counterpoint to Muslim women's subordination, the continuing grip of gendered forms of patriarchal control in the western context goes unchecked.[30]

26 Signe Arnfred, 'Simone de Beauvoir in Africa: "woman = the second sex?" Issues of African feminist thought', *JENdA: A Journal of Culture and African Women Studies* (online), no. 3, 2002, at www.jendajournal.com/vol2.1/arnfred.html (viewed 16 May 2009).

27 Josie Appleton, 'Nothing to lose but their burqas', *spiked* (online), 20 November 2001, at www.spiked-online.co.uk/Articles/00000002D2DB.htm (viewed 16 May 2009).

28 Quoted and translated in Norma Claire Moruzzi, 'A problem with headscarves: contemporary complexities of political and social identity', *Political Theory*, vol. 22, no. 4, 1994, 653–72 (653). This view has been echoed by, among others, the feminist group Ni Putes Ni Soumises (Neither Whores nor Submissives) who argue against the wearing of the veil on the grounds that those who do not veil are often subjected to gang rapes, verbal and physical abuse, and labelled 'prostitutes'.

29 This is particularly clear in contemporary western social attitudes towards feminism, which is seen as a 'dirty word', outdated and unnecessary. Chilla Bulbeck, '"Women are exploited way too often": feminist rhetorics at the end of equality', *Australian Feminist Studies*, vol. 20, no. 46, 2005, 65–76.

30 As Chilla Bulbeck notes (ibid., 73): 'As my gender studies students and taxi drivers alike are fond of pointing out, Australia is not a country where women are forced to

Religion is increasingly demonized as a key site of oppression and violence. Many feminist scholars have taken pains to enunciate the many ways in which religion can and does act in this way.[31] While religions may provide the means and justification for the subjection of women, many such critiques proffer a distorted view of religion that ignores certain traditions while focusing on and castigating others. Any engagement with liberal legalism must acknowledge the ways in which liberal traditions are purportedly secular, yet very much Christian in thought, nature and character. In this way, liberal legality facilitates the imposition of criteria that are decidedly Christian in character. Modern liberal society's privileging of secularism over traditional beliefs and values, religious and otherwise, lends itself to the social and legal stigmatization of Islam, and castigates any action undertaken in the name of religion as irrational, unreasonable and defiantly different.[32] Liberal discourse then, be it social, political or legal, is replete with stereotypes and preconceived assumptions and presumptions fixated on perceived cultural and religious differences that aid in the maintenance and preservation of the hierarchy that ranks cultures and religions according to their conformity to the liberal norms and values enshrined in a so-called liberal democracy. This conformity is judged through perceptions, judgements and visualizations of the female body: how 'free' is the body of the Other woman to explore her sex and sexuality? And in what ways is the body of the Other woman constrained by the men of her culture?[33] The body accordingly becomes the measure, enshrining both difference and hierarchy.[34] Perception forms the particular identity and meaning ascribed to and imposed on the bodies of Muslim women, as in the issue of veiling. The image of 'a weak and helpless woman who needs to be saved from barbaric customs and a brutal,

---

wear veils, or confined to the home, visibly oppressed by lack of educational opportunities or denial of political rights.'

31 See, for example, Susan Moller Okin, *Is Multiculturalism Bad for Women?* (Princeton, NJ: Princeton University Press 1999).

32 See, for example, David Aaronovitch, 'I don't mean to be rude . . . : Why are we so scared of offending each other? That is what a civilised society should be able to do', *Observer*, 9 January 2005, which offers a response to those who objected to the depiction of rape and murder in the gurdwara as a representation of male oppression within Sikhism in the play *Bezhti*, and the televised version of *Jerry Springer, the Opera* on BBC2 portraying Jesus wearing a nappy. Similar comments were made following the responses of Muslims to the Danish cartoons. The denigration and equation of religion with oppression was enthusiastically received by commentators while religious protesters were deemed 'fanatics' opposed to free speech.

33 The more 'liberated' a woman, the more civilized the society. 'The grid through which we rank the humanity of the area is based on how *we* perceive their treatment of their women-folk': Laura Nader, 'Orientalism, Occidentalism and the control of women', *Cultural Dynamics*, vol. 2, no. 3, 1989, 323–55 (333).

34 Oyèrónké Oyěwùmi, *The Invention of Women: Making an African Sense of Western Gender Discourses* (Minneapolis: University of Minnesota Press 1997), 7.

all-powerful misogynistic group of men' is constantly deployed in discussions of Islam and its treatment of women,[35] entrenching it deeper and more firmly in the public consciousness so that, in times of need, it can be called upon to justify whatever 'interventionist' measure is deemed necessary to save brown women from brown men.

Honour killings: yet another victim of the Crusades?

Nowhere is this image more evident than in the socio-legal rhetoric on honour killings and forced marriages that is framed by comments such as 'the elephant in the room ... is that "honour killings" are largely a Muslim phenomenon'.[36] The figure of the Muslim woman becomes a central point in the battle between liberal and illiberal cultures.[37] Stereotypes of barbaric Muslim fathers murdering their innocent daughters or forcing them into marriages are evoked to justify blaming (Muslim) culture for the bad behaviour of (Muslim) men,[38] rather than the underlying patriarchal norms and the 'male-dominant cultures of impunity' that exists within *all* cultures and societies.[39] The purpose here is not to deny that honour killings are, without question, horrific and unacceptable. Rather, it is to highlight the ways in which existing approaches to honour killings demonize communities, so preventing a more sensitive and nuanced approach.

The crusade to save Muslim women from the twin horrors of gender inequality and violence permeates the discourse on honour killings yet, while these crimes are castigated and held up as yet another example of the horrors in Other cultures, there is an unwillingness to acknowledge parallel forms of violence within dominant society. Indeed, it is possible to suggest that 'the killing of women by close family members throughout the world can in part be explained with reference to underlying honor/shame systems as a subcategory of patriarchal ideology'.[40] Instead, crimes of passion, 'the killing of women in the heat of passion for sexual or intimate

---

35 Oyèrónké Oyěwùmi, 'Feminism, sisterhood and other foreign bodies', in Oyèrónké Oyěwùmi (ed.), *African Women and Feminism: Reflecting on the Politics of Sisterhood* (Asmara, Eritrea and Trenton, NJ: Africa World Press 2003), 34.

36 Melanie Phillips, 'The lethal reality of Londonistan' (blog), 12 June 2007, at www.melaniephillips.com/diary/?p=1548 (viewed 16 May 2009).

37 Uma Narayan, *Dislocating Cultures: Identities, Traditions and Third World Feminism* (London and New York: Routledge 1997), 17.

38 Leti Volpp, 'Blaming culture for bad behaviour', *Yale Journal of Law and Humanities*, vol. 12, no. 1, 2000, 89–116.

39 Oyèrónké Oyěwùmi, 'There she is: Mama Africa!', *JENdA: A Journal of Culture and African Women Studies* (online), no. 5, 2004, at www.jendajournal.com/issue5/oyewumi.htm (viewed 16 May 2009).

40 Nancy V. Baker, Peter R. Gregware and Margery A. Cassidy, 'Family killings fields: honor rationales in the murder of women', *Violence against Women*, vol. 5, no. 2, 1999, 164–84 (180).

reasons',[41] are constructed as aberrations rather than as emblematic of the violence against women that is endemic in western culture. Provocative headlines—such as 'MUSLIM CUT HIS DAUGHTER'S THROAT FOR TAKING A CHRISTIAN BOYFRIEND', [42] 'FATHER GETS LIFE FOR MURDERING DAUGHTER WHO REJECTED ISLAM',[43] 'COUSIN STABBED MUSLIM WOMAN IN HONOUR KILLING',[44] 'HONOUR KILLINGS, AND WHY MY MUSLIM FATHER WANTS ME DEAD'[45]— construct honour crimes as evidence of the violence and misogyny associated with Islam. In the words of MP Ann Cryer:

> So-called 'honour crimes' should not be confused with the concept of 'crimes of passion'. Whereas the latter is normally limited to a *crime* that is committed by one partner (or husband and wife) in a relationship on the other as a *spontaneous* (emotional or passionate) reply (often citing a defence of 'sexual provocation'), the former may involve *the abuse or murder* of (usually) women by one or more close family members (including partners) in the name of individual or family honour [emphasis added].[46]

The shift in terminology and language is revealing. While honour crimes are emotively connoted as 'abuse or murder', crimes of passion are neutrally described as 'crimes'. The spontaneity of crimes of passion appears to be a mitigating factor, suggesting that subconscious or unacknowledged beliefs in the male right of ownership over the female body are less of a sin than vocalized acknowledgements of a proprietary interest. I would suggest that they are rather more insidious, as overt misogynistic beliefs are more easily challenged than latent ones. The distinctions drawn between 'honour killings' and 'crimes of passion' obscure the fact that both are acts of femicide, and instead posit 'honour killings' as a violent aberration predicated on misguided notions of honour and female propriety distinctly confined to the (Muslim) Other. What such stereotypes ignore is the similar occurrence of 'misogynous killings of women by men' in a non-cultural context. The phrase 'crime of passion' is used to denote 'the killing of women in the heat of passion for sexual or intimate reasons',[47] and appears to be confined to those killings perpetrated by ethnic majority

---

41 Lama Abu-Odeh, 'Comparatively speaking: the "honor" of the "East" and the "passion" of the "West"', *Utah Law Review*, no. 2, 1997, 287–308 (289).
42 Sue Clough and Sean O'Neil, *Telegraph*, 30 September 2003.
43 *The Times*, 5 July 1989.
44 Danielle Demetriou, *Independent*, 7 October 2003.
45 Lina Das, *Daily Mail*, 2 October 2003.
46 Council of Europe, Parliamentary Assembly, Doc. 9720, Report, Committee on Equal Opportunities for Women and Men, 7 March 2003, available on the Council of Europe website at http://assembly.coe.int/Main.asp?link=http%3A%2F%2F assembly. coe.int%2FDocuments%2FWorkingDocs%2Fdoc03%2FEDOC9720.htm (viewed 16 May 2009).
47 Abu-Odeh, 'Comparatively speaking', 289.

(in the main) male actors. Once again, the question arises: is the distinction merely semantic or is there a more fundamental difference between honour killings and crimes of passion? In a House of Lords debate on the subject, Anthony Giddens suggested that the compulsions and motivations that underlie honour killings can also be found in western society.[48] Bhikhu Parekh discussed the historical occurrence of race-related killings in the United States, where the law in the southern states took a somewhat permissive view of white men who killed their wives or daughters on suspicion of them having had a relationship with a black man.[49] Parekh built on this scenario, drawing parallels with a situation in which a white racist justifies the murder of a black or Asian man for having a relationship with a white woman on grounds of them having tarnished the honour of his country and race.[50] Meditations such as these highlight the value of reformulating and reconceiving of the notions of honour and shame, facilitating the conceptualization of 'honour' as a synonym for male pride and ego similar to the way in which the law understands 'passion'. Conceiving of honour in this broader sense helps to cut through the colour line that runs through the apparent distinction between honour and passion.

This disparity in conceptualization is simultaneously predicated on, and reinforcing of, stereotypes about the brutality of Muslim men and the subordination of Muslim women, so preventing seeing both kinds of violence as forms of womanslaughter.[51] Exoticizing honour killings instead renders them as part of the racial, religious and cultural savagery of the Other, rather than as one of the cross-cultural sites of male violence against women. Muslim women are accordingly cast as the victims of a cruel religion in a move that fails to acknowledge the concrete reality of the two (non-Muslim) women killed every week by their partners or ex-partners in the United Kingdom.[52] What appears to be a cultural divide is nothing more than a synthetic segregation of the same phenomenon: violence against women based on an underlying belief in male ownership of the female body.

Sexual relations of male dominance and female passivity (enforced or nominal) are arguably seen only in relation to the (Muslim) Other and rarely if ever in relation to the (non-Muslim) Self. The sexual relations of Muslim men and women are conceived in terms of control and subordination. So construed, this particularly patriarchal relationship is often invoked as the

---

48 Hansard (HL), vol. 676, 15 December 2005, col. 1423.
49 Ibid., col. 1432.
50 Ibid.
51 Jill Radford, 'Womanslaughter: a license to kill? The killing of Jane Asher', in Jill Radford and Diana E. H. Russell (eds), *Femicide: The Politics of Woman Killing* (Buckingham: Open University Press 1992).
52 Amnesty International, 'A global outrage: global and UK statistics', 13 February 2006, available on the Amnesty International UK website at http://hardy.amnesty.org.uk/svaw/vaw/global.shtml#uk (viewed 7 May 2008).

justification for 'forcing' women to be free.[53] In constructing Muslim women as 'passive targets of oppressive [and discriminatory] practices',[54] liberal discourse utilizes sexist stereotypes to reinforce racially imbued conceptualizations of the Muslim Other. The power of liberal thinking to infect the social and normative cosmos with this 'hegemonic homogenisation'[55] of conceptions of women's freedom derives from an inherent sense of positional superiority,[56] wherein the liberal West has appropriated the power to construct itself and its values as universal standards.[57] The 'racing' of norms and space requires a fixation with the bodies of the Other without a parallel in dominant society. New markers of civilized and uncivilized behaviour have taken the place of the old, but with one key similarity. Gender equality remains the mobilizing force for the contestations around race and religion, implying that both offer little or no opportunity for equality. Thus situated, Muslim women forever lack agency, autonomy and the capability or ability to make free and informed choices, breathing life into the histories of liberal colonial constructions of the unreasonable savage.

Forced marriages: consenting to oppression

As with the discourse on honour killings, norms of gender equality and the need to protect women from 'cultural' violence are once again invoked with regard to forced marriages as a means of dehumanizing the Other. Tabloid articles—with headlines like 'MURDERED FOR LOVING OUR VALUES',[58] or 'CORONER SAYS "ARRANGED MARRIAGE" GIRL WAS "VILELY MURDERED". BUT WILL ANYONE EVER STAND TRIAL?'[59]—identify forced marriages and honour killings with Islam, rather than deconstructing these acts as emblematic of a dangerously patriarchal and proprietary attitude towards women that is manifested in various forms that transcend religion, race and culture. The purpose here, again, is not to deny the unacceptable horror of forced marriages, or the need for effective strategies to stop them. Rather, the aim is to expose the way that concern over forced marriages and the lack of choice and consent is arguably, as in the case of honour killings, one-sided, belying the fact that sexual relations of dominance, control and violence exist within

53 Mojúbàobolú Olúfúnké Okome, 'What women, whose development? A critical analysis of reformist feminist evangelism on African women', in Oyěwùmi (ed.), *African Women and Feminism*, 70.
54 Patricia Stamp, 'Burying Otiena: the politics of gender and ethnicity in Kenya', *Signs*, vol. 16, no. 4, 1991, 808–45 (845).
55 Leslye Amede Obiora, 'Feminism, globalisation and culture: after Beijing', *Indiana Journal of Global Legal Studies*, vol. 4, 1997, 355–64 (358).
56 Edward W. Said, *Orientalism* (London: Penguin 2003), 7.
57 Kapur, 'Human rights in the 21st century', 673.
58 Allison Pearson, *Daily Mail*, 21 June 2006.
59 Jaya Narain and James Tozer, *Daily Mail*, 11 January 2008.

'liberal' cultures and societies. The ineffectiveness of socio-legal attitudes towards violence against women in the western context, which is manifested in the 5.6 per cent conviction rate for rape,[60] and the 3.6 per cent conviction rate for domestic violence,[61] is rarely viewed as being symptomatic of a patriarchal culture that condones violence against women. Neither is there recognition of the parallels between a legal system that, through such a low conviction rate, implicitly conveys the impression that women routinely lie about being raped, and the much-demonized *hudood* laws (enacted in Pakistan in 1979) that required four men as eyewitnesses for a charge of rape. In both systems, the testimony of women is deemed unworthy while the word of men is taken as gospel. The issue here is one of consent, and the ways in which this is understood. A juxtaposition of the ways in which conceptions of choice and consent operate in the context of forced marriage and rape reveals the ways in which modern liberal legality conceals sexist attitudes towards violence against women in a 'non-cultural' context.

Political and legal responses to forced marriage centre on the issue of consent.[62] Recent judgements by the English courts have significantly relaxed the legal construction of duress as a ground for vitiating consent to marriage: from a stringent need to show one's 'will was overborne by *genuine fear induced by threats of immediate danger to his life, limb, or liberty*',[63] to 'threats, pressure or whatever it is, such as to *destroy the reality of consent and overbear the will of the individual*',[64] to the vague and indeterminate offering of 'social expectations which can of themselves impose emotional pressure'.[65] This final construction highlights the difficulty in distinguishing forced from arranged marriages; it also posits the *possibility* of individuals taking advantage of loose definitions and stereotypes of coerced Asian women. Again, the aim here is to tease out the double standards that permeate contemporary liberal discourse. In so doing, a more balanced approach can be effected that might facilitate a more meaningful right of exit that takes account of the importance of consent, but also recognizes that different individuals, groups, cultures and communities conceive of consent in a variety of ways. The label 'forced marriages' evokes images of violence and brutality, and connotes physicality—the exercise of violence—yet what is

60 Liz Kelly, Jo Lovett and Linda Regan, *A Gap or a Chasm? Attrition in Reported Rape Cases*, Home Office Research Study 293 (London: Home Office 2005), 25.
61 Women's Aid, 'Saving lives. Reducing harm. Protecting the public. An action plan for tackling violence 2008-11', 5 March 2008, available on the Women's Aid website at www.womensaid.org.uk/domestic-violence-articles.asp?section=000100010022004300 01&itemid=1548 (viewed 16 May 2009).
62 Working Group on Forced Marriage, *A Choice by Right: The Report of the Working Group on Forced Marriage* (London: Home Office Communications Directorate 2000).
63 *Singh v. Singh* [1971] 2 All ER 828, 226.
64 *Hirani v. Hirani* (1983) 4 FLR 232, 234.
65 *Re SK (An Adult) (Forced Marriage: Appropriate Relief)* [2006] 1 W.L.R. 81 (83).

clear is that often the duress is the result of social and familial influence or expectations.[66] In such instances, then, the issue is not force *per se*, but the absence of *consent*. Nowhere is consent more problematic than in rape, where considerations of force and duress feature heavily. The definition of consent—when a person 'agrees by choice, and has the freedom and capacity to make that choice'[67]—is of little help when one considers the problem of determining what constitutes 'freedom' and 'capacity'. Rather, the concept of consent in the context of rape embodies and reflects a broader socially internalized understanding of consent that plays to particular sexist stereo-typical assumptions of women who 'ask for it'.[68]

Consent within rape is thus very much a gendered concept that perpetuates the gendered nature of law,[69] and reinforces the madonna/whore distinction. The exceptionally low conviction rate suggests, among other things, a blatant gender bias in the law that deploys the concept of consent as its key weapon in discriminating against women. Similar to forced marriages, 'the gravamen of rape remains the conjunction of force and non-consent'.[70] Consent then, serves a strategic purpose: it legitimizes sexual violence against women through automatic presumptions about the conduct of rape victims, whereas, in forced marriages, the desire to protect Other women from similar violence means the absence of consent is more readily believed. This racist and sexist deployment of consent acts as a double-edged sword, playing to stereotypes of the Other woman as a weak and helpless victim in need of saving from her savage and barbaric culture, while simultaneously condoning or, at the very least, ignoring or downplaying violence against women in the ethnic majority context. This contradiction is partly attributable to the racism that informs the discourse on forced marriages and partly to discursive and definitional confusion surrounding consent, which operates to the detriment of rape victims yet works in favour of women who have been compelled to marry. Rape exists as a gendered harm, another manifestation of male violence against women. In contrast, forced marriages, though seemingly constructed as a gendered harm, are not in fact conceived as such. Instead, forced marriages are viewed as a cultural harm, perpetrated by Other men against Other women, and another weapon in the battle against illiberal Islam. As with crimes of passion, violence against

66 Ibid.
67 Sexual Offences Act 2003, section 74.
68 ICM, 'Sexual assault research: summary report', 12 October 2005, available on the Amnesty International website at www.amnesty.org.uk/uploads/documents/doc_16619.doc (viewed 16 May 2009).
69 Paul Reynolds, 'Rape, law and sexual consent: the scope and limits to sexual regulation by law', *Contemporary Issues in Law*, vol. 6, no. 1, 2002/3, 92–102.
70 Donald A. Dripps, 'Beyond rape: an essay on the difference between the presence of force and the absence of consent', *Columbia Law Review*, vol. 92, no. 7, 1992, 1780–809 (1784). While it is not necessary for force to have occurred to prove rape, convictions are much harder to establish where the victim displays no signs of violence.

women within a western or non-othered context is tacitly ignored and conceived of as an aberration, while violence within the realm of (Islamic) Otherness is confronted as emblematic of the deviance of Islam as a whole.

Bringing an end to the Crusades

The purpose of this article is not to solve the problems facing women who *are* oppressed by patriarchal norms and modes of practice. Rather, it seeks to reveal the ways in which certain stereotypes and prejudices colour the rhetoric surrounding particular practices that are constructed as being part of Islamic tradition, by custom if not by religion. The constant deployment of Islamphobically informed norms to justify the crusade against Islam on grounds of women's equality works to disguise the operation of similar traditions of violence and inequality within dominant 'white' western liberal culture. The division of the world into polarized factions—Islam/West, us/them, liberal/illiberal—has resulted in gross distortions that negate any attempts at a useful and constructive dialogue about the rights of women in *all* cultures.

Instead, what we are left with is a framework that forces Muslim women into the category of victim. This victim-status is dependent on veiling being seen as a symbol of gender inequality and oppression: a walking *purdah* that symbolizes the control of Muslim men over the sexuality and being of Muslim women. Furthermore, in aligning the veil with hostility to democracy and the fear of fundamentalism, the language of violence weaves its way into the very fabric of the hijab. This insistence on the violence of Muslim men reappears in discussions on honour killings and forced marriages, so linking Islam to brutal thought and action. Contrasting the lenient approach to perpetrators of crimes of passion with the severity with which honour killings are viewed and treated lays bare those particular norms and stereotypes that view religion as a violent and oppressive force that seeks to control and suppress female personhood through the murder of women for perceived transgressions of 'honour'. Accordingly, the concern with violence against Muslim women is revealed as little more than a facade for the demonization and exclusion of the racialized Muslim Other. The consequent effect of this semblance of concern is that violence against women within a 'non-cultural' context becomes an aberration, and that within 'cultural' contexts becomes the norm. Casting honour killings as specifically 'cultural' thus negates any opportunity for formulating credible strategies for dealing with violence against women.[71] The discussion of forced marriages draws out more clearly the ways in which constructions of cultural harm against women have been deployed within the liberal narrative of equality for all as

---

71 Ratna Kapur, *Erotic Justice: Law and the New Politics of Postcolonialism* (London: Glass House Press 2005), 115.

a justification for homogenization and exclusion. The very use of the term 'force' is arguably a strategic misapplication that brutalizes the Other and posits them as

> a violator of rights … and the "British" cultural standard as the civilised measure against which the cultural Other must be assessed. Championing women's rights in the subaltern community and family … becomes a way of delegitimising the community and its familial structures.[72]

Part of this delegitimization requires the depiction of Other women as agency-less victims. The language of force fulfils this requirement by imagining the female victim as bruised and battered. The articulation of force is thus the language of violence, submission and control over the female body. It is this image of cultural violence and control that permeates the discursive crusade currently being waged.

How then to end the battle? Or, at the very least, to even out the lines of battle? What is needed is a dismantling of the latent racism in liberal socio-political thought so that issues of sexism and gender-based oppression can be considered other than through the prism of racism and Islamaphobia. Such a de-racialization of discursive frameworks requires a re-reading of gender-based cultural practices that carves out a space, for example, for viewing veiling in some circumstances as an assertion of identity and resistance to the global forces of homogenization, and even as a form of feminism that resists (male) notions of female sexuality as centred around the body. Creating this space would enable the possibility of viewing these practices through a non-racialized non-coloured lens. In order truly to dismantle the racism inherent within liberal structures, there is a need to create a framework of analysis that enables cultural dissent from within communities without perpetuating the racism from without. Tackling harm against women, as, for example, in forced marriages or honour killings, requires strategies that are free from racial bias and that embody a conception of culture as fluid and ever-changing, rather than the (deliberate) construction of culture as fixed and static that permeates much of the (racist) discourse on multiculturalism. Such a space would thus enable a move away from the logic of paradigm and polarity that permeates western liberal discourse.[73]

To facilitate a genuine end to the so-called 'clash of civilizations', we need to unpack, acknowledge and begin to dismantle the prejudicial stereotypes that have become so much the norm. As long as we continue to play into stereotypes, we miss the opportunity to move forward to a time of true acceptance and recognition that allows *all* voices to be

72 Ibid., 156.
73 Kathi Weeks, *Constituting Feminist Subjects* (Ithaca, NY: Cornell University Press 1998), 48–69.

heard, and *all* religions, cultures and societies to be fairly and neutrally critiqued.

Muslim headscarves in France and army uniforms in Israel: a comparative study of citizenship as mask

LEORA BILSKY

ABSTRACT On 15 March 2004 the French government passed a law that banned the wearing of 'conspicuous signs' of religious affiliation in public schools. The ban was the result of an ongoing controversy in France about the admissibility of the hijab worn by Muslim schoolgirls. On 8 November 2007 Professor Nizar Hassan, a Palestinian citizen of Israel, asked a Jewish student of his, who came to class wearing his army uniform, to refrain from wearing it to his classes in the future. Following the incident a public storm erupted in which high-ranking officers in the Israeli army participated. Considering these two very different controversies involving individuals belonging to minority groups can provide a new perspective on current debates about citizenship and difference. It can shift the focus of the investigation from the Islamic Other as an object of enquiry to the interaction between the state and the individual as participants in a complex symbolic conversation. The two controversies should be read against the background of two contrasting conceptions of the public sphere and its relations to equality: while the French republic insists on creating a neutral public sphere as a pre-condition for equality, in Israel the possibility of equality is connected to guaranteeing a separation between the public and the private sphere. Comparing the two controversies, Bilsky considers one recurrent theme that dominated them both, the accusation of hypocrisy, and she analyses the ways in which this accusation distorted the public debate. She argues that the focus on hypocrisy reveals an important aspect of citizenship that was misinterpreted in both cases, namely, 'citizenship as mask'. Without a proper understanding of the role of masks in democratic citizenship, we witness the transformation of a debate about equality and plurality into a competition for the exposing of hypocrites. Bilsky returns to Hannah Arendt's reflections on citizenship as a way to understand the limits of a theory of equality based on sameness, and uses the two controversies to demonstrate the need to develop a theory of citizenship that can better respond to both equality and plurality.

I would like to thank Liat Kozma, Pnina Lahav and Daphne Barak-Erez for their readings and comments. I thank Rottem Rosenberg, my research assistant, and my students in the Tel Aviv Law Faculty for discussing earlier drafts of this article. I also thank the Cegla Center for the grant that enabled this research.

Covering and uncovering

On 15 March 2004 the French government passed a law that banned the wearing of 'conspicuous signs' of religious affiliation in public schools. The ban was the result of an ongoing controversy in France about the admissibility of the hijab worn by Muslim girls to school. France is not the only European country to worry about girls or women wearing the Muslim headscarf. Similar legislation has been proposed in Belgium, Holland and Bulgaria. In this article I will focus on the controversy in France since it represents what we can call an 'ideal type' of the republican model of accommodating minority religious groups, one based on a commitment to secularism, abstract individualism,[1] and the integration of minorities through assimilation. I will contrast this model with the Israeli model of a 'Jewish and democratic' state. The Israeli system is based on the opposite values of non-separation between church and state, on collectivism and on the *millet* system for accommodating the religious differences of minority groups. As a point of comparison with the French controversy over the hijab, I will use a less well-known Israeli controversy over army uniforms. Specifically, I will consider one recurrent theme that dominated the two controversies, the accusation of hypocrisy, and analyse the ways in which this accusation distorted the public debate. I will then offer a theory of citizenship that can explain this peculiar choice of rhetoric. I argue that the focus on hypocrisy reveals an important aspect of citizenship that underpins both debates, namely, 'citizenship as mask'. Without a proper understanding of the role of masks in promoting democratic citizenship, we can witness, as we did here, the transformation of a debate about equality and plurality into a competition for the exposing of hypocrites.[2]

On 3 December 2007 the Israeli Knesset education committee published a statement condemning Professor Nizar Hassan of Sapir College in Sderot. Hassan, a filmmaker, is a Palestinian citizen of Israel. He was denounced for insulting an Israeli army officer in uniform. The incident occurred on 8 November 2007 when a film student who came directly from his military service appeared in Hassan's classroom in army uniform. Hassan asked the student to avoid coming to his class in uniform in the future. Following the incident a public storm erupted in which high-ranking officers in the Israeli army participated. Lieutenant General Gabi Ashkenazi, Chief of General

1 The notion of 'abstract individualism' assumes that essential human characteristics are properties of every individual regardless of particular circumstances. For more on 'abstract individualism' in the context of the French controversy over the hijab, see Joan Wallach Scott, *The Politics of the Veil* (Princeton, NJ: Princeton University Press 2007), 124–50.
2 See Leora Bilsky, 'Uniforms and veils: what difference does the difference make?', *Cardozo Law Review*, vol. 30, no. 6, 2009, 101–29 (forthcoming), for a full comparison of the two controversies. Here, I focus on the theme of hypocrisy, and develop a theory, based on Hannah Arendt's writings, that can explain its role in the two debates.

Staff, demanded an explanation. General Stern, in charge of human resources in the army, required an apology. After a Knesset committee condemned him, Sapir College suspended Hassan and appointed a hearing committee that published its report on 31 January 2008. The committee, consisting of three academics, recommended that Hassan's further employment should be on condition that he apologize to the student. Subsequently, the president of Sapir College, Zeev Tzahor, wrote a letter to Hassan in which he required, in addition to the apology, that Hassan submit a statement in which he declared his commitment to honouring the uniform of the Israel Defence Forces (IDF). Hassan refused to apologize under such conditions. These events received broad media coverage and caused a public uproar. Hassan threatened to sue the college in the labour court. Later, he reached an agreement with the college according to which he would be re-employed after one semester, and compensated for the time in which he was suspended; in return, he withdrew his legal suit. The college never officially withdrew its requirement that Hassan apologize.

The debate over the hijab in France and the one over the uniform in Israel evinced some basic similarities. Both dealt with the accommodation of individuals belonging to a minority group. Both involved the education system (secondary schools in France, higher education in Israel). They both focused on the use of symbols, specifically, the wearing of certain 'conspicuous' articles of clothing in the public sphere. Both ignited a public storm, condemnations, identifications and a heated debate that included even the national parliaments. These similarities notwithstanding, a basic difference remained: the diametrically opposite ways in which individuals belonging to a minority group chose to challenge the terms of citizenship offered to them by their respective political systems. In France, some schoolgirls chose to question the principles of abstract individualism and secularism by showing up at school after the ban wearing the hijab. This act challenged the republican model whereby one's social, religious, ethnic and other origins remain invisible in the public sphere. In Israel a Palestinian professor moved in the opposite direction. He challenged the political system—which routinely labels and classifies people according to their religious, ethnic and national origins—by excluding the 'mark' from his classroom. Hassan required that any 'conspicuous' sign, in particular, army uniforms of any kind, be removed in order to create a neutral space in his classroom, a space in which a dialogue could be conducted between teacher and student as equal human beings.

The two controversies should be read against the two different conceptions of the public sphere and its relations to equality. While the French republic insists on creating a neutral public sphere as a precondition for equality, in Israel the possibility of equality is provided by the guarantee of a separation between public and private spheres. That is, the public sphere might be a non-neutral space, shaped by the symbols of the dominant Jewish group, but the individual rights of people belonging to religious minority groups are protected by law.³ Moreover, while the Israeli public sphere is shaped by Jewish symbols, individuals belonging to different religious and ethnic groups are welcome to enter it with their group markers, be it hijab or *kaffiyeh*. Notwithstanding this difference, in both cases, the challenge of the individuals seemed to pierce the 'mask' of equality presented by the state. The official reaction to this challenge was to adopt further masks by redirecting the blame back on to the individuals, by accusing them of being political extremists—of 'covering up' radical Islamist or nationatlist beliefs—and by narrowing the boundaries of freedom of speech. The accusation of hypocrisy became a focal point in both debates.

How can a comparison of the two controversies advance our thinking about the accommodation of religious, ethnic or national minorities by a democratic state? I argue that it can help us to go beyond the essentialist understanding of Islam that is inherent in the 'clash of civilizations' paradigm, and to develop a more contextual understanding of the terms of citizenship offered to minorities. This allows for a shift in focus away from individuals (their choices, family backgrounds, religious beliefs) to the interrelations between an individual belonging to a minority group and the citizenship regime constructed by a political community. A comparison of these two cases can shed light on the way individuals belonging to minority religious and ethnic groups fare under very different organizations of a public space (republican and ethno-democratic).⁴

Both debates, about pieces of clothing, were quickly turned into debates about hypocrisy. The arguments on both sides in both debates engaged the opposition between authenticity and hypocrisy. Each side tried to pierce the 'mask' of the other side, exposing him/her as a hypocrite. In order to make sense of this recurrent rhetorical move and the emotional charge that it produced, I turn to theory. Specifically, to the writings of the political thinker Hannah Arendt on hypocrisy, and her subsequent articulation of an ideal of citizenship based on the metaphor of the Greek theatrical mask. I suggest that Arendt's writings on the subject offer a key to understanding the pathologies of the two controversies. In particular, I argue that contemporary theories of citizenship are locked in the tension between two ideals that push in opposite directions: 'equality as sameness' and 'authenticity as difference'. But, before getting to the theory, it's worth describing the contexts in which the charge of hypocrisy was raised in the French and Israeli controversies.

3 For an elaboration on the view that there is no necessary contradiction in Israel's being simultaneously 'Jewish' and 'democratic', see Ruth Gavison, 'The Jews' right to statehood: a defense', *Azure*, vol. 15, 2003, 70–108.
4 See Ruti Teitel, 'Militating democracy: comparative constitutional perspectives', *Michigan Journal of International Law*, vol. 29, no. 1, 2007, 49–70 (58–62). Teitel suggests focusing on the different conceptions of public space in the United States (libertarian) and in Europe (militant) in order to understand the differing approaches to church–state relations.

Context

My analysis begins with an unexpected commonality between the two controversies. Both debates about articles of clothing were quickly turned into debates about hypocrisy and the terms of citizenship offered to minority groups. It is the charge of hypocrisy, I claim, that can offer a key to understanding the significance of wearing symbolic pieces of clothing in the public domain. The occasion for the accusation of hypocrisy and 'cover-up' was the act of veiling (hijab) in the one case, and the demand for unveiling (uniform) in the other. The accusation of hypocrisy points to a complex association of democratic citizenship to the concept of the mask. On the one hand, democratic citizenship promises equality, and this is to be achieved first and foremost by offering a legal mask (legal persona) to all citizens alike. On the other hand, the foundation of a democratic culture is transparency, whereby deceit is seen as threatening the very foundation of public debate. Moreover, democracy is also based on individualism, and this, in turn, points to the need to recognize the uniqueness of each individual. These contradictions are reflected in contemporary debates about the conflicting values of assimilation and multiculturalism as two paradigms for the public sphere and citizenship.[5] Those that express surprise that an 'innocent' piece of cloth like a headscarf can cause so much anxiety and emotion miss this dimension of the controversy. In my view, the symbolic power of the hijab or the uniform relates to the unresolved tension at the heart of democratic culture between 'covering' and 'transparency'. Before developing this idea, I will outline the contexts in which the accusations of hypocrisy were raised. As the French controversy is more familiar, I will dedicate more space to the Israeli case.

France

Historian Joan Wallach Scott, in her recent book *The Politics of the Veil*, maintains that the significance of the French controversy over the hijab in public schools cannot be explained by numbers alone since it did not involve a significant number of students.[6] She poses the question: 'What is it about the headscarf that makes it the focus of controversy, the sign of something

5 Rogers Brubaker, 'Immigration, citizenship, and the nation state in France and Germany', in Gershon Shafir (ed.), *The Citizenship Debates: A Reader* (Minneapolis: University of Minnesota Press 1998), 131–67; Charles Taylor, 'The politics of recognition', in Charles Taylor, *Multiculturalism: Examining The Politics of Recognition*, ed. Amy Gutmann (Princeton, NJ: Princeton University Press 1994), 25–75.
6 Scott, *The Politics of the Veil*, 3. As Scott points out, only 14 per cent of French Muslim women wore the hijab before the law was passed. See also the case of *Dogru* v. *France* [2008] ECHR 1579, in which the European Court of Human Rights upheld the decision to expel a French Muslim student from her public school on the grounds that she insisted on wearing her hijab. In the decision, it is noted that, in the year 2004–5, when the law was passed, a total of 639 religious signs were recorded in French public

intolerable?' She rejects the formal answer that presents the conflict in terms of a cultural clash between Islam and the values of French republicanism, in particular secularism, abstract individualism and gender equality. Scott argues that the controversy was not about the separation between church and state, and instead attributes its origins to racism, immigration problems and France's colonial past.

According to Scott, the headscarves that the Muslim girls wear exposes a symbolic veil of abstract republicanism behind which unresolved problems of French citizenship are hidden. The act of wearing the hijab in public schools challenges at a symbolic level the republican ethos of equality by demonstrating that it cannot accommodate difference. That is, a woman who claims that the very demand to 'unveil' unequally burdens her makes the promise of equal citizenship a sham.

Scott's analysis exposes the layers of hypocrisy shaping the debate. In particular, she raises doubts about claims that the ban defends the ideals of French universalism and gender equality. Indeed the first layer of hypocrisy she describes relates to the ideal of universalism. The 'universality' entailed by the republican ideal has been presented as a demand for the creation of a religiously neutral public sphere. The ban on the hijab demonstrates the intention of legislators to ensure that France is a unified nation, and its public sphere is secular. However, since the Muslim and Jewish religions, for instance, are at once religious and cultural, the effect of this intention is to create a culturally homogeneous public sphere. Those supporting the ban vehemently deny that the demand for neutrality might also be discriminatory against certain religious groups, and might even be racist. For example, they ignore the fact that the legislation originally excluded the hijab from schools and only later was reformulated to include all religious signs. Scott dedicates a chapter to exploring the long history of French racism during which North African Muslims were the target.[7] She argues that the rush to ban the hijab avoided dealing with the more complicated problem of the social and economic integration of immigrants from former colonies by targeting the victims of discrimination as the cause of the problem.[8]

Scott's second layer of hypocrisy relates to the role of gender in the debate. The hijab is considered by supporters of the ban to be inimical to the French

---

schools, and that this total was less than 50 per cent of the signs that were recorded during the year before. This means that about 1,300 cases were noted in the year before the law had been passed.

7 Scott, *The Politics of the Veil*, 42–89.

8 Ibid., 85–9. Likewise, Ruti Teitel argues that, behind the arguments in defence of equality, one can find religious discrimination: 'the language of the proposed garb law suggests it is designed not to equalize, but rather to cover up present discrimination against millions of France's Muslim citizens': Ruti Teitel, 'Through the veil, darkly: why France's ban on the wearing of religious symbols is even more pernicious than it appears', *FindLaw's Writ* (online), 16 February 2004, at http://writ.news.findlaw.com/commentary/20040216_teitel.html (viewed 21 May 2009).

republican principle of equality because it signifies the subordination of Muslim women. However, in a chapter dedicated to exploring gender relations in France, Scott demonstrates how the ideal of an abstract individual upheld by French republicanism is hard to square with gender equality, and with the need to accommodate the difference that gender (and in particular female sexuality) makes in the public sphere. The very focus on the hijab is interpreted by Scott as a sign of a hypocritical political discourse that avoids discussing the issues of racism, gender equality, and economic and social discrimination, all hiding behind the veils of a few Muslim girls.

Hypocrisy plays a central role in Scott's analysis of the failures of the French controversy. She suggests that the main justification for the support of the ban, the republican ideals of universalism, secularism and equality, cannot withstand close scrutiny. These ideals are hypocritical in the sense that they are masks that hide deeper problems of French citizenship, namely, racism, the unsuccessful integration of immigrants and gender inequality, and that they fail to accommodate differences (religious, ethnic or gender). A genuine debate on French citizenship would have to defend the assumption that equality requires 'similarity' or assimilation to a dominant norm, against the argument that it is precisely these requirements that entrench inequality and discrimination against groups deemed 'unassimilable' or groups that insist on being treated as equals without hiding away their differences.

Israel

The uniform controversy in Israel erupted over the actions of an individual Palestinian Arab professor. As in the French case, we can ask: 'What is it about the army uniform that makes its exclusion from the public sphere a sign of something intolerable?' The search for an answer leads us to examine the problems of citizenship under the terms of the Jewish and democratic state.

While in France the accusation of hypocrisy was mainly raised against the defenders of the ban, in Israel it was first directed at the individual who triggered the debate.[9] Following the public outcry over Hassan's treatment of an officer in uniform, Sapir College appointed a hearing committee on 25 November 2007 to investigate the incident and make recommendations. The committee published its report and recommendations on 31 January 2008. The report begins by stating the 'facts': 'The clash between Professor

9 This difference can be connected to the public perception of the different agents involved. In France the teenage girls were depicted as lacking free agency or real choice; hence, the concept of 'hypocrisy', which depends on a distinction between outside/inside, between internal motives and external explanations, cannot apply to them. Nevertheless, we can find a variation on the accusation of hypocrisy when wearing the hijab is taken to represent a commitment to radical Islam. However, as Scott notes, this type of accusation contradicts the depiction of the girls as lacking meaningful agency: Scott, *The Politics of the Veil*, 124–50.

Nizar Hassan and the student Eyal Cohen concerned the request by the lecturer to the student, who arrived directly from his military service wearing his uniform, not to appear in uniform in class in the future.'[10] This statement is not contested. However, its interpretation by the two parties diverges dramatically. Hassan explained to the hearing committee that his request stemmed from his commitment to the values of humanism and universalism. He explained that he wanted to meet his students in the classroom as individual human beings, not as soldiers, neither as Jews nor as Arabs. He did not mean to humiliate the student. He saw the uniform as an expression of violence and militarism, and reacted against it.

The committee dismissed Hassan's explanation: 'Even though Nizar [*sic*] attempted to present his behaviour as motivated by purely humanistic values, the committee thinks that it was actually a result of his deep reservations about unambiguous symbols of Israeli existence.'[11] In place of humanist values, the committee saw radical nationalism. The language of 'cover-up' and play-acting was repeated throughout the report. The committee saw Hassan as attempting to provide cover for himself with anti-militaristic rhetoric. It concluded:

> Nizar [*sic*] abused his status and authority as a professor in order to display his views, feelings and frustrations, as a son of the Arab minority in Israel, while disguising himself [literally, *covering himself in a cloak*] as a 'humanist' holding a 'universalist' world-view. In truth, he adopted an aggressive position with a clearly nationalist character, analogous to other radical nationalist views common in Jewish Israeli society.[12]

The report first set out to strip away the mask of humanism that Hassan purportedly took on by pointing to the underlying 'truth' about his nationalism. The work of the committee was presented as an act of unveiling: it pierced the mask of abstract individualism adopted by Hassan, and discovered behind it the frustrations of someone belonging to the 'Arab minority'. In short, Hassan was presented as a hypocrite: a nationalist disguised as a humanist. It is interesting to note that, by means of this unveiling, the committee was able not only to fit Hassan into the familiar category of 'Palestinian nationalist', but also to assign to itself the role of the moderate centrist, threatened alike by radical Jewish and Palestinian nationalists. The accusation of hypocrisy thus helped to avoid dealing either with Hassan's position as a Palestinian citizen of Israel or his individual

10 'Duah ha-vaada li-vdika ve-shimua le-berur ha-tluna neged ha-martse Nizar Hassan', 31 January 2008, available on the Sapir College website at http://college.sapir.ac.il/ sapir/News/shimua.pdf (viewed 22 May 2009). All excerpts from the Hebrew report are translated by the author.
11 Ibid.
12 Ibid.

claim to humanism. Moreover, it helped to avoid discussion of the central issue Hassan raised about the non-neutrality of the public sphere of education in Israel undermining the possibility of equality.

In an interview with *Haaretz*, Hassan conveyed his response to the committee's report. It was the accusation of hypocrisy that enraged him the most.

> First of all I am not the 'son of a minority'. I am a Palestinian and proud of it. Second, how could they decide that I don't hold humanist values, and that it is not my principled view? They did not even ask me how I would treat a Jordanian or Lebanese or French or any other soldier. The committee had no doubt that I am acting out of frustration. But how can they talk about the experience of the Arab minority in Israel when they don't have a clue what it is? They don't even understand Arabic.[13]

The hearing committee accused Hassan of hypocrisy, and he in turn accused the committee of being hypocritical. He took issue in particular with the committee's characterization of the wearing of army uniforms. The report stated that 'reserve service in Israel cannot be separated from civilian life. This is a fundamental fact that cannot be denied or repressed, and it is unique to Israeli life ... This is a civilian army in the full sense of the word.' It was to this characterization of the IDF as an 'army of civilians', neither separate nor separable from Israeli civic society, that Hassan objected:

> Say that you are a militaristic society that cannot live without weapons and uniforms and we'll end the story. What do you want from me? Take me out of the game and build yourself a college in your image, a Jewish and Zionist college, with the values that the hearing committee talks about, and a precondition for working in it will be a promise to honour the uniform. But stop with this double standard. It is not acceptable to me that a student will enter my classroom wearing a uniform and weapons ... not out of a feeling of frustration, as the committee claims, but out of a belief that a complete separation is needed between the two systems.[14]

Hassan's complaint about the 'Jewish and Zionist' college echoes (in a distorted way) Israel's self-characterization in its foundational laws as 'Jewish and democratic'.[15] He argued that, behind the veil of democracy,

---

13 Tamara Traubman and Yuval Azulai, 'Hayal, shaper hofaatha!', *Haaretz Magazine*, 23 April 2008.
14 Ibid.
15 Israel is defined as a 'Jewish and democratic state' in its basic laws. See 'Basic Law: Human Dignity and Liberty', clause 1, passed by the Knesset on 17 March 1992; 'Basic Law: Freedom of Occupation', clause 2, passed by the Knesset on 9 March 1994.

lay the reality of ethnocracy.[16] His employment at Sapir College served as a fig-leaf, a gesture meant to show the equality enjoyed by Palestinian citizens in Israel. However, it was not a real commitment to democracy since the moment he attempted to exercise his academic freedom (trying to shape his classroom as a neutral space free of uniforms), he was suspended and his employment became expressly conditional on his commitment to honour the Israeli army uniform. In other words, his act triggered a hidden contract, one that put the 'Jewish' before the 'democratic' whenever the two collided.[17]

According to Hassan, Israeli democracy is flawed in another way. Behind the presentation of the IDF as a 'civilian army' lies the reality of a militaristic society. Since its inception the Israeli army has been presented as a key instrument in Israel for achieving *mamlachtiyut*.[18] According to this ethos, compulsory and nearly universal service is central to the army's assimilatory and equalizing role.[19] The army is understood, alongside the public school, to be a central component in the national and democratic revolution

16 The term 'ethnocracy' was first used in the Israeli context by Oren Yiftachel, who argued that Israel should be defined as an 'ethnocracy', a regime that is neither authoritarian nor democratic since, although it exhibits several democratic features, it facilitates a non-democratic seizure of the country by one ethnic group (the Jews). In this regime, there cannot truly be equal citizenship for those who are not part of the dominant ethnic group, i.e. non-Jews: Oren Yiftachel, '"Ethnocracy": the politics of Judaizing Israel/Palestine', *Constellations*, vol. 6, no. 3, 1999, 364–91 (364). Similarly, but with some difference, Sammy Smooha characterizes Israel as an 'ethnic democracy', a democratic regime that gives individual civil and political, as well as some collective, rights to minorities, while attempting to create a homogeneous nation–state, a state of and for a particular ethnic community. In this type of regime minorities are treated as second-class citizens, but are allowed to engage in democratic struggles to improve their status: Sammy Smooha, 'Ethnic democracy: Israel as an archetype', *Israel Studies*, vol. 2, no. 2, 1998, 198–241 (199–200).

17 For more about the conflict between 'Jewish' and 'democratic' as it was played out in the trial of Yigal Amir, the assassin of Prime Minister Yitzhak Rabin, see Leora Bilsky, *Transformative Justice: Israeli Identity on Trial* (Ann Arbor: University of Michigan Press 2004), 201–36.

18 There is no English equivalent of *mamlachtiyut*. Hebrew-English dictionaries translate the term as 'statehood' or 'sovereignty'. However, as legal historian Nir Kedar points out, this could be misleading as it misses the important normative aspect of the term. Kedar suggests that *mamlachtiyut* 'is a contemporary political ideology that copes simultaneously with the form and substance of two basic characteristics of the modern state: sovereignty and norm … the term not only implies sovereignty (i.e. power) and formal state machinery but is a normative expression that stresses "state consciousness", i.e. society's ability to construct a sovereign polity based on the respect of democracy, law and civic values': Nir Kedar, 'Ben-Gurion's *mamlkhtiyut*: etymological and theoretical roots', *Israel Studies*, vol. 7, no. 3, 2002, 117.

19 For more on the role of the army in Israeli democracy, mainly in the country's early years, see Uri Ben-Eliezer, *The Making of Israeli Militarism* (Bloomington: Indiana University Press 1998), 193–206. For the implication of the construction of citizen-as-soldier for the citizenship of women, see Niza Berkovitz, '"Eshet hail mi imtsa": nashim ve-ezrahut be-Israel', *Sociologia Israelit* (Israeli Sociology), vol. 2, no. 1, 1999, 277–317.

envisioned by the founding Zionist movement. Hassan challenged this understanding by advancing a critical reading of the role of the army in Israeli society. Where others see democratization, he sees militarization. The contrast between these two interpretations is particularly revealing when Hassan demands the exclusion of the army uniform (that is, the uniform as worn by students) from the classroom in the name of democratization.[20] Instead of seeing both military and educational institutions as harmonious components of the Israeli democratization project, each stands in contradiction to the other. Hassan claims that only by separating the army from the system of education can democracy be achieved.[21] In other words, Hassan attempts to show that, behind the mask of a 'civilian army' that seems to be harmonious with democratic ideals, lies the reality of militarism, of the penetration of the army into Israeli civil society and the subsequent unequal distribution of power to different groups according to their relation to the army.[22]

Interestingly, Hassan refrains from complaining about the discrimination against Arabs in Israel's higher education system. For example, he does not point to the very small percentage of Arab professors teaching in Israeli universities and colleges.[23] In fact, in his interview, Hassan argued that, if he had taken upon himself the assigned role of 'son of a minority' asking for

20 It is interesting to compare this notion to the argument over whether the draft of women into combat units promotes democratic values and equality. For more on this argument, see Daphne Barak-Erez, 'Al tayasot ve-sarbaniot matspun', in Daphne Barak-Erez (chief ed.), *Iyunim Be-Mishpat, Migdar VeFeminism* (Srigim-lion: Nevo 2007), 65–98. For a critical view of the military draft's ability to promote democratization and gender equality, see Hassan Jabareen, 'Likrat gishot bikortiot shel ha-miut ha-Palestini: ezrahut, leumiut ve-feminism ba-mishpat ha-Israeli', in Daphne Barak-Erez (ed.), *Tsava, Hevra ve-Mishpat* (Tel Aviv: Ramot Press 2002), 53–93.

21 For a discussion of the different meanings of 'militarism', see Baruch Kimmerling, 'Militarism ba-hevra ha-Israelit', *Teoria ve-Bikoret* (Theory and Criticism), vol. 4, 1993, 123–40. Kimmerling rejects the argument, posed by several political scientists, that militarism has not developed in Israel despite the army's central role. Kimmerling distinguishes between different types of militarism and argues that Israel is characterized by 'civil militarism', which is manifested by a penetration of the army into civil spheres such as education and politics.

22 For more on the army as an instrument of stratification between various social groups in Israel, see Gershon Shafir and Yoav Peled, *Being Israeli: The Dynamics of Multiple Citizenship* (Cambridge: Cambridge University Press 2002), 101–3, 126, 143–5; Yagil Levi, *Tsava Aher Le-Israel: Militarism Homrani Be-Israel* (Tel Aviv: Yedioth Ahronoth Books 2003); and Orna Sasson-Levy, 'Constructing identities at the margins: masculinities and citizenship in the Israeli army', *Sociological Quarterly*, vol. 43, no. 3, 2002, 357–83.

23 According to research conducted by Sikkuy (The Association for the Advancement of Civic Equality in Israel), in 2007 Arabs constituted only 1.4 per cent of the senior academic staff of universities in Israel, and 13.8 per cent of the senior staff of colleges: Yaser Awad, 'Yetsug ha-ezrahim ha-Aravim be-maarehet ha-haskala ha-gvoha 2008', December 2008, available on the Sikkuy website at http://www.sikkuy.org.il/docs/haskala2008.doc (viewed 21 May 2009).

special consideration and understanding of his personal problem with IDF uniforms, there would have been no problem. And, indeed, it is apparent from the report that what the committee found most difficult was taking Hassan's position at face value, as a principled objection to the non-separation between the army and the educational system in Israel.[24] For this reason the committee characterized his views and opinions as psychological in nature, as the feelings and frustrations of 'a son of the Arab minority', assuming that his group affiliation explained everything there was to explain about his views.

Hassan attempted to shape the space of his classroom based on the French republican principles of abstract individualism, universalism and humanism. In the name of these principles, Hassan justified his exclusion of the IDF uniform. He explained that he wanted to teach in a space free of national symbols, uniforms of any kind, in order to be able to meet his students as equal human beings. While Muslim students in France ask that the enforced neutrality of the public sphere be limited to accommodate their religious difference, Hassan asks that this neutrality be adopted in order to correct the conditions of inequality. His problem stems from the fact that, in Israeli public space, individuals are constantly labelled according to their social/ethnic/religious group, and are not offered a neutral mask of citizenship. Hassan's ban on uniforms was a private one, and did not have the force of law. It was the initiative of an individual, an act that tried to expose the non-separation of the various sectors of society (educational, political, military) as a failure of Israeli democracy. For this intervention, he was disciplined and publicly condemned.

Theory

The charge of hypocrisy is based on a demand for uncovering, for the mask to be pierced to reveal the 'truth' about the politics behind it. Although the French Muslim schoolgirls and Nizar Hassan made diametrically opposing demands—to cover on the one hand, and to uncover on the other—both were accused of hypocrisy. One way to articulate the injury that they suffered is offered by the American law professor Kenji Yoshino in his book *Covering*. Yoshino engages in exposing a hidden type of discrimination that is formulated as a demand for 'covering' or 'ton[ing] down a disfavored identity to fit into the mainstream'.[25] We see that neither the Muslim students nor Hassan experience the classical type of discrimination. They are

24 Henriette Dahan-Kalev and Udi Lebel, 'Generalim be-batei ha-sefer: al ha-kesher ha-mitatsem bein tsava ve-politica', *Politika: Ktav-Et Le-Mada Ha-Medina ve-Yahasim Bein-Leumiim* (Politika: Journal of Political Science and International Relations), vol. 11/12, 2004, 27–40.
25 Kenji Yoshino, *Covering: The Hidden Assault on Our Civil Rights* (New York: Random House 2006), ix.

not asked to 'convert' or to 'pass', that is, to conceal their identities as members of a religious or ethnic minority group. In both cases, individuals belonging to such minority groups are accepted as participants in the system of education, either as students or as teachers. Moreover, no special demand is directed at them as members of that group: they ask for a dress code, or are asked to comply with one, that is or would be universally applied. So, of what does the discrimination consist? Yoshino suggests the term 'covering' to explain the injury, a demand that is directed at individuals belonging to minority groups, pressuring them to assimilate or disguise their different appearances. Yoshino maintains that gays, people of colour and women are faced with pressure to cover their different appearances and that anti-discrimination law should protect them against such pressure.

We can interpret the demand directed at the Muslim girls in France to unveil as a demand to cover their difference (their religious dress code) by 'uncovering', to arrive at school without a hijab. The demand is not to negate their religious belief, but only to cover its conspicuous representation, to cover its public manifestation.[26] The 'covering' demand is more subtle in Hassan's case since his appearance is no different than that of any other Israeli. His difference stems from his attitude to the army uniforms of Jewish students. In the eyes of an Israeli Jew, these army uniforms are virtually invisible since they appear everywhere. Accordingly, Hassan's demand that they be excluded from his classroom directs our attention to his 'difference': he refuses to 'cover' and to treat the uniforms as invisible. His refusal reveals the symbolic meaning of army uniforms, a meaning that is not universally shared throughout the society. He thus contests the problematic equation (or identity) made between a citizen and a soldier in Israel.

Understanding the demand for 'covering' as an unequivocal injury depends on further assumptions: first, the existence of an 'authentic self', prior to any social interaction; and second, the negative evaluation of the demand for assimilation. Both assumptions are contested. They are informed by a liberal, atomistic understanding of self-identity.[27] Moreover, they presuppose a weak public sphere, and a minimal role of the state in shaping equal citizenship through the mechanisms of assimilation and integration. The American type of multiculturalism assumes that the main threat to religious freedom comes from the state and is, accordingly, based on a weak public sphere. On the other hand, the French republican system sees the main threat as coming from religious groups and is, accordingly, based on a strong public sphere actively constructed as religiously neutral by the state. Republican systems conceive of civic equality as a political achievement in which assimilation plays a central role. Israel offers a more complicated

26 Judith Resnik, 'Living their legal commitments: paideic communities, courts, and Robert Cover', *Yale Journal of Law and Humanities*, vol. 17, no. 1, 2005, 17–55.
27 Paul Horwitz, 'Uncovering identity', *Michigan Law Review*, vol. 105, no. 6, 2007, 1283–300.

model since it endorses a strong public sphere in which the state engages in the construction of Israeli Jewish citizenship by various processes of assimilation. However, the state is not committed to a 'neutral' public space and equality for minority groups is to be achieved by respecting the rights of individuals.

Yoshino acknowledges that seeing all demands for 'covering' as a hidden act of discrimination stands in tension with approaches to civic equality based on a positive evaluation of assimilation.[28] In order to create or enhance civic solidarity and social mobility in a plural society we often need public education, a common language and the sharing of a basic corpus of literature. All of these require different degrees of 'covering'. Considering the very demand for 'covering' as an act of civil discrimination can therefore undermine the very project of achieving equal citizenship and social solidarity. It seems that, without interrogating more closely the demand for assimilation and its relation to equal citizenship, a demand for 'covering' cannot be taken as illegitimate in and of itself.

The political philosopher Charles Taylor explains the dilemma as stemming from two contrasting ideals that are fundamental to modern democratic cultures.[29] On the one hand, equal respect for each citizen requires that we do not look beyond the 'mask' of citizenship, that we ignore salient group markers that set us apart. On the other hand, the principle of individualism requires recognition of the uniqueness of each human being, a recognition that often leads to the acknowledgment of differences. How do we reconcile these two ideals?

Yoshino's call to understand 'covering' as discrimination highlights this tension. American anti-discrimination law is based on the recognition that certain groups whose 'difference' is apparent (such as African Americans or women) should enjoy stronger protection by the court. 'Strict scrutiny' is a legal doctrine that recognizes difference as irrelevant, and asks us to ignore it in order to treat people as equals. Demands for 'covering' ease the tension between difference and sameness, helping the majority accept individuals belonging to minority groups by toning down their differences. The legal blindness can create its own discrimination: because it does not recognize difference, it does not allow it an equal footing in the public sphere. Making the very demand to 'cover' part of anti-discrimination law responds to this problem by enhancing the ideal of 'uniqueness'. The demand for equality is also a demand for the acceptance of difference. Does Yoshino expose a blind spot in American anti-discrimination law, or does he merely come up against the conceptual limit of anti-discrimination law?

28 Accordingly, Yoshino acknowledges that not every demand for covering should be rejected but should, instead, trigger a conversation in which good reasons are given for supporting the demand, balancing them against the loss of liberty on the part of the individual.
29 Taylor, *Multiculturalism*.

Yoshino remains ambivalent with respect to the legitimacy of assimilation, precisely because he does not offer an alternative understanding of equality. Arguing against 'covering' seems to stand at odds with the basic assumption that 'similar people' should be treated alike. In other words, under the assumption that equality presupposes similarity (or legal blindness to immutable difference), it is very hard to formulate a demand for 'covering' as discrimination. In order to proceed, we should consider whether the two ideals that Taylor identifies at the core of modern democracies contradict each other, or whether there is a way to reconcile them under a different conception of equality. Yoshino's theory helps us expose the tension between 'equality as similarity' and 'authenticity as difference'. By articulating the harm of 'covering', he points to the dark side of assimilation, and seems to tilt the balance in favour of 'authenticity'. However, when we try to engage the question with regard to political systems that endorse robust republicanism, this accommodation breaks down. When a 'civic mask' is upheld as the main mechanism for achieving equality, arguments for the harm of 'covering' often sound nonsensical. This might explain why hypocrisy, and the relation between masks and identities, became central to the debates in France and in Israel.

Citizenship as mask

In her analysis of the French Revolution and the wave of terror that followed it, Hannah Arendt points to a puzzle: 'It must seem strange that hypocrisy—one of the minor vices, we are inclined to think—should have been hated more than all the other vices taken together.'[30] In trying to explain this, Arendt offers an analysis of the relation of the public sphere to citizenship, and the way in which hypocrisy undermines it.

The clearest expression of the ideal of 'citizenship as mask' can be found in Arendt's book *On Revolution*. Here she borrows from the original meaning of 'persona' as a mask, explaining that it functioned both to cover the face and to allow the voice of the speaker to be heard.[31]

> In its original meaning, it [*persona*] signified the mask ancient actors used to wear in a play ... The mask as such obviously had two functions: it had to hide, or

---

30 Hannah Arendt, *On Revolution* (New York: Viking Press 1963), 96.
31 See also George Kateb, *Hannah Arendt: Politics, Conscience, Evil* (Totowa, NJ: Rowman and Allanheld 1983), 10: 'Arendt presents the political actor as one who hides much in order to reveal more. He wears a mask. But the mask in the ancient theater hid the face yet allowed the actor's true voice to come through ... To wear a mask is to sustain a persona, a role, a position, an identifiable character. It is not a distortion of Arendt's meaning to say that she believes that it is the highest responsibility of the citizen to protect his mask so that in the artificial composure of his appearance the truth of his words may sound.'

rather to replace the actor's own face and countenance, but in a way that would make it possible for the voice to sound through. At any rate, it was in this twofold understanding of a mask through which a voice sounds that the word *persona* became a metaphor and was carried from the language of the theater into legal terminology.[32]

Adopting the theatrical Greek mask as her political ideal, Arendt sets out to criticize a liberal understanding of equality that is based on 'sameness', and to develop an understanding of equality that can respond to the tension between sameness and difference. The ideal of citizenship as mask helps Arendt give metaphorical expression to the two ideals we have posited as being at the core of democracy: equality and plurality.[33]

The mask equalizes by covering the face of the actor, hiding those attributes (ethnicity, race, gender and so on) that should not be considered relevant when she/he speaks and acts as a citizen. This understanding of political equality is an inversion of the modern understanding of equality as a natural condition of human beings. Arendt rejects the view that attributes the source of equality to nature, to the fact that we are all born equal (that is, as human beings). For Arendt, equality is not something that is natural, nor is it a pre-political fact. Rather, it is a political artefact that can only be achieved in public, through political organization, through the adoption of the 'mask' of citizenship. The dark side of allowing difference to enter the public realm without the protection of the mask of citizenship is captured in Arendt's discussion in *The Origins of Totalitarianism*:

> Our political life rests on the assumption that we can produce equality through organization, because man can act in and change and build a common world, together with his equals and only with his equals. The dark background of mere givenness, the background formed by our unchangeable and unique nature, breaks into the political scene as the alien which in its all too obvious difference reminds us of the limitations of human activity—which are identical with the limitations of human equality. The reason why highly developed political communities, such as the ancient city–states or modern nation–states, so often insist on ethnic homogeneity is that they hope to eliminate as far as possible those natural and always present differences and differentiations which by themselves arouse dumb hatred, mistrust, and discrimination because they indicate all too

32 Arendt, *On Revolution*, 106–7.
33 This is different from modern writings on citizenship that focus on the equalizing effect of national closure that makes citizenship conditional on a process of political assimilation; see, for example, Rogers Brubaker, *Citizenship and Nationhood in France and Germany* (Cambridge, MA: Harvard University Press 1992). For Arendt, the ideal of political equality granted to citizens is accompanied by the ideal of plurality (and not assimilation). It is for this reason that she is critical of assimilation as the cornerstone of national citizenship.

clearly those spheres where men cannot act and change at will, *i.e.*, the limitations of the human artifice. The 'alien' is a frightening symbol of the fact of difference as such, of individuality as such, and indicates those realms in which man cannot change and cannot act and in which, therefore, he has a distinct tendency to destroy.[34]

How can a political mask allow for difference and uniqueness to appear while retaining a commitment to equality? When difference appears without any mediation, it is frightening, abrupt, and provokes a tendency to destroy. However, the attempt to hide all difference is equally dangerous since it denies the fact of human uniqueness. Using the mask as simply a means of hiding can be just as dangerous to the viability of a plural political sphere.

It is precisely to this danger that Arendt turns in her discussion of the hunting down of hypocrites during the 'reign of terror' that followed the French Revolution. Hypocrisy, as Arendt notes, literally means 'play-acting'. However, the hypocrite is not Arendt's ideal actor. The hypocrite's acting, rather, takes up the whole space of the self, not leaving any for duality, for the internal dialogue of actor and spectator. In order for the mask to help constitute the political realm of equality and plurality, it has to both conceal and reveal, and not consume the actor's whole identity. If it does so consume the actor, it reveals nothing but the mirror-image of whatever social role the hypocrite is playing.[35] Arendt explains:

> Psychologically speaking, one may say that the hypocrite is too ambitious; not only does he want to appear virtuous before others, he wants to convince himself. By the same token, he eliminates from the world, which he has populated with illusions and lying phantoms, the *only core of integrity from which true appearance could arise again, his own incorruptible self.*[36]

Thus, Arendt arrives at the conclusion that what makes hypocrisy the vice of vices is that it threatens the integrity of the political realm. The reaction of those involved in the French Revolution to the problem of hypocrisy was to try to eliminate the mask altogether. Arendt warns against this simplistic solution, which may have accounted for the deterioration of the revolution into the 'reign of terror'. Such a response ignores the important role played by the mask in constituting a political realm of equality and plurality. 'The Reign of Terror eventually spelled the exact opposite of true liberation and

34 Hannah Arendt, *The Origins of Totalitarianism* (New York: Meridian Books 1958), 301.
35 Arendt, *On Revolution*, 103 (emphasis in the original): '... the unmasking of the hypocrite would leave nothing behind the mask, because the hypocrite is the actor himself in so far as he wears no mask. He pretends to *be* the assumed role, and when he enters the game of society it is without any play-acting whatsoever.'
36 Ibid., 99 (emphasis added).

true equality; it equalized because it left all inhabitants equally without the protecting mask of a legal personality.'[37]

We seem to be caught in a vicious cycle between a need of masks in order to tone down difference, and the spectre of hypocrisy that makes us suspicious of masks as such. The hunting down of the hypocrite tends to strip away all masks and leave us with dumb difference. The way out of this cycle lies in Arendt's interpretation of the Greek mask, as already quoted: 'The mask as such obviously had two functions: it had to hide, or rather to replace the actor's own face and countenance, but in a way that would make it possible for the voice to sound through.' She suggests a different understanding of the mask in that its function is not simply to hide the face but rather to 'replace' the face while allowing the voice 'to sound through'. The mask becomes, in other words, a metaphor for representation. It allows us to introduce a plurality of voices into the public sphere by giving us the means to represent them. Such understanding dismantles the dichotomy between artifice and truth, since it is only through artifice that the true voice can be recognized and become part of a common public sphere. Authenticity or recognized uniqueness does not precede the public appearance but is, rather, its result. It is dependent on the play of actors and spectators within a public realm. With this understanding of citizenship as Greek mask, we can return to our contemporary debates.

Contemporary masks

How can Arendt's ideal of the mask help us understand the contemporary debates in Israel and France? How does it help explain the prevalence of the accusation of hypocrisy in both debates? The accusation that was raised against the individuals who refused the demand to 'cover' seemingly helped shift the blame back on to them. It challenged the authenticity of their demand. In France the schoolgirls were depicted as lacking any freedom of choice, as yielding to family or peer pressures. In the name of 'freedom of religion', they were perpetuating traditional, oppressive and patriarchal norms. Likewise, in Israel, the Sapir College committee could not accept Hassan's explanation about promoting the values of individualism and humanism. It refused to hear Hassan's unique voice and rushed to subsume it under group politics, attributing his position to Palestinian nationalism.

In both controversies we witness a failure to listen to the individual who was taken to be 'representative' of a group. Although the debate revolved around the right to freedom of speech and expression, the individuals were not heard, and mute symbols were presented as 'clear' and in no need of

37 Ibid., 104.

interpretation or explanation. Joan Wallach Scott argues that, although the debate revolved around the meaning of the hijab, the voices of the schoolgirls who wore it were almost entirely missing from the public sphere. The meaning of the veil was taken to be self-evident, as representing the subordination and discrimination of women under Islam. It was presumed that the students were coerced or forced by their families to wear the hijab since, by definition, the wearing of the headscarf could not signify any meaningful individual choice.[38]

In contrast, studies of and interviews with the schoolgirls that were published after the enactment of the ban reveal a multiplicity of meanings (often contradictory) in their choosing to wear the hijab. These girls' choices, Scott explains, did not easily conform to the notion of an abstract individual presumed by French republicanism to be worthy of respect. She argues that, in order to understand the students' choices, one should envision an alternative concept of the person, a relational rather than an unencumbered self. Seyla Benhabib also argues that, in many cases, it was not coercion but a matter of choice, but, in order to see this, we must overcome the tendency to oppose freedom of choice to tradition. Benhabib offers the term 'democratic reiteration'—an act that gives new and modern meaning to a traditional custom—to capture the meaning of contemporary Islamic veiling.[39] The girls comply with the traditional dress code of women under Islam but, in using it to challenge the terms of equality offered them by French public schools, they transform its meaning. By excluding their voices from the debate, the complexity and even the contradictory meaning of their act disappeared. Their choice was understood as stemming from family and peer pressure; their politics were seen as obedience to a patriarchal tradition. Thus, the legal ban on wearing the hijab, an act of coercion by the state against the freedom of the individuals, was perceived to be not only justified but also liberating, when applied to the Muslim schoolgirls.

The voices of the individuals involved in the Israeli controversy were also missing or misrepresented during the public debate. It is important to note that the whole controversy began with an act of silencing. Nizar Hassan refused to allow Eyal Cohen, the student in uniform, to explain his position. He postponed the discussion of the incident to the following class, when the student arrived without his uniform. Thereafter, Hassan's own voice is

---

38 Scott, *The Politics of the Veil*, 124–5.
39 Seyla Benhabib, *The Rights of Others: Aliens, Residents, and Citizens* (Cambridge and New York: Cambridge University Press 2004), 187, 193. Benhabib explains that 'democratic reiterations' are linguistic, legal, cultural and political repetitions-in-transformation, invocations that are also revocations. They not only change established understandings but also transform what passes as the valid or established view of an authoritative precedent. See also Seyla Benhabib, 'What is that on your head? Turkey's new legislation concerning the "headscarf"', 5 March 2008, available on the *Reset Dialogues on Civilization* website at www.resetdoc.org/ EN/Benhabib-Headscarf.php (viewed 26 May 2009).

distorted in public, and he is not even invited to the Knesset committee that discussed the matter.[40] The college's hearing committee rejected his explanation that he acted to promote humanist values. Instead of trying to listen and understand the unique position of a Palestinian citizen who opposed the wearing of army uniforms in class out of a principled commitment to humanism, the committee attributed his act to sinister political motives, to radical nationalism.

As we have seen, in both cases the accusation of hypocrisy dominated the debate, directing observers to look behind the mask to expose the 'authentic self' that it was hiding. The participants in the debates assumed, contra Arendt, that identity, or the 'true self', was to be found in the private realm by piercing the public mask. The voices of the individuals were to be ignored because they were regarded as inauthentic. Conversely, political equality was understood as achievable by forcing a unitary mask on the individuals, one that did not allow their unique voices to sound through. In other words, it seems that both conversations failed precisely because they were caught between the need to enforce sameness and the fear of absolute difference, with no middle ground.

How does Arendt's ideal of the mask move us beyond this binary? What conversational move does it allow? Arendt's mask allows us first to take seriously the tension between equality (as sameness) and authenticity (as difference), and to engage it. What does it mean to understand the citizen's mask as something tailored to achieve equality, while at the same time allowing it to represent difference? Such an ideal changes the direction of the investigation and raises new questions. Instead of looking for the 'authentic' self behind the mask, engaging in a competition of exposing hypocrites, we can understand the complaint of the individual as a critique of the current mask of citizenship offered by the political system. According to Arendt the important question is not 'what is the "truth" or the essence hidden behind the mask'. The mask can only hide uniqueness that precedes representation and, as such, can only raise fears. The self, according to Arendt, should not be understood as the 'essence' behind the mask, but rather the result of an interplay between revealing and hiding. It is not an essence (a what) but a performance (constituted through action and corresponding narratives).[41] When it works, the mask allows re-presentation of the unique voice so that it can become part of a social web of stories. When the schoolgirls in France come to school wearing the hijab, they are telling us something important

---

40 He was interviewed by newspapers and his views were reported but, as I shall show, he was not given a proper 'hearing' in parliament when his act was discussed and condemned.

41 See Bonnie Honig, 'Toward an agonistic feminism: Hannah Arendt and the politics of identity', in Bonnie Honig (ed.), *Feminist Interpretations of Hannah Arendt* (University Park: Pennsylvania State University Press 1995), 135–67. Honig criticizes Arendt for stopping at the 'private' and challenges the idea that the 'body' defies representation.

about the failure of the current mask of French citizenship. Their symbolic act can indicate that the demand to uncover does not allow them any way to re-present their difference as part of a public conversation. They challenge the French political system to offer a mask that can allow difference to be re-presented, to be heard as different voices, to be acknowledged in the public sphere.

Likewise, when Hassan demands that the student take off his army uniform, he seems to say that there is something wrong with the mask of citizenship in Israel. The uniform currently functions as the *de facto* mask of the citizen in Israel. This mask is only available to some, while excluding the rest. Hassan's refusal points to the degree to which citizenship itself is currently equated with the army uniform. Such a mask does not allow the representation of individuals who do not serve in the army. It defines the Palestinian citizen who is excluded from army service as the Other. In other words, the uniform indicates the lack of a neutral mask that can allow the individual and unique voices of Palestinian citizens to sound through.

The absent feminists

Changing the perspective from piercing the mask to evaluating the current mask of citizenship according to the double function it is supposed to serve also points to an important difference. If we use the metaphor of the ancient Greek mask, it seems that the French mask of citizenship blocks the voices of some groups (that is, it hides too much), while the Israeli mask is not offered to all citizens (exposes too much). It challenges us to begin a serious conversation about the adequacy of the citizen mask in both political systems. It also challenge us to interrogate the way the Us–Them binary has been constructed. Interestingly, in both debates, it is the lack of criticism (or even active support) of women belonging to the hegemonic group that enables such dichotomous thinking. Feminists in both societies have long criticized the terms of citizenship offered to women, and the way the civil mask does not adequately protect or represent them. Seeing continuity between their claims and the complaints made by individuals (women and men) belonging to minority religious and ethnic groups might move the discussion on to an evaluation of the general terms of citizenship. Lacking such intervention, it has been easy to ignore the criticism and instead blame the individuals who ignite the debates.

In her analysis of the hijab controversy, Scott refers to an interesting phenomenon: the inversion of issues. She detects this inversion in relation to the issue of gender equality. The consensus of the French public was that the hijab represented the subordination of women under Islam and their inequality. A commitment to gender equality required, therefore, a ban on wearing the hijab in public. However, as Scott demonstrates, the support given by French feminists to the ban helped to uphold a myth of sexual equality rather than to further the goal of real gender equality. First, this support overwhelmed feminist criticism about the terms of equality afforded to French women, particularly the inability to accommodate gender difference (female sexuality) in the public sphere. In fact, French feminists have long argued that 'women's liberation' has been falsely equated in France with 'sexual liberation' and contributed to the sexual objectification of women.[42] However, during the debate on the hijab, this criticism disappeared. The focus on the headscarf created an inversion: instead of looking at the shortcomings of the French republican model in accommodating difference, in relation to women, both secular and religious, the blame was redirected at the minority. Islam (in its stereotypical depiction) was blamed as the sole cause for the difficulties of integrating immigrant minorities. The role of the law in denying Muslim girls access to public education and thus pushing them back to private religious schools was obscured. The Muslim minority was blamed for its exclusion and the discrimination it faced. This inversion undermined the possibility of finding a common ground between women across religious differences. The ban solidified an opposition between two 'cultures', depicting Islam as resistant to assimilation. By setting aside the feminist critique of French citizenship, it was easy to present the issue as an unavoidable clash between irreconcilable cultures instead of an interrogation of the terms of the public sphere.

Israeli feminists did not join the public debate about Hassan's refusal to allow students in uniform into his classroom. This abstention is strange, given that one of the defining campaigns of Israeli feminists during the 1980s was that against the exclusion of women from army combat units.[43] One of the most famous legal cases revolved around the struggle of a young Israeli woman, Alice Miller, to compel the IDF to recruit women to be trained as air force pilots.[44] Her legal victory opened the way for other women to enter various combat units. As a result of this struggle the law was changed to prohibit the exclusion of women from combat units. These cases provoked a

---

42 See Scott, *The Politics of the Veil*, 151–75.

43 In fact, two of the defining struggles of Israeli feminists (against the army and religious authorities) were based on the claim that, while men have a central role in the Israeli public sphere, women tend to be excluded from it. The feminist struggle can therefore be characterized as an attempt to include the female body in the public sphere by making the latter a gender neutral space. For an interpretive essay on the struggle of Jewish religious women to pray at the Western Wall with a Torah scroll and prayer shawls, see Lea Shakdiel, 'Women of the wall: radical feminism as an opportunity for a new discourse in Israel', in Hanna Naveh (ed.), *Israeli Family and Community: Women's Time* (London and Portland, OR: Vallentine Mitchell 2003); and Phyllis Chesler and Rivka Haut (eds), *Women of the Wall: Claiming Sacred Ground at Judaism's Holy Site* (Woodstock, VT: Jewish Lights 2003).

44 *Miller* v. *Minister of Defense* HCJ 4541/94. See Daphne Barak-Erez, 'The feminist battle for citizenship: between combat duties and conscientious objection', *Cardozo Journal of Law and Gender*, vol. 13, 2007, 531–60; Yofi Tirosh, 'Alice be-erets ha-(ham)raa: hirhurim al hishtakfuiot ha-guf ha-nashi ba-siah al shiluv nashim be-tafkidei lehima', in Barak-Erez (chief ed.), *Iyunim Be-Mishpat, Migdar VeFeminism*, 885–940.

debate among feminists about the centrality of army service to women achieving equality in Israel. Following the legal reform, the sociologist Orna Sasson Levi investigated the way in which women soldiers negotiated their 'feminine' identity, given the 'masculinity' of the new positions opened to them. She was struck by the way women soldiers chose to adopt a mask of masculinity. Sasson Levi further demonstrated the way this mask was, in some ways, subversive (challenging the unquestioned link between male identity and certain military roles), but in other ways seemed to solidify gender roles. This sophisticated discussion of women's citizenship and the central role of the army in shaping it could have shed light on Hassan's act of excluding army uniforms from his classroom in the name of equality.[45] More importantly, it could have raised questions about the legitimacy of the interpretive move made by the college committee and the Knesset committee, depicting Hassan's action as a clear and unambiguous sign of Palestinian nationalism. Bringing the two debates together could have added force to Hassan's claim about the lack of 'neutral' space for the practice of equal citizenship, and the adverse impact it has on those designated as the Other.

Epilogue

The two debates led in each case to a logical conclusion: a ban in France; a demand for a letter of apology in Israel. The individuals' protests were met by an act of force that was meant to end the debate. In France, the ban failed to respond to those Muslim students who claimed that the hijab was part of their identity and should not be set aside. In Israel, the hearing committee demanded that Hassan apologize. However, this was no simple personal apology. It involved a symbolic bow to the uniform of the Israeli army, as the letter of Professor Tzachor, the president of Sapir College indicated:

> As a condition for your continued employment, you are requested to apologize to the student for hurting and disparaging him. I will ask to see the apology within a week of the day you receive this letter. In your apology, you must refer to your obligation to be respectful of the IDF uniform and the full right of every student to enter your classroom in uniform. I won't accept an apology that is not unequivocal. I won't accept an apology that does not refer to respecting the IDF uniform or that has any haggling political nuances ... and obviously, until the apology is received, you are not permitted to lecture at the college.

45 Indeed, some explanation as to why the two debates were not connected can be found in an earlier article by Hassan Jabareen, who criticized the feminist struggle to join combat units as lacking a larger perspective about its impact on strengthening the centrality of the army with regard to Israeli citizenship, and its concomitant adverse effect on Palestinian citizenship; see Jabareen, 'Likrat gishot bikortiot shel ha-miut ha-Palestini'.

Thus, the two struggles ended in failure. In both cases the subversive act of the individual was disciplined, the boundaries that had been breached repaired and reinforced. However, in both cases, the subversive act that had been silenced returned to disrupt public order, indicating that the closure had not been as complete as it had seemed. In France, Cennet Doganay, a young Muslim woman of fifteen, who had been banned from class for wearing the hijab, responded by appearing in school with her head shaved. Doganay explained that the ban left her no other choice if she was to respect both the French law and the Islamic dress code that required the covering of her hair.[46] This act of protest rekindled the debate. It challenged the basic assumption of the supporters of the ban that the hijab was not an integral part of the wearer's identity. And that its removal did not constitute an injury to civil rights, and did not amount to discrimination. The act was subversive in that it presented the hair itself, the symbol of secular femininity, as the 'mask' that the Muslim girls refused to wear. This undermined the distinction between nature and artifice, body and culture, distinctions that made the ban look as if it was not interfering with the civil liberties of the individual woman. Why was it more difficult to accept the act of shaving one's head than the ban on covering one's hair? What can explain the public reaction to the shaving? I believe that, with this subversive act, Doganay was able to perform the way in which the French mask of citizenship failed to represent the voices of Muslim girls. The exaggerated obedience to the ban on head-covering, leading to complete exposure—the entire removal of the female's hair—returned the discussion to the repressed question: the place of the female Other in the public sphere, and the ability of the French mask of citizenship to ensure equality to those considered Other.

In December 2007 a media campaign was launched in Israel under the slogan 'A True Israeli Does Not Dodge the Draft'. The campaign's goal was to criticize the ongoing decline in army enrolment in Israel. Interestingly, this campaign was not initiated or funded by the IDF or any governmental body, but was rather the initiative of a private advertising company, funded by contributions from business people and the media.[47] With this campaign, Hassan's argument regarding the dangerous conflation between Israeli citizenship and military service returned to centre stage. However, this time, it was not due to the subversive act of an excluded Palestinian citizen, but rather to events set in motion by those identifying with the ruling elite. The purpose was not to take off the 'mask' (of the uniform army), but rather to expose the Others, those who do not serve in the army. They were

46 'Muslim girl shaves head over ban', 1 October 2004, available on the *BBC News* website at http://news.bbc.co.uk/1/hi/world/europe/3708444.stm (viewed 26 May 2009).

47 'Campaign "Israeli amiti lo mishtamet'", 15 December 2007, available on the *Promomagazine* website at http://www.promomagazine.co.il/pages/show/1995 (viewed 26 May 2009).

denounced and identified as non-citizens or, rather, as not truly Israeli citizens. The campaign stirred a public debate. The same disturbance caused by Hassan's refusal to accept students wearing uniforms in his classroom returned from the opposite direction, in the form of an attempt to exclude those who did not wear army uniforms by defining them as non-citizens. The campaign did not indicate who was the target of condemnation. Did it include ultra-religious Jews? Arabs? Nonetheless, it underlined the question that was first raised by Hassan and then silenced: have military uniforms become the Israeli mask of citizenship? What is the risk of adopting such a restrictive citizenship mask for the possibility of developing a democratic civil society?

The 'return of the repressed' in both cases is instructive. It urges us to look deeper, and articulate our theories of citizenship and our conception of masks in order to enhance equality in plural and democratic societies.

Revisiting Lepanto: the political mobilization against Islam in contemporary Western Europe

HANS-GEORG BETZ AND SUSI MERET

ABSTRACT In recent years, the place of Islam in Western European society has become a central political issue, particularly on the far right of the ideological spectrum. Parties as diverse as the Schweizerische Volkspartei (SVP), the Lega Nord, the Dansk Folkeparti and the Vlaams Belang have mobilized against the 'Muslim invasion', launching campaigns against the building of mosques and minarets, the integration of Muslim immigrants and the recognition of Islam as a religion of equal status. Betz and Meret discuss how parties such as the SVP have framed the question of Islam in terms of culture, values and identity. This has allowed them to put themselves forward as defenders of fundamental liberal values, such as individualism, secularism and gender equality. Betz and Meret also advance an analytical framework that might allow us to put contemporary Islamophobia in Western Europe in a larger historical and transnational context. Their central argument is that the current political mobilization against the 'Islamization' of Western European societies is part of a larger 'quest' for a European identity.

In the spring of 2007, leading politicians of Switzerland's largest political party, the Schweizerische Volkspartei (SVP), together with representatives of a small religious party, launched a signature campaign in support of a popular initiative for a constitutional ban on the construction of minarets in Switzerland. The promoters argued that minarets represented a symbol of victory and conquest, and therefore posed a fundamental threat to the survival of Swiss national and cultural identity. A minaret ban would not only 'slow down the propagation of Islam', but also allow Switzerland to 'reinforce' its Christian and western values. A year later, Filip Dewinter, the *eminence grise* of the Belgian Vlaams Belang, invited the leaders of several right-wing populist parties—among them Heinz-Christian Strache of the Freiheitliche Partei Österreichs (FPÖ)—to Antwerp to launch a transnational project to resist the 'Islamization' of Europe's cities, a European network against the construction of mosques. A few days later, Jean-Marie Le Pen travelled to Vienna to consult with the leadership of the FPÖ about the foundation of a new European 'patriotic' party bringing together various right-wing populist formations, such as the Vlaams Belang and Bulgaria's

Ataka, around the common themes of resistance to 'EU centralism' and the defence of Europe's Christian traditions and values against Islam.[1]

The leading role of Jean-Marie Le Pen's Front National (FN) in this project was quite remarkable. Unlike other parties on the populist right in recent years, the FN has for the most part refrained from mobilizing against Islam, largely because of Le Pen's esteem for those Muslim French of Maghrebi origin who fled to France, in fear of their lives, after fighting for the French state during the Algerian war.[2] After the failed presidential campaign of 2007, however, the party apparently concluded that it was politically expedient to revive its hard-line ethno-nationalist positions of the early 1990s that were based on the notion that Europe was both white and Christian. This meant, above all, as the party put it in its fifty anti-immigration measures of 1991, resisting 'the implantation of Islam in France', a religion fundamentally alien to 'its identity'.[3] A Front National pamphlet from 1992 on immigration laid out the party's position in greater detail, distinguishing between immigrants from predominantly Catholic countries, such as Italy, Spain and Poland, whose integration posed few problems, and those from North Africa, Turkey and other parts of the developing world, whose ethnic and religious background made integration virtually impossible. In fact, the authors maintained, if history taught anything it was that there had never been 'lasting peaceful coexistence' between Christian Europe and the Muslim world.[4]

The FN's ethnocentric arguments have proven a potent 'master frame', which diffused in the course of the late 1990s throughout the populist right in a process of 'cross-national learning'.[5] This frame derives its ideological force to a large extent from an ethno-national discourse that explicitly rejects an association with traditional racism. No longer are there references to postulates of racial hierarchy; instead, the emphasis is on 'difference'. Filip Dewinter, the leader of the Belgium Vlaams Belang, has summed up the new orthodoxy: 'everyone is equal but not all the same.'[6] For the contemporary

1 Peter Lattas, '"Patrioten aller Länder, vereinigt euch!" EU-Rechte: Europäische Freiheitspartei und Städtebündnis gegen Islamisierung', *Junge Freiheit*, 1 February 2008; 'Nationalist leaders to form new European "patriotic" party by November', *EUbusiness.com*, 25 January 2008, at www.eubusiness.com/news-eu/1201274222.43 (viewed 26 March 2009). Translations, unless otherwise stated, are by the authors.

2 See Hans-Georg Betz, 'Culture, identity, and the question of Islam: the nativist agenda of the radical right', in Peter Davies with Paul Jackson (eds), *The Far Right in Europe: An Encyclopedia* (Oxford: Greenwood World Press 2008), 114–15.

3 Bruno Mégret, 'Cinquant propositions', *Présent*, 22 November 1991, 7.

4 Jean-Yves Le Gallou and Philippe Olivier, *Immigration: le Front national fait le point* (Paris: Éditions nationals 1992), 20–3.

5 See Jens Rydgren, 'Is extreme right-wing populism contagious? Explaining the emergence of a new party family', *European Journal of Political Research*, vol. 44, no. 3, 2005, 413–37.

6 Interview with Filip Dewinter, 'Belgium's far right resurgence,' 11 October 2000, formerly available online at http://news.sbs.com.au/dateline/belgiums_farright_resurgence_129821 (viewed 20 January 2009).

radical right, what differentiates individuals from each other is their cultural background, their values, beliefs, attitudes and identity. The defence of the right to difference, together, in turn, with the preservation of cultural pluralism, is central to the radical right's identitarian project, which serves as a powerful justification for radical right-wing policies of exclusion.

Nativism: historical roots

This type of identitarian politics has a long pedigree. Among the politically most important examples is nativism, which originated in the United States in the early nineteenth century in response to the arrival of new immigrants from Europe.[7] In his influential study of American modernism in the early twentieth century, Walter Benn Michaels argues that nativism was an attempt to establish a collective national identity via the invention of a distinct American cultural identity. For Michaels, nativism marked a decisive shift from earlier forms of universalist racism to a new form of cultural pluralism (or multiculturalism), based on the assumption that different cultures were of equal value but essentially incompatible with each other. The nativist goal was 'to transform American identity from the sort of things that could be acquired (through naturalisation) into the sort of thing that had to be inherited (from one's parents)'.[8]

From this it followed that there were differences that could neither be bridged nor overcome. For if 'to belong to a culture you must be able to encounter it in the form of memory, as a tradition that is already yours, then no one can ever cease to belong to his or her culture or begin to belong to some other culture'.[9] This opened the door for exclusion on the basis of cultural—and ethnic—identity, couched in terms of 'assimilability'. For, as Michaels insists, the nativist conception of culture, albeit superficially a repudiation of racism, in fact represented a new form of racism.[10] A case in point is *United States* v. *Thind*, argued before the Supreme Court in 1923, involving an immigrant from India who had been refused naturalization. The Supreme Court upheld the decision based on nativist logic:

> The children of English, French, Germany, Italian, Scandinavian, and other European parentage, quickly merge into the mass of our population and lose the distinctive hallmarks of their European origin. On the other hand, it cannot be

---

7   For an excellent overview of the literature on nativism, see Tyler Anbinder, 'Nativism and prejudice against immigrants: a historiographic essay', in Reed Ueda (ed.), *A Companion to American Immigration* (Oxford and Malden, MA: Blackwell 2006), 177–201.
8   Walter Benn Michaels, *Our America: Nativism, Modernism, and Pluralism* (Durham, NC: Duke University Press 1995), 8.
9   Ibid., 80.
10   Ibid., 129.

doubted that the children born in this country of Hindu parents would retain indefinitely the clear evidence of their ancestry. It is very far from our thought to suggest the slightest question of racial superiority or inferiority. What we suggest is merely racial difference, and it is of such character and extent that the great body of our people instinctively recognize it and reject the thought of assimilation.[11]

Others would go even further, reviving fears of a purported internal subversion of the American creed by groups (such as, in particular, Catholic immigrants from Germany and Ireland in the 1820s and 1830s) 'remaining strangers in the land', 'tenaciously adhering to the customs and usages of their own country', inassimilable and therefore a fundamental and constant threat to America's established 'ideals, institutions, and mission'.[12] By couching their 'war against the immigrant' in these terms, the nativists managed to present themselves as defenders of Americanism, protecting their country against the 'social, political, and economic evils which seemed inevitably linked to the immigrant invasion'.[13]

The centrality of culture in contemporary European nativism

The anti-Islamic arguments advanced today by Western European political parties bear a striking resemblance to the rhetoric employed by American nativists in the nineteenth and early twentieth centuries.[14] And for good reason. Nativism's primary concern was the question of assimilability, that is, to what degree 'aliens' were culturally compatible with the majority community and thus likely to be absorbed by it. This presupposed a strong sense of what Charles Taylor has called 'civilizational identity', the notion 'people have that the basic order by which they live, even imperfectly, is good and (usually) is superior to the ways of life of outsiders'.[15] From this perspective, nativism represents a mechanism of 'cultural defense' in response

11 US Supreme Court, *United States* v. *Bhagat Singh Thind* 261 U.S. 204 (1923), available online at http://vlex.us/vid/20020912 (viewed 26 March 2009).
12 The quotations are from the opinion of Justice Stephen Field in the Chinese Exclusion Case (*Chae Chan Ping* v. *United States* 130 U.S. 581 (1889)), quoted in Hoang Gia Phan, '"A race so different": Chinese exclusion, the *slaughterhouse cases*, and *Plessy* v. *Ferguson*', *Labor History*, vol. 45, no. 2, 2004, 133–63 (155). See also Michael W. Hughey, 'Americanism and its discontents: Protestantism, nativism, and political heresy in America', *International Journal of Politics, Culture and Society*, vol. 5, no. 4, 1992, 533–52 (542).
13 Ray Allen Billington, *The Protestant Crusade 1800–1860: A Study of the Origins of American Nativism* (Chicago: Quadrangle Books 1964), 322.
14 See Tariq Modood, *Multicultural Politics: Racism, Ethnicity, and Muslims in Britain* (Minneapolis: University of Minnesota Press 2005).
15 Charles Taylor, 'Religious mobilizations', *Public Culture*, vol. 18, no. 2, 2006, 281–300 (286).

to processes that appear to pose a fundamental challenge to this civilizational order: a 'political-identity mobilization' in its support.[16] In the United States, as Taylor and others have noted, this has meant above all a defence of a particular combination of Anglo-Protestantism and republicanism, derived from the 'seventeenth century Puritan ideal of a covenant as a voluntary association of qualified saints'.[17] In contemporary Western Europe, by contrast, civilizational order and identity are no longer bound up with religion. In fact, in sharp contrast to the United States, Christianity is in sharp decline in Western Europe, making the Old World the 'closest thing to a godless civilisation the world has ever known'.[18] This might help explain why the response in Western Europe to Islam has been markedly different than in the United States. Take, for instance, the findings of a recent report on Islam and the West, commissioned by the World Economic Forum in Davos. When asked, in 2007, whether greater interaction between the West and the Muslim world should be seen as a benefit or as a threat, 70 per cent of American respondents considered it a benefit; against that, in Western Europe, on average two-thirds of respondents thought greater interaction represented a threat (ranging from 59 per cent in Belgium to 70 per cent in Denmark). For the authors of the report this reflected 'a growing fear among Europeans—driven in part by rising immigration from predominantly Muslim regions—of a perceived "Islamic threat" to their cultural identities'.[19]

Hardly surprising, then, that nativist parties mobilizing against Muslim immigrants and Islam in contemporary Western Europe have framed their discourse largely in terms of the defence of difference and identity. From their perspective, Western Europe shares a distinct cultural heritage, which represents, in the words of the Lega Nord, a 'culture of reference'. Immigrants either 'follow the customs—or get out of the country', as the Dansk Folkeparti has, rather blatantly, put it.[20] The result is what Jean-Marie

16 Ibid., 293. At the same time, nativism in the United States was 'the expression of an identity-anxiety, which was the fear that the "American" identity—however this might be conceptualized—was in jeopardy': Martin E. Spencer, 'Multiculturalism, "political correctness," and the politics of identity', *Sociological Forum*, vol. 9, no. 4, 1994, 547–67 (550).

17 Hughey, 'Americanism and its discontents', 535.

18 Mark Lilla, 'Europe and the legend of secularization', *International Herald Tribune*, 31 March 2006.

19 *Islam and the West: Annual Report on the State of Dialogue* (Geneva: World Economic Forum 2008), 139. According to a German survey from 2006, 56 per cent of German respondents thought that there was a 'cultural war' between Christendom and Islam; 61 per cent thought peaceful coexistence between the West and the Muslim world was impossible; 56 per cent thought the construction of mosques should be forbidden as long as there were Muslim countries that banned the construction of churches: see Elisabeth Noelle and Thomas Petersen, 'Eine fremde, bedrohliche Welt', *Frankfurter Allgemeine Zeitung*, 17 May 2006.

20 Editorial, 'Vaskeægte værdifast', *Dansk Folkeblad*, no. 4, 2007, 2.

Le Pen has described as a policy of 'assimilation in the name of the right to difference'.[21] This type of assimilation, however, entails not only the willingness, but also the ability, on the part of the immigrant, to absorb the host culture. Assimilability, in turn, presupposes cultural commensurability with respect to the foundational values that define Western Europe's cultural heritage. For the nativist right, Muslim immigrants lack both the basic ability and the willingness necessary for assimilation, for the simple reason that Islam itself is entirely incompatible with the principles of western civilization. Worse still, in the nativists' eyes, Islam poses a fundamental threat to western values and culture, which renders any effort to integrate Muslim immigrants not only futile but highly dangerous.

The Dansk Folkeparti is an exemplary case in point. Appeals to national, ethnic and cultural explanations have always played an important role in its anti-immigrant rhetoric and discourses.[22] As early as 1999, the party's leader Pia Kjærsgaard charged that immigrants, today for the most part with a Muslim background, had 'absolutely no wish to be part of Danish society'. On the contrary, they often had the 'deepest disrespect for all that is western, Danish, Christian'.[23] One year later, the party began to harden its position against Islam significantly, playing to popular concerns about the threat posed by Muslim countries. The party's 2001 book *Danmarks fremtid: dit land, dit valg ...* (Denmark's Future: Your Country, Your Choice ...) largely amplified those fears. Pictures, interviews, statistics on crimes and violence committed by ethnic minorities and examples from other countries were used in the book to illustrate what the party considered the obvious result of three decades of failed immigration policy in Denmark. Danish society was described as being under serious threat. How Denmark might end up looking was described in a chapter devoted to a case study of the district of Kreuzberg in Berlin. The German residents were described as an isolated minority in their own country where, in schools, shops and mosques, Turkish was the spoken language, Islam was the dominant religion and women wore the hijab. The message was even more blatantly expressed by the party's youth organization, which distributed a flyer with an image of three blond Danish girls captioned 'Denmark today' and, next to it, an image of three hooded and blood-splattered Muslims captioned 'Denmark in ten years: rapes, violence, insecurity, forced marriages, oppressed women, gang

21 Jean-Marie Le Pen, 'Discours à l'occasion du meeting du Cercle National des Combattants', 26 October 2007, available on the FN website at www.frontnational.com/doc_interventions_detail.php?id_inter=91 (viewed 26 March 2009).
22 The 1997 party manifesto ('Dansk Folkepartis Principprogram') explicitly referred to 'our warm and strong national soul' as the basis for the party's nationalist principles: 'The Danish People's Party is proud of Denmark: we love our fatherland and we feel a historical obligation to protect the Danish heritage.'
23 Pia Kjærsgaard at the party's fourth annual congress in Vissenbjerg, Fyn: see 'Vi i DK satte vort folk og fædreland over alt andet', *Dansk Folkeblad*, no. 5, November 1999, 4–5.

crimes. This is what a multi-ethnic society will give you. Is this what you want?'[24]

The ideological reconstruction of Islam

In making their case against Muslims, the nativist right relies to a large extent on confounding Islam with radical 'Islamism'. The events of 9/11 provided the perfect justification for the assertion that there was no difference between the two. The Dansk Folkeparti was the first to use the terrorist attack as an opportunity to depict Islam as a totalitarian and violent ideology whose destructive effects posed a deadly threat to western democratic principles and values from within. Thus, the party's then MEP, Mogens Camre, charged, only a few days after 9/11, that Muslims had 'infiltrated all western countries'. If some of them spoke 'nicely to us', it was only because they were waiting to comprise a large enough number 'to get rid of us', as had happened 'in Sudan, Indonesia, Nigeria and the Balkans'. There was no real difference between ordinary Muslims and the 9/11 terrorists. Both shared 'a hatred founded on a sick ideology'.[25] Other party officials echoed Camre's views.

Within a few years, the Dansk Folkeparti's characterization of Islam had spread throughout the nativist right. In 2005 Andrea Gibelli, then head of the Lega Nord's group of deputies in the Italian parliament, made headlines when he charged that a 'moderate Islam' did not exist. The truth was that 'so-called moderate Islam' was nothing but a 'screen' behind which Muslims were hiding their real objective, namely 'the cultural colonization' of the West.[26] In response, the Lega announced it was prepared to wage a 'cultural war against Islam' in order to resist the 'Islamic invasion' and defend Italy's 'Catholic identity'.[27] The Lega's position was hardly original. As early as 2002, Filip Dewinter, in a programmatic speech on Islam, had charged that Islam was a 'totalitarian' ideology, a 'religion of conquest' (*veroveringsgodsdienst*), seeking to colonize Europe. Three years later, in a speech on Muslim terrorism, Dewinter went even further. Characterizing Islam as 'the Trojan horse of Islamic fundamentalism', and Islamic fundamentalism as 'the Trojan horse of

24 In 2002 criminal charges were brought against three leading members of the party's youth organization for distributing the flyer. They were later sentenced to seven days in prison.
25 Speech by Mogens Camre, delivered at the sixth annual congress of the Dansk Folkeparti, Vejle, 15–16 September 2001.
26 Adalberto Signore, 'Lega all' attacco: "L'Islam moderato è il paravento del fondamentalismo"', *Il Giornale*, 28 July 2005.
27 'Contro l'Islam guerra culturale', *Qui Lega Parlamento*, 30 July 2005; interview with Mario Borghezio (Lega Nord MEP), "'Nous sommes des soldats politiques dans la tradition européenne'", *Le Choc du Mois*, no. 6, November 2006, 20–1. On the evolution of Islamophobia in the Lega Nord, see Giuseppe Scaliati, *Dove va la Lega Nord: radici ed evoluzione politica di un movimento populista* (Milan: Zero in Condotta 2006).

terrorism', he suggested that there was a direct link between Islam and terrorism.[28]

Today, the notion that Islam is not only a religion but a totalitarian ideology has become a central staple of the nativist right's case against Western Europe's Muslim community. Some have gone so far as to compare Islam to Nazism. Geert Wilders, for instance, the flamboyant leader of the Dutch Partij voor de Vrijheid, created a stir in 2007 when he called for banning the Qur'an on the grounds that it was the source of a 'sick', 'fascist' ideology inciting 'death and destruction', comparable to Hitler's *Mein Kampf*, and that it 'wants to kill everything we stand for in a modern western democracy'.[29] Wilders reiterated his view of the Qur'an in his short film *Fitna*, released online in both a Dutch and English version at the end of March 2008; within the first twenty-four hours of its release on LiveLeak.com, the film had attracted six million viewers.[30] Similar comparisons were made by the pastor and Dansk Folkeparti MP Søren Krarup during a parliamentary debate in 2007. In his view, the Qur'an, like Hitler's *Mein Kampf* and Marx's *Das Kapital*, was a 'holy book that wants to dominate everything—and that is totalitarianism'.[31] In Austria, FPÖ leader Heinz-Christian Strache has also gone on record characterizing Islam as 'not only a religion, but a totalitarian legal and social system', and radical Islamism as 'the fascism of the twenty-first century'. At the same time, Strache referred to immigration from Muslim countries as a 'third Turkish siege' that had to be resisted by any means possible.[32]

28 Filip Dewinter, 'Het groene totalitarisme: De kolonisatie van Europa!', speech delivered at a conference in Antwerp, 20 November 2002, available online at http://forum.politics.be/showpost.php?s=2b1282399c53719aeb977df9a2c7e8a8&p=19766&postcount=77 (viewed 1 April 2009); Filip Dewinter, 'Stop Islamterreur', speech at a demonstration outside the British embassy in Brussels following the 7/7 bombings in London, 14 July 2005. See also his interview with Bas Paternotte, '"Multicultureel betekent multicrimineel"', *Metro*, 15 June 2005, 18.

29 Geert Wilders, 'Genoeg is genoeg: verbied de Koran', *de Volkskrant*, 8 August 2007; Gregory Crouch, 'A Dutch antagonist of Islam waits for his premiere', *New York Times*, 22 March 2008; see also Wilders's interview with Arian Faal, '"Koran ist ein faschistisches Buch" Geert Wilders erläutert Hintergründe seines umstrittenen Islam-Films', *Wiener Zeitung*, 20 February 2008, in which he reiterates his position that Islam is a 'dangerous ideology' and the Qur'an a 'fascist book' promoting violence.

30 The film was removed from the site shortly thereafter. However, a 'new version' of the film is available on LiveLeak.com at www.liveleak.com/view?i=216_1207467783 (viewed 3 June 2009).

31 Jeppe Bangsgaard and Morten Henriksen, 'Krarup: Koranen svarer til Mein Kampf', *Berlingske Tidende*, 24 May 2007.

32 Strache's remarks were made in a speech at the 28th FPÖ party congress in Innsbruck on 2 June 2007, and at a press conference two days later; the former is quoted in '28. Bundesparteitag der FPÖ in Innsbruck', available on *Wiener Nachtrichten Online* at http://wienernachrichten.com/newpages/par17i.html (viewed 28 March 2009); the latter in 'Strache: "Islamismus ist der Faschismus des 21. Jahrhunderts"', *Die Presse*, 4 June 2007.

This was in line with the FPÖ's larger nativist position, advanced since the late 1990s. This maintains that the advance of a 'radical Islam' in Europe poses a fundamental threat to the 'spiritual foundations of the West' and its 'value consensus' with regard to human dignity, basic freedoms, democracy and solidarity.[33] During the past several years, this line of argument has been adopted by virtually all nativist parties.[34] It has allowed even the most radical parties, such as the Vlaams Belang, to promote themselves as defending liberal values and democracy against Islam. The argument rests on the premise that Islam is incompatible with liberal democracy and that, as a result, Muslim immigrants cannot be assimilated and will invariably form a community apart, a constant source of 'strategic subversion'.[35]

The nativist right advances a number of reasons why Islam is incompatible with western liberal democracy. For one, as the Dansk Folkeparti claimed as early as 2001, Islam propagates 'mediaeval' ideas, fundamentally at odds with modern social values.[36] The charge was made famous by Pim Fortuyn who, in an interview in early 2002, characterized Islam as a 'backward culture', a reflection of his strong conviction that Western Europe was quickly becoming the main stage for a clash between the two dominant cultures in the world: modernity and Islam.[37] Pia Kjærsgaard, the leader of the Dansk Folkeparti, went even further, denying that the post-9/11 confrontation represented a conflict between civilizations. For, as she put it, this would imply that there were two civilizations, which was not the case. 'There is only one civilization, and that is ours.'[38]

In the years that followed, the Dansk Folkeparti repeatedly reaffirmed their disdain for Islam and Muslims. Thus, in 2002, the party's official newspaper concluded a report on the murder of a Kurdish teenager by her own father (for having a Swedish boyfriend) by stating that Denmark should never have opened its doors to 'the Middle Ages'. Three years later, Kjærsgaard—responding to the suggestion of a local imam that it was acceptable, in the aftermath of a murder, to pay money in order to avoid blood revenge—asked who would have imagined, a hundred years earlier,

33 FPÖ, *Das Programm der Freiheitlichen Partei Österreichs* (Vienna 1998), 13.
34 Tjitske Akkerman and Anniken Hagelund, '"Women and children first!" Anti-immigration parties and gender in Norway and the Netherlands', *Patterns of Prejudice*, vol. 41, no. 2, 2007, 197–214.
35 The term 'strategic subversion' is from Lukas Reimann (SVP): see his 'Islam: Aufklären statt verschleiern!', *Schweizerzeit*, 11 May 2007.
36 Dansk Folkeparti, *Danmarks fremtid: dit land, dit valg ...* (Copenhagen: Dansk Folkepartis Folketingsgruppe 2001), 191.
37 Pim Fortuyn interviewed by Frank Poorthuis and Hans Wansink, '"De islam is een achterlijke cultuur"', *de Volkskrant*, 9 February 2002. See also Lijst Pim Fortuyn, 'Politiek is Passie', 2003, quoted in Cas Mudde, 'A Fortuynist foreign policy', in Christina Schori Liang (ed.), *Europe for the Europeans: The Foreign and Security Policy of the Populist Radical Right* (Aldershot: Ashgate 2007), 216.
38 Pia Kjærsgaard, statement made during the opening debate of the Danish parliament, 4 October 2001.

that many Danish cities and towns would be full of people with 'a lower level of civilization, with traditions brought from their home countries, such as honour killing, male chauvinism, halal slaughter—and blood revenge'. Yet, she claimed, this was exactly what had happened. Denmark, despite having 'left the Middle Ages hundreds of years ago', had in 2005 become home to tens of thousands of people who 'live in the year 1005', both culturally and mentally, and who import undemocratic and illiberal practices into Denmark and try to impose them on the Danish majority.[39] In 2007, two years later, Kjærsgaard vowed that her party would never bow to their 'mediaeval traditions'.[40]

In defence of democracy and western values

The Dansk Folkeparti was among the first of the nativist parties to make the question of Islam's incompatibility with liberal democracy an important electoral issue. As early as 2001, one of its campaign publications maintained that Islam and democracy represented an 'impossible combination': in Islam, unlike in Christianity, there is no space for individual free will; the Qur'an determines everything, from how the individual is supposed to live to how society is supposed to be organized.[41] This was in line with the party's earlier efforts to champion liberal values and, in particular, the rights of women in Muslim cultures. Thus, as early as 1997, the party was among those supporting a bill not only to prohibit female genital mutilation in Denmark but to make it a crime to take girls or young women outside the country so that the procedure could be performed. In the years that followed, the party increasingly adopted related issues, such as forced marriage, honour killing and the hijab. In the process, it increasingly depicted Muslim women as oppressed victims of a backward culture while, at the same time, portraying young Muslim men as aggressive and prone to violence (see Figure 1).

Other nativist parties were quick to integrate these arguments into their programmes, and to add new items to the list. Following Fortuyn's example, they started to portray themselves as defenders of liberal values and principles: the separation of church and state, freedom of expression and, above all, gender equality and women's rights. In Denmark, for instance, where the Dansk Folkeparti has had considerable influence on government policy regarding integration, the party has insisted that minorities embrace 'real Danish values', such as open-mindedness, tolerance, equality, solidarity and diligence.[42] In Norway, the Fremskrittspartiet has used 'the

39 Pia Kjærsgaard, 'Blodhævn', *Pia Kjærsgaards ugebrev* , 6 June 2005.
40 Pia Kjærsgaard, quoted in Troels Henriksen, 'DF: Bliv integreret eller tag hjem', *Jyllands-Posten*, 2 August 2007.
41 Dansk Folkeparti, *Danmarks fremtid*, 28.
42 'Vi har gjort Danmark lidt mere Dansk', *Dansk Folkeblad*, no. 5, October 2007, 6–7.

THI KENDES FOR RET

UNDERKASTELSE

Det islamiske hovedtørklæde er symbolet på kvindens underkastelse. Islamisterne bruger det som
stærkt og tydeligt tegn på troens dominans over både mand og kvinde, muslimer og ikke-muslimer.
Det drejer sig ikke om "30 gram stof"! Det drejer sig om tyranni og underkastelse.
Et flertal i Folketinget vil acceptere det i folketingssalen. Og Domstolsstyrelsen har besluttet,
at du som borger fremover skal acceptere, at du i retten møder en dommer indhyllet i tyranniets slør.
Stop det. Nu!

www.danskfolkeparti.dk Tlf. 3337 5199 E-mail: df@ft.dk

Figure 1   Dansk Folkeparti poster, May 2008: 'The Judgement of the Court: Submission'

emancipation of immigrant women' to defend assimilationist policies intended to force immigrants to adopt 'Norwegian values'.[43]

However, as Tjitske Akkerman has recently argued, this is a liberalism turned inward, driven by fear.[44] It allows the nativist right to advocate a situation in which the Muslim immigrant community has no influence in society by, among other things, rejecting its demands for basic rights. Thus, a prominent SVP politician, Ulrich Schlüer, has accused Muslims of using freedom of religion to justify the denial of fundamental rights to others, such as the equality of men and women before the law. Since Islam supposedly places religion and the instruction derived from it above the state, it is in direct contradiction to the 'democratically created legal system' as well as

43 Akkerman and Hagelund, "'Women and children first!'", 206.
44 Tjitske Akkerman, 'Anti-immigrant parties and the defence of liberal values: the exceptional case of the List Pim Fortuyn', *Journal of Political Ideologies*, vol. 10, no. 3, 2005, 337–54 (346–7).

the 'liberal constitutional state *(freiheitliche Rechtsstaat)*'.[45] It is hardly surprising that Schlüer has been one of the most vocal advocates of a transnational alliance of nativist parties and movements against the 'silent Islamization' of Western Europe, that is, the intention of Muslim immigrant communities—by exploiting the liberal democratic order—to change fundamentally the rules of the game, one example being, as another leading SVP politician has put it, the 'creeping introduction of sharia law'.[46] This transnational alliance, Städte gegen Islamisierung/ Cities against Islamization—an attempt to bring together various nativist parties, such as the Vlaams Belang, the FPÖ and the German Bürgerbewegung pro Köln (created to oppose the construction of a mosque in Cologne) in pursuit of a common goal—has adopted the same line of reasoning. It holds, among other things, that Islam represents a social order based on sharia law, and is 'therefore incompatible with our central European values and norms, which form the foundation of our pluralist democracy'.[47]

Strategies of exclusion

The nativist right has advanced numerous ideas, demands and policy proposals that would impede and ultimately reverse the integration of Muslims in Western European society. The intermediate goal of these initiatives has been to render Muslims—and Islam itself—invisible. This is reflected, for instance, in the campaign against the 'Muslim headscarf'. As early as 1989, Bruno Mégret charged that the wearing of the hijab (by Muslim girls in school) was a visible sign of the Islamic 'invasion' of France, with Islam 'implanting itself symbolically' on French soil.[48] Recently, Heinz-Christian Strache and Filip Dewinter made a similar point when they called for a ban of the hijab in schools, universities and the public services. Such a ban would, they argued, not only free young women from the archaic tribal thinking of their parents but also, and more importantly, be a visible sign that European societies were prepared to defend their social values and

---

45 Ulrich Schlüer, 'Minarette gehören nicht in die Schweiz', 3 May 2007, available online at www.minarette.ch/index.php?id=75 (viewed 28 March 2009).

46 See 'Regeln gelten für alle!', *SVP International Newsletter*, 31 March 2006, 4; Christoph Mörgeli, 'Auswüchse einer falschen Einwanderungspolitik', *SVPja*, no. 12, 17 December 2004, 7.

47 Statement by Judith Wolter (Bürgerbewegung pro Köln) in the Cologne city council in support of her party's demand that Cologne become a member of Städte gegen Islamisierung/ Cities against Islamization, 4 March 2008, available online in 'Auseinandersetzung um "Städtebündnis gegen Islamisierung"', at www.pro-koeln-online.de/artikel08/ratssitzung.htm (viewed 28 March 2009).

48 Jane Freedman, 'Women, Islam and rights in Europe: beyond a universalist/ culturalist dichotomy', *Review of International Studies*, vol. 33, no. 1, 2007, 29–44 (33).

norms. For, as Dewinter put it, the hijab—together with the chador—was the 'ultimate sign of radical Islam's rejection' of the West and everything it stood for.[49] Søren Krarup of the Dansk Folkeparti went even further, characterizing the hijab as a 'symbol of tyranny and slavery', the external sign of a totalitarian system comparable to the swastika and the hammer and sickle.[50]

The debate over the hijab has become increasingly heated, particularly with regard to the question of how to regulate its use in the public sector. When in 2007 the Danish parliamentary presidium allowed the wearing of the hijab in parliament, the Dansk Folkeparti MP Søren Espersen called the decision 'a black day for democracy and equal opportunities'. For the hijab was 'not just a piece of cloth' but a symbol of the Islamic uprising and a clear manifestation of Muslim women's oppression.[51] When the Board of Governors of the Danish Court Administration (*Domstolsstyrelsen*) came out in favour of the hijab, Pia Kjærsgaard warned that it was a big mistake, given the advance of 'aggressive interpretations of Islam' throughout the western world and 'daily challenges to the western values of equality, liberty and democracy'.[52]

The nativist right's efforts to render Islam invisible, however, have been most forceful and sustained with respect to the construction of mosques, Muslim cultural centres and minarets (see Figure 2). In Switzerland, for instance, in 2007, the SVP started a signature campaign in support of a popular initiative to ban the construction of minarets. The initiative argued that minarets were 'symbols of conquest' on the grounds that Islam claimed to be the only 'true religion' and thus posed a fundamental threat to the survival of Western Europe's cultural identity.[53] From this perspective, the demands of Muslim communities in Denmark, Germany, Italy, Switzerland and elsewhere to have their own mosques with 'gigantic minarets' are an expression of the growing self-confidence of these communities, reflected in their desire to mark their presence with 'aggressive symbols of Islamic power', as pro Nordrhein-Westfalen (pro NRW), a new anti-Islam party in

49 'Österreich: Strache will Kopftuchverbot', *Die Presse*, 17 July 2007; Filip Dewinter, open letter to Patrick Janssens, mayor of Antwerp, 1 June 2007, available on *Politics.be* at www.politics.be/persmededelingen/15243 (viewed 28 March 2009).

50 Søren Krarup, quoted in 'Tørklædet som symbol', *Nyhedsavisen*, 20 April 2007. Krarup's statement was supported by Pia Kjærsgaard who maintained that the hijab was a 'provocative political symbol' used by some Muslim women to make a political statement: Morten Henriksen, 'Pia K. enig i hagekors-udtalelser', *Berlingske Tidende*, 20 April 2007.

51 'En sort dag for folkestyre og ligestilling—symbolet på underkastelse tillades i Folketingssalen', Dansk Folkeparti press release, 8 April 2008, available on the Dansk Folkeparti website at www.danskfolkeparti.dk/En_sort_dag_for_folkestyre_og_ligestilling_-_symbolet_på_underkastelse_tillades_i_Folketingssalen.asp (viewed 28 March 2009).

52 Pia Kjærsgaard, 'Domstolene skal holdes fri fra politik og religion', *Pia Kjærsgaards ugebrev*, 28 April 2008.

53 Lukas Reimann, 'Minarett = Symbol der Eroberung', *impuls* (SVP Canton St Gallen), no. 3, 2006, 6.

Figure 2   Logos for the anti-minaret campaigns of the SVP (left) and pro NRW (right)

Germany, has recently put it.[54] Others have argued that highly visible (grand) mosques facilitate the recruitment of future terrorists, and allow for the circulation of radical literature and the spreading of extremist ideas. The inevitable consequence of allowing the Muslim community to construct a grand mosque is, as Pia Kjærsgaard put it in late 2007, the creation of a 'parallel society' and a dangerous radicalization of the Muslim community, not only in Denmark, but throughout Western Europe.[55]

During the past several years the nativist right has launched numerous campaigns seeking to prevent and/or stop the construction of new mosques (such as in Cologne, Linz and Bologna). In Denmark and Norway, the mobilization against mosques and minarets had already begun in the late 1990s. In 1998, for instance, the Dansk Folkeparti voiced its opposition to the construction of a mosque in Aarhus, arguing that Denmark was a Christian country and that 'the Muslim way of life' was 'incompatible with the Danish Christian way of thinking'.[56] Two years later, Carl Hagen, the former leader of the Norwegian Fremskrittspartiet, introduced a parliamentary motion intended to ban the use of loudspeakers to call the faithful to Friday prayers from Norwegian mosques and thereby protect Norway's Christian values and culture, which, in the party's view, were already under threat.[57]

54 'Nein zu Großmoscheen, Minaretten und Muezzinruf!', pro NRW petition, 9 February 2008, available on the party's website at www.pro-nrw-patriot.de/pdf/nrwpetition.pdf (viewed 31 March 2009).

55 Pia Kjærsgaard, 'Ingen stormoské i Danmark', *Pia Kjærsgaards ugebrev* , 31 December 2007.

56 Pia Kjærsgaard, 'Nej og atter nej til islamisk stormoské', *Dansk Folkeblad*, no. 8, 1998, 3.

57 'Innstilling fra kommunalkomiteen om forslag fra stortingsrepresentant Carl I. Hagen om nytt prinsipp for integrering av innvandrere samt lovregler slik at det ikke gis adgang til å fremføre bønnerop gjennom høyttaler fra moskeer', Dokument nr. 8:34, 19 October 2000, available on the Norwegian parliament's website at www.stortinget.no/Global/pdf/Innstillinger/Stortinget/2000-2001/inns-200001-009.pdf (viewed 31 March 2009).

In the same year, the Lega Nord launched a campaign against the construction of a mosque in the town of Lodi in Lombardy. The party went so far as to pour pig urine on to the land set aside for the planned mosque, thus rendering it unclean, before having a priest 'reconsecrate' the terrain by celebrating a mass where the mosque was supposed to be built.[58] In the following years, the Lega Nord increasingly promoted itself as Italy's most anti-Islamic party, particularly by opposing the planned building of mosques (in, for example, Modena, Cesena and Ravenna). During the most recent anti-mosque campaign (Bologna), Roberto Calderoli, a former minister under Berlusconi, proposed the introduction of a 'pig-day against Islam' with contests to find the 'most beautiful pigs' to be walked across the site of the planned mosque.[59] In other cases, the Lega Nord has followed the advice given by the Vlaams Blok in 2001, namely to use the municipal building code to stop the construction of mosques.[60] The SVP and the FPÖ have tried to adopt the same strategy, albeit not always successfully.[61] The goal of this strategy is, as the head of the FPÖ in Vorarlberg has explained, 'to drag out the building authorization process as long as possible so that the plans for a minaret will never be realized'.[62]

In the spring of 2007, Heinz-Christian Strache launched a new project, SOS-Abendland (SOS Occident), aimed at counteracting the advance of Islam (see Figure 3). For Strache, western society was experiencing a dramatic erosion of values that, he argued, created a vacuum to be filled by 'radical ideologies' such as 'Islamism, which openly promoted the destruction of Western society'.[63] Strache has hardly been alone in evoking Europe's Christian heritage. As early as 2002, the Lega Nord introduced a motion in the Italian parliament making it mandatory to display the crucifix in all public places, from schools to railway stations. In the years that followed, the party made similar demands at the regional and community level, arguing that the crucifix was not only a religious icon but also

58 Chantal Saint-Blancat and Ottavia Schmid di Friedberg, 'Why are mosques a problem? Local politics and fear of Islam in Northern Italy', *Journal of Ethnic and Migration Studies*, vol. 31, no. 6, 2005, 1083–104 (1089–90).

59 'Bologna, si infiamma lo scontro sulla moschea. Calderoli: "Un maiale-Day contro l'Islam"', *La Repubblica*, 13 September 2007.

60 Vlaams Blok, *Aanpassen of terugkeren* (Brussels 2001), 9. See also Andrea Gibelli, 'Islam, terrorismo e sicurezza', speech delivered at the Scuola Politica Federale, Bellaria Igea Marina, 5–6 November 2005, available on the Padania Office website at www.padaniaoffice.org/pdf/scuola_politica_federale/bellaria_sestri/Bellaria_Gibelli. pdf (viewed 31 March 2009).

61 'Kein Verbot von Minaretten im Kanton Bern', *Neue Züricher Zeitung*, 6 September 2007.

62 Andreas Dünser, 'FPÖ will Minarette verhindern', *Vorarlberger Nachrichten*, 21 February 2008.

63 'SOS Abendland: Strache warnt vor Werteverfall und Verlust der Freiheit', FPÖ press release, 16 March 2007, available online at www.ots.at/presseaussendung.php?ch= politik&schluessel=OTS_20070316_OTS0150 (viewed 31 March 2009).

Figure 3 FPÖ's rhyming EU election poster, 2009: 'Our course is clear: The Occident in Christian Hands'

'indisputably the symbol of our cultural identity, of fraternity, peace and justice, that distinguishes a whole cultural community, epitomizing the essence of western "thought"'.[64] Other leading nativist parties, such as the Vlaams Belang, the Dansk Folkeparti and the SVP, have begun to emphasize the assertion of Christian values and Christian culture in speeches, party programmes and election pamphlets. The implied argument is that Europe will only be able to face the challenge posed by the advance of Islam if, as the newly elected head of the Vlaams Belang recently put it, Europe aggressively defends its 'culture of reference' based on Europe's 'centuries-old western Christian humanist values and norms'.[65]

In the long run, however, the only way to prevent the Islamization of Europe, apparently, is the complete closing of Europe's borders to Muslim migrants. For, as the charter of Cities against Islamization warns, the 'fast demographic increase of the Islamic population in the West threatens to result in an Islamic majority in a lot of Western European cities within a few decades'.[66] For Geert Wilders, who is among the most vocal advocates of a

64 'Il crocifisso sia esposto in tutti gli edifici pubblici', Lega Nord Regione Lombardia press release, Milan, 14 February 2006, available on a party website at www. regionelombardia.leganord.org/Comunicati_stampa/2006/2006%2001_03/ 2006_02_14%20COMUNICATO%20STAMPA%20CROCIFISSO.htm (viewed 31 March 2009).

65 Bruno Valkeniers, 'Recht door zee!', 4 March 2008, available on the Vlaams Belang website at www.vlaamsbelang.be/6/75 (viewed 31 March 2009).

66 Charter of Cities against Islamization, available online at www.citiesagainst islamisation.com/En/2 (viewed 31 March 2009).

complete 'immigration halt from non-western countries', this has already become reality in Amsterdam, at least with respect to the younger generation.[67] For Wilders and other nativists, the problem is one of numbers. They argue that, given Europe's low birth rates (a concern that has always been central to radical right-wing populist parties such as the Front National and the Vlaams Blok) and the continued influx of immigrants who purportedly refuse assimilation, it is only a matter of time until the immigrant community will be strong enough to pose a fundamental challenge to Europe's values and culture. A Swiss 'committee against mass naturalization', organized by Ulrich Schlüer, suggested as early as 2004 in a newspaper advertisement that, if current trends continued, within less than forty years, more than two-thirds of the Swiss population would be Muslims.[68] The Dansk Folkeparti has expressed similar concerns. In order to make the point, in spring 2001, the party went so far as to publish an ad in a leading Danish newspaper, including the names of all newly naturalized citizens, and pointing out that a majority of them were of Middle Eastern origin.[69]

Some on the nativist right have pointed to the case of Kosovo as an example of what might happen in Western Europe if immigration from Muslim countries were allowed to continue. As early as 1999, Umberto Bossi argued that the conflict in Kosovo was a struggle between Christian Serbs, desperate to defend their culture and values, and Muslim Albanians, the vast majority of whom had come as immigrants and now demanded independence and annexation to their Albanian motherland.[70] In the same year, the Dansk Folkeparti characterized the Kosovo conflict as an 'inverted crusade',[71] and charged that the Danish army's presence in the province was helping the Muslims in their fight against Christians. The support for the Muslim Kosovo-Albanians was also considered in stark contrast to the historical significance of the region, where Christian Serbs had already tried to contain the advancement of the Ottomans in the famous battle of Blackbird Plain in 1389.[72] In 2008 Heinz-Christian Strache wrote an open

---

67 See Moritz Schwarz's interview with Geert Wilders, '"Ich lebe in Todesangst"', *Junge Freiheit*, 7 September 2007.

68 On the ensuing controversy, see Markus Schär, 'Ein Kreuz mit dem Islam', *Weltwoche*, no. 38/04, 15 September 2004. The ad appeared in Switzerland's respected *Neue Züricher Zeitung*, 14 September 2004; its content was severely criticized by the Ethikrat der öffentlichen Statistik der Schweiz (Ethics Board of Swiss Public Statistics).

69 'Årets 4.743 nye danskere (indtil nu . . .)', [2001], available on the Dansk Folkeparti website at www.danskfolkeparti.dk/pdf/file-53-6412-24499.pdf (viewed 31 March 2009).

70 Bossi's statement in a session of the Camera dei deputati, Legislatura XV, Seduta no. 513, 26 March 1999, transcript available on the Italian government website at http://legxv.camera.it/_dati/leg13/lavori/stenografici/sed513/s090r.htm (see page 51) (viewed 31 March 2009).

71 Editorial, 'Det omvendte Korstog . . .', *Dansk Folkeblad*, no. 4, September 1999, 2.

72 Karsten Holt, 'Myten om den kærlige krig', *Dansk Folkeblad*, no. 1, February 2008, 24–5.

letter to Austria's Serbian community expressing his outrage over Austria's official recognition of Kosovo's independence, which he characterized as an attack not only on Serbia's sovereignty but also its identity. At the same time Strache made clear that his support for the Serbian position was part of his campaign against Islamization. For, as he put it in an interview, 'we are Europeans, we are Christians... and all European nations have to be united in rescuing our European Christian Occident'.[73] Otherwise, as the logic of the argument implies, Europe is likely to experience the same fate as Kosovo.

A similar logic is behind the nativist right's position on Israel, which several parties, such as the Lega Nord and the Vlaams Belang (which traces its roots to Nazi collaborators), see as a bastion of 'western civilization' and democracy fighting for survival.[74] Carl I. Hagen, for instance, declared in a speech in 2004 delivered to a Christian congregation that defence meant, above all, the defence of the values of democracy, freedom and Christianity. Abandoning Israel would mean there was little 'hope for Europe'.[75] The Dansk Folkeparti, too, has been outspoken in its support for Israel. As early as 2002, the Israeli ambassador Carmi Gillon was invited to participate in the Dansk Folkeparti annual meeting, despite the fact that Gillon had been harshly criticized by a number of NGOs for his support for using torture as a proper means of 'self-defence against terrorism'. For the Dansk Folkeparti, his participation affirmed the party's 'solidarity with the Israeli people in their fight against Muslim terrorism'.[76] More recently, the party's official paper has extolled the work of Danish volunteers in Israel while, at the same time, chastising the West for ignoring the fact that anti-Jewish 'hatred is flourishing in Arabia'.[77]

73 Interview with Heinz-Christian Strache by Ivana Cucujkic, 'Der Tschuschen-Freund', *biber*, 2 January 2008.
74 Interview with Filip Dewinter by Adi Schwartz, 'Between Haider and a hard place', *Haaretz*, 29 August 2005. See also Dewinter's 2005 letter to the Flemish Jewish community in which he distanced himself and his party from Holocaust deniers, noting that the 'genocide against the Jewish people by the Nazi regime cannot and must not be forgotten': 'Open Brief van Vlaams Volksvertegenwoordiger Filip Dewinter aan de Joodse gemeenschap', Brussels, 28 January 2005, available on the Vlaams Belang website at http://vlaamsbelangvlaamsparlement.org/2/134 (viewed 31 March 2009). For the Lega Nord, see Giuseppe Baiocchi, 'Gli ebrei morti, gli ebrei vivi', *La Padania*, 6 November 2001.
75 For the July 2004 speech, see 'Carl I. Hagen infame tale hos Levende Ord', at www.youtube.com/watch?v=c12XeNljACM (viewed 31 March 2009). The present Fremskrittsparti leader, Siv Jensen, however, has moderated this position; see Jensen's petition at a meeting in support of Israel outside the Danish parliament, 'Siv Jensens appell', 8 January 2009, available online at www.frp.no/Innhold/FrP/Les+Siv+Jensens+appell.d25-TgtnIYJ.ips (viewed 31 March 2009).
76 'Besøg af Israels ambassadør', *Dansk Folkeblad*, no. 5, October 2002, 4.
77 See Karsten Holt, 'Danske ildsjæle i kamp for Israel', and Kenneth Kristensen, 'Jødehadet florerer i Arabien', both in *Dansk Folkeblad*, no. 3, July 2007, 8–9 and 10–12, respectively.

The new nativism

In his classic analysis of American nativism, John Higham argues that what distinguished nativists was their belief that 'some influence originating abroad threatened the very life of the nation from within'.[78] The mass immigration of populations culturally alien to the 'American way of life' was seen as part of a vast conspiracy dedicated to the subversion, if not the destruction, of the United States. For this reason, Richard Hofstadter included nativism among the prime examples of the 'paranoid style in American politics', reflected, for instance, in the exemplary title of the 1835 anti-Catholic pamphlet, *Foreign Conspiracies against the Liberties of the United States*, by Samuel Morse.[79] Morse, for whom Catholic immigrants were agents and tools of an international conspiracy (organized by the Holy Alliance), insisted that 'a war of principles' was under way pitting liberty against despotism.[80]

The contemporary nativist right's case against Europe's Muslim community rests on similar arguments. Reminiscent of the charges advanced by American nativists in the 1830s and 1840s, today's nativist right characterizes Europe's Muslim immigrants as a Trojan horse serving the interests of foreign powers seeking the destruction of European culture and civilization as a first step towards the realization of 'a kind of Eurabia'.[81] In order to support their claim, the nativist right quotes remarks made by prominent Muslims, such as Recep Tayyip Erdoğan, Turkey's prime minister and ex-mayor of Istanbul, who said 'the mosques are our barracks, the minarets our bayonets, the domes our helmets, and the believers our soldiers'.[82] Others have quoted Muammar al-Qadhafi's prediction that the 'fifty million Muslims in Europe' will turn Europe into a 'Muslim continent' within a few decades.[83] And they have repeated purported claims by European Muslim leaders that the day will come when Belgium, Italy or Germany will

78 John Higham, *Strangers in the Land: Patterns of American Nativism, 1860–1925*, rev. edn (New Brunswick, NJ: Rutgers University Press 2002), 4.

79 Richard Hofstadter, 'The paranoid style in American politics', *Harper's Magazine*, November 1964, 77–86.

80 David H. Bennett, *The Party of Fear: From Nativist Movements to the New Right in American History* (Chapel Hill: University of North Carolina Press 1988), 41.

81 Filip Dewinter, '"Forza Europa"', speech delivered at the party congress of the German Republikaner, 8 October 2007, available on the Republikaner website at www.rep-hagen.de/content.aspx?ArticleID=412d695e-d0a9-4ad2-b0f4-5a14c92eb2ee (viewed 1 April 2009).

82 Quoted by SVP politicians in support of their initiative to ban the construction of minarets: see 'Moscheen ohne Minarette', *Neue Zücher Zeitung*, 3 May 2007, and also Patrick Freudiger, 'Keine Islamischen Machtsymbole auf Schweizer Boden!', *SVP Pressedienst*, 4 June 2007, 8.

83 Quoted in Eros N. Mellini, 'Einige Anmerkungen zur "islamischen Gefahr"', *SVP Pressedienst*, no. 41, 9 October 2006. Mellini was the leader of the SVP in the Italian-speaking Swiss canton of Ticino.

be 'a Muslim country'.[84] For the nativist right, these and similar statements represent clear evidence that there is 'a precise plan' for Islam to gain 'religious hegemony' in and over Europe, a plan well known to those 'immigrants who are its accomplices, even if the majority of them are unsuspecting instruments for the accomplishment of the project'.[85] Thus Filip Dewinter charged in January 2009, on the occasion of a visit by Erdoğan to Belgium, that the Turkish prime minister obviously regarded 'the Turks living in Belgium as colonizers (*kolonisten*) entrusted with the colonization of Europe by Turkey and Islam'.[86]

It is hardly a coincidence that the nativist right has adopted Samuel Huntington's *The Clash of Civilizations and the Remaking of World Order* as their favourite work of reference.[87] Not only is Huntington, as Michael Shapiro has pointed out, an 'articulate exemplar' of those who think that the West is threatened by the 'increasing presence of cultural Others'.[88] He and his followers also subscribe to the notion that some cultures are superior to others in nurturing values, attitudes and beliefs that facilitate democratic governance, social justice and prosperity.[89] Geert Wilders made the same point when he maintained that, in his view, there was 'no equality between cultures': Islamic culture is 'inferior to European culture, because it is backward'.[90] For Wilders and the nativist right in general, the campaign against the Islamization of Europe represents first and foremost a war in defence of western 'civilizational superiority', at a time when western civilization has lost its claim to universality.[91] As Wilders put it in December 2008 at a conference entitled 'Facing Islam': 'The tide is turning against us. We are losing on every front.' The reason, he continued, was that Europe today was in danger of succumbing to the 'disease' of cultural relativism,

84 See, for instance, Dewinter, 'Het groene totalitarisme'.
85 Mellini, 'Einige Anmerkungen zur "islamischen Gefahr'"; see also Eros N. Mellini, 'L'Islam che preoccupa', *Il Paese*, 28 July 2006.
86 'Turkse premier op meeting in Hasseltse Grenslandhallen—Dewinter: "Erdogan heeft hier niets te zoeken"', 15 January 2009, available on Filip Dewinter's website at www.filipdewinter.be/zondag-grote-meeting-met-turkse-premier-erdogan-in-hasseltse-grenslandhallen (viewed 4 April 2009).
87 Samuel P. Huntington, *The Clash of Civilizations and the Remaking of World Order* (New York: Simon and Schuster 1996). The FPÖ, for instance, states in a position paper on Islam that Huntington's predictions 'have already come true in many areas': FPÖ, 'Wir und der Islam', Vienna, 22 January 2008, 2, available on the FPÖ Freiheitlicher Parlamentsklub website at www.fpoe-parlamentsklub.at/fileadmin/Contentpool/Parlament/PDF/Wir_und_der_Islam_-_Freiheitliche_Positionen.pdf (viewed 1 April 2009).
88 Michael J. Shapiro, 'Samuel Huntington's moral geography', *Theory & Event*, vol. 2, no. 4, 1998, 5–12 (5).
89 Lawrence E. Harrison, 'The end of multiculturalism: the US must be a melting pot—not a salad bowl', *Christian Science Monitor*, 26 February 2008.
90 Faal, '"Koran ist ein faschistisches Buch"' (interview with Wilders).
91 William E. Connolly, 'The new cult of civilizational superiority', *Theory & Event*, vol. 2, no. 4, 1998, 2–3.

with disastrous consequences: if Europe failed to defend 'the ideas of Rome, Athens and Jerusalem' and stop the process of Islamization, 'we will lose everything; our cultural identity, our democracy, our rule of law, our liberties, our freedom'.[92]

Today, even in highly secularized societies such as Denmark and Norway, the nativist right promotes a return to, and defence of, the authentic Christian values and principles that form the basis of these countries' heritage and history.[93] At the same time, these parties have started to put themselves forward as defenders of liberal values and principles with respect to gender equality and women's rights among ethnic minorities. As such, they advocate freedom of expression, open-mindedness, tolerance, solidarity and diligence as central values to be respected, accepted and adopted by ethnic minorities wishing to become part of European society. On behalf of these values, the nativist right seeks to establish barriers preventing ethnic—particularly Muslim—minorities from gaining full access to some civic and social rights. Playing the role of protectors of Western Europe's Christian roots has also allowed the nativist right to embrace questions of morals and ethics, such as homosexuality, abortion and civil marriage. In some cases, the result is rather ironic. The Lega Nord, for instance, was originally stridently anti-clerical and highly critical of the Vatican, and now describes Pope Benedict XVI as 'a strong and resolute Pope', determined to defend Christianity, 'its values and millenarian tradition', fearless in the face of Islamic fundamentalism.[94]

Promoting secular liberal values together with traditional Judaeo-Christian ones has allowed the nativist right to appeal to both secular and religious voters. Empirical evidence suggests that the populist right recruits its supporters predominantly among the non-religious (in terms of church attendance). According to the most recent European Values Survey, for instance, 98 per cent of Dansk Folkeparti voters attend church rarely or never. At the same time, however, some parties have made moderate but still noticeable inroads among religious voters. In the most recent Austrian

92 The conference, organized by Arieh Eldad, member of the Knesset, was held at the Begin Heritage Center, Jerusalem, on 14 December 2008. Wilders's speech is available online on a number of anti-Islam websites, such as http://gatesofvienna.blogspot.com/2008/12/geert-wilders-speech-in-jerusalem.html (viewed 1 April 2009). In January 2009, the Amsterdam court of appeal ruled that Wilders be put on trial for inciting hatred towards Muslims by comparing Islam to Nazism: see 'OM moet Wilders alsnog vervolgen', *De Telegraf*, 21 January 2009.

93 See, for instance, the Lega Nord's most recent election manifesto, which has a section entitled 'Le nostre radici cristiane' (Our Christian roots), available on the party's website at www.leganord.org/elezioni/2008/lega/ue/radici_cristiane.pdf (viewed 1 April 2009). For an analysis of the Lega's use of Christianity, see Renzo Guolo, 'Chi impugna la croce? Lega, Chiesa e Islam', *Religioni e Società*, vol. 20, no. 52, 2005, 39–45.

94 Federico Bricolo, 'Con questo Papa l'Occidente bloccherà l'espansionismo islamico', 25 March 2008, available on the Lega Nord website at www.leganord.org/dblog/articolo.asp?articolo=948 (viewed 1 April 2009).

election, for instance, the defection of a significant number of religious voters to the FPÖ and Jörg Haider's Bündnis Zukunft Österreich (BZÖ) was one, albeit minor, reason for the dramatic comeback of the populist right in that country.[95]

Yet the populist right's nativist turn is not primarily the result of strategic considerations. Rather, it is a reflection of its core ideological position, its distinct focus on identity, reiterated most recently by Jean-Yves Le Gallou in his statement at last year's 'annual university' of the Club de l'Horloge on the role of populism in contemporary European politics.[96] It is this programmatic combination of immigration, Islamization and identity, evoked by Le Gallou, that distinguishes the contemporary nativist right in Western Europe and that explains, at least in part, its impact and influence inside and beyond the political arena. For, as the Lega Nord put it in 2004, at a moment in time when the world is facing the global threat of Islamic terrorism, Europe has to reassert its cultural identity, founded on the Christian values that are the basis of 'European and Western civilization'.[97] Only when it has regained its identity will Europe be able to throw Islam 'back where it came from, on the other side of the Mediterranean', in a replay of the famous battle of Lepanto of 1571, once again pitting 'the cross against the crescent'.[98]

95 See 'ÖVP verzeichnet starke Verluste bei strengen Katholiken', *Der Standard*, 2 October 2008.

96 See Jan-Yves Le Gallou, 'Europe: le temps joue pour le populisme', 3 December 2008, available on the *Polémia* website at www.polemia.com/article.php?id=1806 (viewed 1 April 2009). Among the participants at the conference were Frank Vanecke (Vlaams Blok) and Mario Borghezio (Lega Nord).

97 Lega Nord, Segreteria politica federale, 'Oggetto: sintesi posizioni Lega Nord sull'Unione europea', Prot. no. 0440/2004/RM, Milan, 10 March 2004, available on the Padania Office website at www.padaniaoffice.org/pdf/affari_istituz/doc_politici/Punti_LN_Europa.pdf (viewed 1 April 2009).

98 The Mediterranean image was first advanced by Filip Dewinter in Dewinter, 'Het groene totalitarisme'. In the spring of 2008 it was adopted by Susanne Winter of the FPÖ during a speech a few days before the municipal election in Graz. For an example of the Lega Nord's use of Lepanto, see 'Lepanto: la battaglia che salvò l'Europa', *La Padania*, 7 October 2004.

Refutations of racism in the 'Muslim question'

NASAR MEER AND TARIQ MODOOD

ABSTRACT   Meer and Modood identify a variety of reasons why the notion that Muslim minorities could be subject to racism by virtue of their real or perceived 'Muslimness' is met with much less sympathy than the widely accepted notion that other religious minorities in Europe, particularly Jewish groups, can be the victims of racism. They begin by elaborating the relationships between Islamophobia, anti-Muslim sentiment and cultural racism, before turning to the results of interviews with journalists who make allegedly formative contributions to our understanding of anti-Muslim sentiment. Meer and Modood delineate and discuss four tendencies. The first is the conceptualization of racism that assumes that the protections afforded to racial minorities conventionally conceived as involuntarily constituted should not be extended to Muslims because theirs is a religious identity that is voluntarily chosen. The second is that the way that religion *per se* is frowned upon by the contemporary intelligentsia invites the ridiculing of Muslims as being salutary for intellectual debate and not, therefore, an issue of discrimination. Third, while ethnic identities are welcomed in the public space, there is much more unease about religious minorities. Finally, some find it difficult to sympathize with a minority that is perceived to be disloyal or associated with terrorism, a view that leads to a perception of Muslims as a threat rather than as a disadvantaged minority, subject to increasingly pernicious discourses of racialization. Each of these tendencies could benefit from further study, underscoring the need for a greater exploration of anti-Muslim discourse.

I believe we can learn a lot from the history of the Jews of Europe. In many ways they are the first, the oldest Europeans. We, the new Europeans, are just starting to learn the complex art of living with multiple allegiances ... The Jews have been forced to master this art since antiquity. They were both Jewish and Italian, or Jewish and French, Jewish and Spanish, Jewish and Polish, Jewish and German. Proud of their ties with Jewish communities throughout the continent, and equally proud of their bonds with their own country.

—Romano Prodi[1]

1 Romano Prodi, 'A union of minorities', speech delivered at the 'Seminar on Europe—Against Anti-Semitism, for a Union of Diversity', Brussels, 19 February 2004.

In marked contrast to the once seemingly intractable 'Jewish question' that haunted the continent of Europe throughout the eighteenth, nineteenth and twentieth centuries, and that periodically facilitated episodes of persecution and genocide, there is evidence to suggest that the contemporary representation of Jewish minorities within European public discourses has undergone a process of 'normalization'.[2] The affirmations of Romano Prodi, former president of the European Commission, made during his tenure and elaborated above, perhaps exemplify 'the ways in which leaders today champion the preservation . . . of Europe's Jewish communities'.[3] And it comes as some relief to learn that 'no European party of any significance and this includes the various extreme right-wing movements on the continent, currently champions a specifically anti-Semitic agenda'.[4] An optimistic interpretation of this state of affairs would be to posit the existence of something like a mainstream consensus on the current unacceptability of public articulations of antisemitism.[5]

Of course, this should not be read as suggesting that European societies are free from antisemitism in all its guises.[6] Even in Britain, where far-right political parties have never flourished as they have on the continent, partly due to an electoral system that squeezes out smaller parties, survey evidence compiled by Clive Field in 2006 shows that hostility to British Jews continues to exist and often stems from the view that 'the loyalty of British Jews to

2 Matti Bunzl, *Anti-Semitism and Islamophobia: Hatreds Old and New In Europe* (Chicago: Prickly Paradigm Press 2007).

3 Matti Bunzl, 'Between anti-Semitism and Islamophobia: some thoughts on the new Europe', *American Ethnologist*, vol. 32, no. 4, 2005, 499–508 (502).

4 Ibid. The same cannot be said of these European parties' attitudes to Muslims in Europe. See, for example, statements issued by the Austrian Freiheitliche Partei Österreichs (FPÖ) on the prospect of Turkey's accession to the EU; the Belgian Vlaams Belang's comment that 'Islam is now the no. 1 enemy not only of Europe but of the world'; and the Front National (FN) literature on the 'Islamization of France': see Bunzl, *Anti-Semitism and Islamophobia*, 1–47. Parallels can be found in the leading (but much less mainstream) far-right party in Britain, the British National Party (BNP), which frequently campaigns on what it describes as 'the Muslim problem': see Nasar Meer, 'Less equal than others', *Index on Censorship*, vol. 36, no. 2, 2007, 114–18. For examples of less flagrant, more coded, but equally alarming comments made by British politicians and intellectuals, see Nasar Meer, '"Get off your knees!" Print media public intellectuals and Muslims in Britain', *Journalism Studies*, vol. 7, 2006, 35–59; Nasar Meer, 'The politics of voluntary and involuntary identities: are Muslims in Britain an ethnic, racial or religious minority?', *Patterns of Prejudice*, vol. 42, no. 1, 2008, 61–81; and Nasar Meer and Tehseen Noorani, 'A sociological comparison of anti-Semitism and anti-Muslim sentiment in Britain', *Sociological Review*, vol. 56, no. 2, 2008, 195–219.

5 Esther Benbassa, 'Xenophobia, anti-Semitism, and racism: Europe's recurring evils?', in Bunzl, *Anti-Semitism and Islamophobia*.

6 Jerome A. Chanes, *Antisemitism: A Reference Handbook* (Santa Barbara, CA: ABC-CLIO 2004).

Israel transcends their allegiance to Britain'.[7] Such findings may be added to others in support of the view that Britain is experiencing a resurgence of antisemitism.[8] This is a concern that has resulted in a report by the All-Party Parliamentary Group against Anti-Semitism (2006) that has been taken up in public and media discussions incorporating the concerns of some leading Jewish spokespeople and intellectuals.[9] What appears to have gone unnoticed, however, is that a number of surveys have consistently found that

> Islamophobic views in Britain would appear easily to outstrip anti-Semitic sentiments in terms of frequency (more than double the size of the hard core), intensity and overtness ... somewhere between one in five and one in four Britons now exhibits a strong dislike of, and prejudice against, Islam and Muslims ...[10]

While quantitative surveys do not always provide the best accounts of prejudice and discrimination, they can be useful in discerning trends, alerting us in this case to the widespread prevalence of an anti-Muslim feeling.[11] Indeed, recent large-scale comparative studies conducted by the Pew Global Attitudes Project found that one in four Britons expressed attitudinal hostility to Muslims.[12] What makes this more alarming, however,

7   Clive D. Field, 'Islamophobia in contemporary Britain: the evidence of the opinion polls, 1988–2006', *Islam and Christian–Muslim Relations*, vol. 18, no. 4, 2007, 447–77 (465).

8   For example, the Community Security Trust (CST) recorded 547 antisemitic incidents during 2007, the second highest annual total since it began monitoring antisemitic incidents in 1984. These incidents included cases of extreme violence, assault, damage and desecration of property, threats and abusive behaviour. CST, *Antisemitic Incidents Report 2007* (London: CST 2008), available on the CST website at www.thecst.org.uk/docs/Incidents%5FReport%5F07.pdf (viewed 16 April 2009).

9   All-Party Parliamentary Group against Antisemitism, *Report of the All-Party Parliamentary Inquiry into Antisemitism* (London: Stationery Office 2006), available online at www.thepcaa.org/Report.pdf (viewed 16 April 2009). See also the documentary 'The war on Britain's Jews', broadcast in Britain on Channel 4, 9 July 2007.

10 Field, 'Islamophobia in contemporary Britain', 465 (for a detailed list of surveys, see Appendix I, 472–5).

11 For example, in the first two weeks after the London bombings of 7/7, the Islamic Human Rights Commission (IHRC), a charity that is comparable to the CST, registered over 200 incidents. These included sixty-five cases of violent physical attacks and criminal damage, and one fatal stabbing in which the victim was accosted by attackers shouting 'Taliban'. IHRC, 'Enormous upsurge in anti-Muslim backlash' (press release), 22 July 2005, available on the IHRC website at www.ihrc.org (viewed 16 April 2009).

12 Pew Global Attitudes Project, *Unfavorable Views of Jews and Muslims on the Increase in Europe* (Washington, D.C.: Pew Research Center 2008), summary available online at http://pewglobal.org/reports/display.php?ReportID=262 (viewed 16 April 2009).

is that such findings are frequently met with derision by otherwise self-avowedly anti-racist intellectuals or politicians who either remain sceptical of the scale of the problem,[13] or, indeed, of its racial content altogether.[14] This means that, while Muslims are increasingly the subject of hostility and discrimination, as well as governmental racial profiling and surveillance, and targeting by intelligence agencies,[15] their status as victims of racism is frequently challenged or denied. Indeed, it would be no exaggeration to suggest that, instead of highlighting and alleviating anti-Muslim discrimination,

13 See Randall Hansen, 'The Danish cartoon controversy: a defence of literal freedom', *International Migration*, vol. 44, no. 5, 2006, 7–16; Christian Joppke, 'Limits of integration policy: Britain and her Muslims', *Journal of Ethnic and Migration Studies*, vol. 35, no. 3, 2009, 453–72; and Kenan Malik, 'Are Muslims hated?', broadcast on Channel 4's *30 Minutes*, 8 January 2005, transcript available online at www.kenanmalik.com/tv/c4_islamophobia.html (viewed 16 April 2009).
14 See Diane Abbott, Hansard (HC), 21 June 2005, col. 681; David Davis, Hansard (HC), 21 June 2005, col. 686; Bob Marshall-Andrews, Hansard (HC), 21 June 2005, col. 676; Polly Toynbee, 'My right to offend a fool', *Guardian*, 10 June 2005; and Polly Toynbee, 'In defence of Islamophobia', *Independent*, 23 October 1997.
15 See, for example, calls from the outgoing head of MI5, Dame Eliza Mannigham-Buller, for the police to develop a network of Muslim spies who could provide intelligence on their co-religionists: Richard Ford and Michael Evans, 'Recruit Muslim spies in war on terror, urges new security chief', *The Times*, 9 July 2007. This suggestion followed the disclosure that a number of British intelligence agencies had monitored over 100,000 British Muslims making the pilgrimage to Mecca (see David Leppard, 'Terror watch on Mecca pilgrims', *The Times*, 21 January 2007), and that there had been an unpopular attempt by the Department of Education to encourage universities to report 'Asian-looking' students suspected of involvement in 'Islamic political radicalism' (see Vikram Dodd, 'Universities urged to spy on Muslims', *Guardian*, 16 October 2006). This is compounded by the astonishing number of instances of the 'stop and search' of 'Asians' (categorization by religion is not used for instances of 'stop and search'), which, between 2001 and 2002, increased in London by 41 per cent: Metropolitan Police Authority (MPA), *Report of the MPA Scrutiny on MPS Stop and Search Practice* (London: MPA 2004), 21, available on the MPA website at http://www.mpa.gov.uk/downloads/issues/stop-search/stop-search-report-2004.pdf (viewed 16 April 2009). The national figures point to a 25 per cent increase in the 'stop and search' of people self-defining as 'Other': Home Office, *Statistics on Race and the Criminal Justice System—2005: A Home Office Publication under Section 95 of the Criminal Justice Act 1991* (London: Home Office 2006), 24, available on the Home Office website at www.homeoffice.gov.uk/rds/pdfs06/s95race05.pdf (viewed 16 April 2009). (The category 'Other' can include Muslims of Turkish, Arabic or North African ethnic origin, among others; while 68 per cent of the British Muslim population have a South Asian background, the remaining minority are comprised of several 'Other' categories.) These examples would seem to support Junaid Rana's conclusion that 'current practices of racial profiling in the War on Terror perpetuate a logic that demands the ability to define what a Muslim looks like from appearance and visual cues. This is not based purely on superficial cultural markers such as religious practice, clothing, language, and identification. A notion of race is at work in the profiling of Muslims': Junaid Rana, 'The story of Islamophobia', *Souls: A Critical Journal of Black Politics, Culture, and Society*, vol. 9, no. 2, 2007, 148–62 (149).

the complaint of anti-Muslim racism and Islamophobia has, conversely and frequently, invited criticism of Muslims themselves.[16]

In this article we explore some of the reasons why there may be less sympathy for the notion that Muslim minorities might be subject to racism by virtue of their real or perceived 'Muslimness' than there is, rightly, for the idea that Jewish minorities in Europe might be the object of racism by virtue of their real or perceived 'Jewishness'. Or, more precisely, that 'a form of hostility towards Jews as Jews'[17] might be paralleled by a form of hostility towards Muslims as Muslims. This parallel is something that goes beyond similarities in negative stereotyping, however, for, as Geoffrey Levey and Tariq Modood insist, the analogy lies in the way in which anti-Muslim sentiment, like antisemitism, 'trades on and reinforces prejudice ... via a process of induction and a process of deduction'.[18] These authors draw on the thinking of Brian Klug to help capture an operative understanding of antisemitism,[19] and to extend its logic to an understanding of anti-Muslim sentiment, one that describes a 'shift from inductive to deductive negative generalisations'. Where 'inductive negative stereotyping can be seen clearly in the security policies of "racial profiling", [in which] security services concentrate their attention on people who look or behave a certain way based on the activities of Islamists',[20] this can crystallize into negative deductions about Muslims that are then applied to Muslims in general. This process can also work in the other direction, and so can alternate, but is either way mutually reinforcing. This is elaborated in the following conceptual section. Thereafter, we draw on primary interviews with journalists to expand on this understanding, before concluding that, taken together, our data are instructive in illustrating how an anxiety over the 'Muslim question' informs the hesitancy to name anti-Muslim sentiment as racism.

16 See Meer, 'The politics of voluntary and involuntary identities'; Meer, 'Less equal than others'; and Meer, '"Get off your knees!"'.

17 Brian Klug, 'The collective Jew: Israel and the new antisemitism', *Patterns of Prejudice*, vol. 37, no. 2, 2003, 1–19 (6).

18 Geoffrey Brahm Levey and Tariq Modood, 'Liberal democracy, multicultural citizenship and the Danish cartoon affair', in Geoffrey Brahm Levey and Tariq Modood (eds), *Secularism, Religion and Multicultural Citizenship* (Cambridge: Cambridge University Press 2008), 216–42 (239).

19 Klug offers the following: 'The logic of anti-Semitism does not work like this: "The Rothschilds are powerful and exploitive, hence Jews in general are." But more like this: "Jews are powerful and exploitive, just look at the Rothschilds." In other words, anti-Semites do not generalize from instances. They are disposed to see Jews in a certain negative light, which is why I call their prejudice "a priori"': Brian Klug, 'Anti-Semitism—new or old?', *The Nation*, 12 April 2004, 20 (Letters).

20 Levey and Modood, 'Liberal democracy, multicultural citizenship and the Danish cartoon affair', 239.

Islamophobia, anti-Muslim sentiment and cultural racism

One of the things that has bedevilled an informed discussion of anti-Muslim discourse has been the debate over terminology.[21] Perhaps the best illustration of this is the term 'Islamophobia', which, while 'emerging as a neologism in the 1970s',[22] became increasingly salient during the 1980s and 1990s, and arguably reached public policy prominence with the report by the Runnymede Trust's Commission on British Muslims and Islamophobia (CBMI) entitled *Islamophobia: A Challenge for Us All* (1997). The introduction of the term was justified by the report's assessment that 'anti-Muslim prejudice has grown so considerably and so rapidly in recent years that a new item in the vocabulary is needed'.[23] 'Islamophobia' was defined by the CBMI as 'an unfounded hostility towards Islam, and therefore fear or dislike of all or most Muslims', and further elaborated by the proposal of eight possible Islamophobic mindsets.[24] This, of course, was before global events had elevated the issue to a level previously only hinted at, resulting in a reconvening of the CBMI that heard testimony from leading Muslim spokespeople that 'there is not a day that we do not have to face comments so ignorant that even Enoch Powell would not have made them'.[25]

We may all be guilty of sometimes spending 'far too much time deconstructing the key terms of social debate and far too little time analysing how they function'.[26] Indeed, such an exercise here could be instructive, not least because one of the difficulties with how the CBMI conceived of Islamophobia stems from the notion of an '*unfounded* hostility towards Islam'. Such a notion clearly entails the interpretative task of establishing hostility as

21 John E. Richardson, 'On delineating "reasonable" and "unreasonable" criticisms of Muslims', *Fifth-Estate-Online*, August 2006, at www.fifth-estate-online.co.uk/criticsm/ondelineatingreasonableandunreasonable.html (viewed 15 April 2009).

22 Rana, 'The story of Islamophobia', 148.

23 Commission on British Muslims and Islamophobia, *Islamophobia: A Challenge For Us All* (London: Runnymede Trust 1997), 4.

24 Ibid. The eight statements are: 1) Islam is seen as a monolithic bloc, static and unresponsive to change. 2) Islam is seen as separate and 'other'. It does not have values in common with other cultures, is not affected by them and does not influence them. 3) Islam is seen as inferior to the West. It is seen as barbaric, irrational, primitive and sexist. 4) Islam is seen as violent, aggressive, threatening, supportive of terrorism and engaged in a 'clash of civilizations'. 5) Islam is seen as a political ideology and is used for political or military advantage. 6) Criticisms made of the West by Islam are rejected out of hand. 7) Hostility towards Islam is used to justify discriminatory practices towards Muslims and exclusion of Muslims from mainstream society. 8) Anti-Muslim hostility is seen as natural or normal.

25 Baroness Uddin, quoted in Commission on British Muslims and Islamophobia, *Islamophobia: Issues, Challenges and Action* (Stoke-on-Trent: Trentham Books 2004), 3.

26 Matti Bunzl, 'Methods and politics', *American Ethnologist*, vol. 32, no. 4, 2005, 534 (a rejoinder to Bunzl, 'Between anti-Semitism and Islamophobia').

'founded' or 'unfounded'.[27] Furthermore, what the CBMI was perhaps naive in not anticipating was how the term would also be *politically* criticized for, among other things, allegedly reinforcing 'a monolithic concept of Islam, Islamic cultures, Muslims and Islamism, involving ethnic, cultural, linguistic, historical and doctrinal differences while affording vocal Muslims a ready concept of victimology'.[28] For other critics, by conceiving of discrimination as a collection of pathological beliefs (also implied by use of the term 'phobia'), the term neglected 'the active and aggressive part of discrimination'.[29] An additional complaint was that the term did not adequately account for the nature of the prejudice directed at Muslims. This was advanced by Fred Halliday, whose thesis is worth examining because it accepts that Muslims experience direct discrimination *as Muslims*.[30] Halliday nevertheless considers the term 'Islamophobia' misleading:

> It misses the point about what it is that is being attacked: 'Islam' as a religion *was* the enemy in the past: in the crusades or the *reconquista*. It is not the enemy now … The attack now is not against *Islam* as a faith but against *Muslims* as a people, the latter grouping together all, especially immigrants, who might be covered by the term.[31]

So, in contrast to the thrust of the Islamophobia concept, as he understands it, the stereotypical enemy 'is not a faith or a culture, but a people' who form the 'real' targets of prejudice. While Halliday's critique is richer than many others, particularly journalistic accounts such as those discussed elsewhere,[32] what it ignores is how the majority of Muslims who report experiencing street-level discrimination recount—as testimonies to the

27 For example, does hostility to *all* religion *ipso facto* make one an Islamophobe?

28 William I. Ozanne, 'Review of Confronting Islamophobia in Educational Practice [ed. Barry van Driel, 2004]', *Comparative Education*, vol. 42, no. 2, May 2006, 283, 283; see also Haleh Afshar, Rob Aitken and Myfanwy Franks, 'Feminisms, Islamophobia and identities', *Political Studies*, vol. 53, no. 2, 2005, 262–83.

29 Martin Reisigl and Ruth Wodak, *Discourse and Discrimination: Rhetorics of Racism and Antisemitism* (London: Routledge 2001), 6.

30 Fred Halliday, '"Islamophobia" reconsidered', *Ethnic and Racial Studies*, vol. 22, no. 5, 1999, 892–902.

31 Ibid., 898 (emphasis in the original).

32 See Meer, '"Get off your knees!"'; Meer, 'Less equal than others'; Meer, 'The politics of voluntary and involuntary identities'; and Nasar Meer and Tariq Modood, 'The multicultural state we're in: Muslims, "multiculture", and the "civic re-balancing" of British multiculturalism', *Political Studies* (forthcoming). See also Malik, 'Are Muslims hated?': in this television documentary, Malik argued that 'the Islamic Human Rights Commission monitored just 344 Islamophobic attacks in the 12 months following 9/11—most of which were minor incidents like shoving or spitting. That's 344 too many—but it's hardly a climate of uncontrolled hostility towards Muslims. . . . It's not Islamophobia, but the perception that it blights Muslim lives, that creates anger and resentment. That's why it's dangerous to exaggerate the hatred of Muslims. Even more worrying is the way that the threat of Islamophobia is now being used to stifle

Runnymede's 2004 follow-up Commission bear witness—that they do so when they appear 'conspicuously Muslim' more than when they do not. Since this can result from wearing Islamic attire, it becomes irrelevant—if it is even possible—to separate the impact of appearing Muslim from the impact of appearing to follow Islam. For example, the increase in personal abuse and everyday racism since 9/11 and 7/7 in which the perceived 'Islamicness' of the victims is the central reason for abuse—regardless of the validity of this presumption, to the point that Sikhs and others with an 'Arab' appearance have been attacked for 'looking like bin Laden'—sug-suggests that discrimination and/or hostility to Islam and Muslims are much more interlinked than Halliday's thesis allows.[33]

One illustration of this may be found in the summary report on Islamophobia published by the European Monitoring Centre on Racism and Xenophobia shortly after 9/11. This indicated a rise in the number of 'physical and verbal threats being made, particularly to those visually identifiable as Muslims, in particular women wearing the hijab'.[34] Despite variations in the number and correlation of physical and verbal threats directed at Muslim populations among the individual nation–states, one overarching feature that emerged in all the fifteen European Union countries was the tendency for Muslim women to be attacked because the hijab signified an Islamic identity.[35] The *overlapping* and *interacting* nature of anti-Muslim and anti-Islamic prejudice directed at Muslims can be further demonstrated in the attitudes revealed in opinion polls of non-Muslim Britons one year after 9/11. These showed that

---

criticism of Islam.' Malik is not alone in holding this view and there are several problematic issues that arise in his analysis that may also be evident elsewhere (see Joppke, 'Limits of integration policy', and Hansen, 'The Danish cartoon controversy'). For example, it is easy to complain that Muslims exaggerate Islamophobia without noting that they are no more likely to do so than others who might exaggerate colour-racism, antisemitism, sexism, ageism, homophobia or many other forms of discrimination. That is, his claim remains a political rather than a reasonably informed empirical one. Second, and more important, Malik limits Islamophobia to violent attacks and ignores its discursive character in prejudicing, stereotyping, direct and indirect discrimination, exclusion from networks and so on, and the many non-physical ways in which discrimination operates. Third, Malik draws on data gathered prior to the events of 7/7; according to the same source (the Islamic Human Rights Commission) and using the same indices, the number of incidents radically increased in the first two weeks after the bombings (see note 11).

33 In all fairness to Halliday, this may not easily have been anticipated in 1999, when his '"Islamophobia" reconsidered' was published.

34 Christopher Allen and Jørgen S. Nielsen, *Summary Report on Islamophobia in the EU after 11 September 2001* (Vienna: European Union Monitoring Centre on Racism and Xenophobia 2002), 16.

35 Ibid., 35.

there could be little doubt from G-2002e[36] that 9/11 had taken some toll. Views of Islam since 9/11 were more negative for 47%, and of Britain's Muslims for 35% (almost three times the first post-9/11 figure in G-2001f.[37] ... Dislike for Islam was expressed by 36%, three in four of whom were fearful of what it might do in the next few years. One quarter rejected the suggestion that Islam was mainly a peaceful religion, with terrorists comprising only a tiny minority ...[38]

What these examples make manifest are the confusions contained within the references presently being used to racial and religious antipathy towards Muslims and Islam. Yet this is not unique to the conceptualization of anti-Muslim sentiment, as debates concerning racism and antisemitism demonstrate.[39] This is illustrated in Modood's description of antisemitism as 'a form of religious persecution [which] became, over a long, complicated, evolving but contingent history, not just a form of cultural racism but one with highly systematic biological formulations'. He continues:

> Centuries before those modern ideas we have come to call 'racism' ... the move from religious antipathy to racism may perhaps be witnessed in post-Reconquista Spain when Jews and Muslims were forced to convert to Christianity or be expelled. At this stage, the oppression can perhaps be characterised as religious. Soon afterward, converted Jews and Muslims and their offspring began to be suspected of not being true Christian believers, a doctrine developed amongst some Spaniards that this was because their old religion was in their blood. In short, because of their biology, conversion was impossible. Centuries later, these views about race became quite detached from religion and in Nazi and related doctrines were given a thoroughly scientific-biologic cast and constitute a paradigmatic and extreme version of modern racism.[40]

This should not be read as an endorsement of the view that all racism can be reduced to a biological racism. Indeed, in the example above, modern

36 'Attitudes towards British Muslims', a survey conducted by YouGov for the Islamic Society of Great Britain, 31 October–1 November 2002 ($n = 1,890$), report available on the Islamic Society website at www.isb.org.uk/iaw/docs/SurveyIAW2002.pdf (viewed 16 April 2009); see also Vikram Dodd, 'Muslims face more suspicion', *Guardian*, 5 November 2002.
37 NOP poll conducted for the *Daily Telegraph*, 8–10 October 2001 ($n = 600$); see Anthony King, 'Briton's views of Muslims unchanged after US attacks', *Daily Telegraph*, 12 October 2001.
38 Field, 'Islamophobia in contemporary Britain', 455.
39 Meer and Noorani, 'A sociological comparison of anti-Semitism and anti-Muslim sentiment in Britain'.
40 Tariq Modood, *Multicultural Politics: Racism, Ethnicity and Muslims in Britain* (Edinburgh: Edinburgh University Press 2005), 9–10.

biological racism has some roots in pre-modern religious antipathy, an argument that is also made by Junaid Rana.[41] As such, we should guard against the characterization of racism as a form of 'inherentism' or 'biological determinism', which leaves little space to conceive the ways in which cultural racism draws on physical appearance as one marker, among others, but is not solely premised on conceptions of biology in a way that ignores religion, culture and so forth. Accordingly, we proceed with the view that terms such as 'anti-Muslim sentiment' and 'Islamophobia' should nest within concepts of cultural racism and racialization.[42] This is because neat and categorical delineations within terminology are made implausible by variations in the social phenomena that they seek to describe and understand, so that a more nimble and absorbent nomenclature is preferred.

Media discourse

While these theoretical linkages illustrate how Islamophobia as anti-Muslim sentiment can constitute a form of racism, the discussion thus far has not offered an explanation as to how and why it may be deemed less problematic than other forms of racism. Contrasting perceptions of anti-Muslim sentiment with antisemitism may, once more, provide a fruitful line of enquiry, for the reasons that Claudes Moraes MEP gives.

> The media and Islamphobia are two of the most potent combinations of recent times. ... You see antisemitism is loaded with a very heightened awareness ... that creates a situation which is very emotive and rightly so. With Islam the difference is that there isn't that historical baggage. The media are not identifying a group of people and saying that this is what they suffered. ... There's also a sense of confusion about Islam versus cult-like behaviour because there hasn't been a very good analysis in the media and popular culture generally (interview with Nasar Meer, 3 January 2008).

To explore these issues we turn our attention to some journalists who make these allegedly formative contributions to our understanding of anti-Muslim sentiment.[43] We detail in depth data from interviews in Britain with

41 Rana, 'The story of Islamophobia'.
42 As should antisemitism, though this is not the primary focus of this article.
43 For a fuller discussion of the role of journalists, see Meer, '"Get off your knees!"'. The *Guardian* is probably the only national newspaper in which the issue of anti-Muslim sentiment is taken seriously. Yet even here prevailing opinions are clearly divided among its columnists, with Madeline Bunting, Gary Younge, Seamus Milne and Jonathan Freedland considering it to be an issue of real concern, and Polly Toynbee, Catherine Bennett and Timothy Garton Ash, among others, considering it to be much less so. This is in contrast to its sister paper, the *Observer*, particularly in the writings of Will Hutton and Nick Cohen, who view it as a misconception.

one senior home affairs broadcast journalist and three senior newspaper commissioning editors (two broadsheets and one tabloid).[44]

A narrow view of racism

Our data suggest that one of the explanations for the ambivalence towards attributions of anti-Muslim sentiment reflects a commonly held, narrow definition of racism that assumes that the discrimination directed at conventionally, involuntarily, conceived racial minorities cannot by definition resemble that directed at Muslim minorities. This reckoning is premised on the assumption that Muslim identities are religious identities that are voluntarily chosen.[45] So it is frequently stated that, while gendered, racial and sexual identities are ascribed or involuntary categories of birth, being a Muslim is about chosen beliefs, and that Muslims therefore need or ought to have less legal protection than these other kinds of identities.[46] What this ignores, however, is that people do not choose to be or not to be born into a Muslim family. Similarly, no one chooses to be born into a society in which to look like a Muslim or to be a Muslim creates suspicion, hostility or failure to get the job they applied for.[47] One frequent reaction to this complaint, however, is the charge that Muslim minorities are quick to adopt a 'victim mentality'. These two separate but interlinked issues are illustrated in the following comments of a senior journalist with editorial and commissioning responsibilities at a centre-right national broadsheet newspaper:

> It [Islamophobia] doesn't mean anything to me. No, it's a device or a construct that's been used to cover an awful lot of people and censor debate . . . The racism

44 This research was funded the by the European Commission and forms part of EMILIE: A European Approach to Multicultural Citizenship: Legal Political and Educational Challenges, Contract no. CIT5-CT-2005-02820.

45 See the case study of incitement to religious hatred legislation in Meer, 'The politics of voluntary and involuntary identities', and Modood's rejoinder in the discussion of the Danish cartoon affair, 'Obstacles to multicultural integration', *International Migration*, vol. 44, no. 5, 2006, 51–62.

46 For example, Polly Toynbee, writing in the *Guardian*, has stated that she reserves the 'right' to offend religious minorities on matters of faith because 'race is something people cannot choose and it defines nothing about them as people. But beliefs are what people choose to identify with . . . The two cannot be blurred into one which is why the word Islamophobia is a nonsense' (Toynbee, 'My right to offend a fool'). Elsewhere she has proclaimed: 'I am an Islamophobe and proud of it!' (Toynbee, 'In defence of Islamophobia').

47 Of course, how Muslims respond to these circumstances will vary. Some will organize resistance, while others will try to stop looking like Muslims (the equivalent of 'passing' for white); some will build an ideology out of their subordination, others will not, just as a woman can choose to be a feminist or not. Again, some Muslims may define their Islam in terms of piety rather than politics; just as some women may see no politics in their gender, while for others their gender will be at the centre of their politics.

thing is a bit difficult to sustain because we are talking about a religion here, not race and you have plenty of people who are not Muslim, if you are trying to equate Muslims with South Asians, obviously that's not necessarily the case at all (interview with Nasar Meer, 22 January 2008).

This extract conveys the view that the term 'Islamophobia' is used politically to silence potential criticism of Islam and Muslims, and is particularly invalid because racism is only plausible in relation to ethnic groups, not ethnically heterogeneous religious groups.[48] The journalist continues:

I think I probably went to the first press conference where the phrase came up, I think it was about five or six years ago ... Since we were the ones that were being accused of it, it just seemed rather difficult for me to get my head around, because if Islamophobia means a fear of, literally, that was not what we were talking about. We were talking about fear of terrorists who act in the name of Islam; it's a different thing altogether.

The first sentence of this extract locates this journalist's first interaction with the term, and their sense of grievance in 'being accused of it', while the second sentence returns us to Martin Reisigl and Ruth Wodak's criticism, outlined earlier, as well as rehearsing some of charges put forward by Fred Halliday.[49] The last sentence, which focuses on terrorism, is particularly instructive and will be addressed separately below.

In the meantime this characterization of Islamophobia may be contrasted with another that emerges in the less definitive account of a senior broadcast news editor with responsibilities across the whole range of broadcast, internet and radio journalism. This journalist expresses a similar anxiety to that of the previous respondent, in reconciling what they consider to be a 'full and frank' account with the potential charge of anti-Muslim bias.

There are certainly quite vocal groups of Muslims who are very quick to stress the problems that Muslims can face in this country and work very hard to encourage journalists like me and others to reflect a particular view which might be described as a victim mentality ... I am personally not persuaded that it [Islamophobia] is a huge issue in Britain. It is, racism in all its forms is a problem ... I think for the most part it's really a very tolerant country so I'm kind of conscious that we mustn't allow

48 Writing in the *Daily Telegraph*, Michael Burleigh has similarly stated: 'Those claiming to speak for the Muslim community have played to the traditional Left-wing imagination by conjuring up the myth of "far-Right extremism". In reality, evidence for "Islamophobia" as distinct from a justified fear of radical Islamist terrorism or a desire to protect our freedoms, institutions and values from those who hold them in contempt is anecdotal and slight': Michael Burleigh, 'Religious hatred bill is being used to buy Muslim votes', *Daily Telegraph*, 9 December 2004.

49 Reisigl and Wodak, *Discourse and Discrimination*; Halliday, '"Islamophobia" reconsidered'.

ourselves for the sake of a good story to start painting a picture of a slice of British society which does suffer more than it really does ... (interview with Nasar Meer, 3 January 2008).

While the latter half of this passage reveals a critical perspective on the prevalence of Islamophobia and anti-Muslim sentiment, it is interesting to note how, in marked contrast to the centre-right national broadsheet journalist, the broadcast journalist comfortably places the issue of Islamophobia alongside issues of racism, which 'in all its forms is a problem'. This may in part be due to the insistence of the 'vocal groups of Muslims' that this respondent refers to, for public broadcasters do have a robust policy of diversity awareness training, but the proactive inclusion of Muslim voices is a moot point (see below for more on this), as is the characterization of Muslim complaints as forming part of an alleged 'victim mentality'. Perhaps unsurprisingly, the most Muslim-friendly attitude is to be found in the words of a senior figure at a leading centre-left national newspaper who describes how treating anti-Muslim sentiment with 'less seriousness' can bias the framing of news items:

> I think it is easy to slip into ... I saw it the other day, and it was three headlines together on one page of the *Daily Telegraph*, and the headline said something like 'Foreigners live in £1.3 million houses' ... Then there was a headline where the word Muslim was being used in a pejorative sense and I thought these things, to my mind, are quite dangerous ... I think that's where some papers make a really big mistake time after time after time (interview with Nasar Meer, 29 January 2008).

One development that might alleviate this tendency is the greater presence of Muslim journalists working on a range of news items on different newspapers. This is a point that is also raised by a correspondent formerly with a leading national tabloid, who contrasts the public service requirement of broadcasters with the commercial imperatives of newspaper—and particularly tabloid—journalism, which is shaped by an aggressive drive for sales.

> Because the way newspapers in particular work, I don't know that that's their job to reflect Muslims *per se*, do you know what I mean? ... In my time at the [newspaper] I remember the *Sun* hired a Muslim commentator not long after 9/11, and she did a lot of discussion about whether she was going to wear her veil in the picture. Anila Baig. That was all a bit self-conscious. [We] had a few first-person pieces and features and so on ... if there was a story that involved Muslim groups being invited to No. 10 then you would call the Muslim group to see how it'd gone but I wouldn't say it would go any deeper than that. ... I just report as I do every story. I'm not self-consciously having to check myself or judge myself (interview with Nasar Meer, 18 January 2008).

This extract illustrates the dynamics involved in nurturing 'Muslim voices' within newspapers in a way that can draw attention to how issues of importance to some Muslims, such as the wearing of the veil, may be reported in an educative manner. So even though it may be perceived as 'a bit self-conscious', it appears much more profound than seeking 'Muslim comment' that—by this journalist's own admission—would not penetrate the framing of a story in much depth. This is then related to the final issue that emerges from this paragraph and that concerning reflexivity in this respondent's conception of journalism, something that is evidently in stark contrast to our respondent from the leading centre-left national newspaper (though there is also a tabloid/broadsheet distinction here).

Religion

The last extract touches on a related issue concerning the ways in which religion *per se* is met with anxiety. One particular implication is that, while curbs on defamation of conventionally conceived ethnic and racial minorities may be seen as progressive, the mocking of Muslims is seen to constitute healthy intellectual debate.[50] This tendency is perhaps heightened when the religion in question takes a conservative line on issues of gender equality, sexual orientation and progressive politics generally, leading some commentators who may otherwise sympathize with Muslim minorities to argue that it is difficult to view Muslims as victims when they may themselves be potential oppressors. As Bhikhu Parekh notes, this can be traced to a perception that Muslims are 'collectivist, intolerant, authoritarian, illiberal and theocratic', and that they use their faith as 'a self-conscious public statement, not quietly held personal faith but a matter of identity which they must jealously guard and loudly and repeatedly proclaim ... not only to remind them of who they are but also to announce to others what they stand for'.[51] It is thus unsurprising to learn that some attitude surveys

50 For a discussion of these sentiments in relation to the Danish cartoon affair, see Modood, 'Obstacles to multicultural integration'.
51 Bhikhu Parekh, 'Europe, liberalism and the "Muslim question"', in Tariq Modood, Anna Triandafyllidou and Ricard Zapata-Barrero (eds), *Multiculturalism, Muslims and Citizenship: A European Approach* (London: Routledge 2006), 180, 181. This is also supported in survey findings that report anxiety over the intensity of Muslim religiosity. Clive Field notes that 'in G-2004h [Populus survey for *The Times*, 'Political attitudes', 2–4 April 2004 ($n = 1,045$)], 70% acknowledged that they seemed to take their faith more seriously than Christians, while in G-2005b [Populus survey for *The Times*, 15–16 April 2005 ($n = 714$)], 28% had a concern about the presence of those with strong Muslim beliefs. In G-2005c [Pew Global Attitudes Project survey, 'Islamic extremism', conducted 25 April–7 May 2005 by NOP ($n = 750$)], 80% felt that British Muslims had a keen sense of Islamic identity, which was still growing (63%) and which had to be reckoned as a "bad thing" (56%), with the potential to lead to violence and loss of personal freedoms and to act as a barrier to integration' (Field, 'Islamophobia in contemporary Britain', 457).

report that 77 per cent of people are convinced that 'Islam has a lot of fanatical followers', 68 per cent consider it 'to have more to do with the middle ages than the modern world', and 64 per cent believe that Islam 'treats women badly'.[52] These assumptions are present in our broadcast journalist's insistence that 'the nature of the debate is such that some Muslims most certainly will be offended'.

The recent furore that accompanied the Archbishop of Canterbury's lecture on civil and religious laws in England—that touched on the availability of recourse to aspects of sharia for Muslims who seek it in civil courts in Britain[53]—provides a good illustration of the implication of this journalist's position. Indeed, at the height of the storm, one of the authors received an email (8 February 2008) from a *Daily Mail* journalist that stated: 'I was wondering if you might talk to us about sharia law in the UK, and the effects it might have on our society. ... What we do need is someone saying that Sharia law would not necessarily be a good thing, so if this is not for you, then don't worry!' This sort of approach is anticipated by our respondent formerly from a leading national tabloid who describes how the emphasis rests on getting a story into circulation:

> If you were being accurate you would be going to communities ... and speaking to people. What we tend to do is report what is happening... someone from the Beeb [BBC] might be [going to the communities] if they are doing a story on whether or not Muslim women should be allowed to wear a veil when they go to see their MP. I would have talked to Jack Straw and someone from the organization.

The optimism informing the view that it should be left to a public broadcaster to play the role of an honest broker in reporting emotive stories concerning Muslims with impartiality is not something justified by our interview data. Indeed, our senior broadcast journalist considers the portrayal of difficult stories concerning religious affairs generally, but particularly stories focusing on Muslims, as constituting a necessary part of a public conversation that, in the example of the veil, proceeds by questioning the very legitimacy of the veil itself. As the extract highlights, this is informed by this journalist's view that visible markers of difference and diversity are intrinsically tied to broader, in this view legitimate, public anxieties over immigration that should not be silenced in the interests of maintaining what the respondent describes as an artificially harmonious depiction of multiculturalism:[54]

---

52 Field, 'Islamophobia in contemporary Britain', 453.
53 See Tariq Modood, 'Multicultural citizenship and the anti-sharia storm', *openDemocracy*, 14 February 2008, at www.opendemocracy.net/article/faith_ideas/europe_islam/anti_sharia_storm (viewed 17 April 2009).
54 In another part of the interview the broadcast journalist states: 'I think the [broadcaster] has been through an interesting phase which echoes that slight change

It needs to be something that we do discuss and think about and have a national conversation about because from it flows all the other discussion about our expectations of those who come from other countries to live and work here. . . . I've talked about the veil endlessly over the last year because I do think it's been a really interesting one . . . suddenly people began to say, well hold on, is it right that somebody can teach a class full of kids wearing a full veil. And I think it's a perfectly reasonable question and one that we need to discuss.

In a significant contrast to the public questioning—as an editorial line—of the visibility and indeed legitimacy of religion, our respondent from a leading centre-left national newspaper describes how their paper seeks to incorporate an educational element in its religious coverage. One example may be found in its comment section, which was recently 'blogging' the Qu'ran in a serialization penned by a prominent Muslim intellectual. Another example is the appointment of a young Muslim woman as its religious affairs correspondent, which 'probably raised eyebrows in one or two places'. The journalist continues:

She went on the hajj and did some video for the website, and what I thought was terrific as well, she was able to report pilgrim voices, and these were young British people, they were from the North of England, from London, and so on and so forth, and what the hajj meant to them, what their Muslim identification meant, i.e. voices you don't normally get in a national newspaper.

While these examples perhaps take us away from a direct discussion of racism and Islamophobia, in the way that was elaborated earlier, it is still worth noting how much importance the paper attributes to the value of embedding plural constituencies within its journalism, perhaps as a prophylactic against unwitting anti-Muslim sentiment. This publication is, then, unique in its approach for not only does it seek to afford space in which to cultivate the representation of religion in public discourse, it does so through a consciously Muslim interlocutor.

---

that I've been talking about in the last few years which is I think there was a belief that we had to promote multiculturalism: that it was our job to try and do lots of stories about how lovely it was to have lots of people from different cultures in Britain and not report too much what tensions there were, certainly not allow the voices of those people who had concerns about the changing nature of their high street or whatever it was. I think that has changed over the last couple of years. I think there has been, quite rightly, a change of view that we do need in the corporation to ensure that we reflect whatever tensions and anxieties and indeed prejudices that may exist within British society and a recognition that for people to question, for instance, the level of immigration into this country is not of itself beyond the pale. That is a legitimate position for someone to hold and, indeed, has become a pretty central political discussion right now.'

Terrorism and the securitization of ethnic relations

Other respondents have a very different interest in what Islam means to its British adherents, and place little importance on garnering an empathetic understanding of the spiritual role of religion. Their focus instead appears to be on an assumed relationship between religion and issues of terrorism: issues that are deemed to be especially pertinent in their coverage of Islam and Muslims. As our former tabloid journalist reiterates: 'there's a global jihad going on that we're all involved in ... everything changed after 9/11 and again after 7/7'. This sentiment is repeated by the centre-right national broadsheet journalist who summarizes how 7/7

> was a surprise because what we were looking at in the late 90s and up to 2004 was the belief that it was going to be imported terrorist attacks ... the big surprise was that they were going to attack their own country which was a bit of a turning point I think. It was a bit of an eye-opener.

There is evidence for supposing that this is a widely held view, with Field concluding that, post-7/7, there has been an increased 'tendency to criticize the inactivity of the Muslim population as a whole, and not just its leaders', arising from a belief that 'the Muslim community had not done enough to prevent support for terrorism in its midst'.[55] Indeed, he reports the alarming finding that this belief has given rise to a widespread view that it is legitimate to target Muslims proactively for reasons of national security.

> Three-fifths argued that Britain's security services should now focus their intelligence-gathering and terrorism-prevention efforts on Muslims living in Britain or seeking to enter it, on the grounds that, although most Muslims were not terrorists, most terrorists threatening the country were Muslims ...[56]

These perceptions are perhaps embodied in terminologies that collapse different issues together, a good example of which may be found in attitudes towards the term 'Islamist terrorism'. Our centre-right national broadsheet journalist, for example, remains convinced that terrorism is an outgrowth of Islamism:

> I think we still edge around certain issues ... For instance the government is reluctant to talk about Islamist terrorism even though somebody like Ed Hussein whose book *The Islamist* makes the point that there is a fundamental difference between Islam and Islamism. Unless you understand the ideological basis of it you don't understand anything.

55 Field, 'Islamophobia in contemporary Britain', 459.
56 Ibid.

It is worth noting how, despite the contested and relational nature of terms such as 'terrorism' and 'Islamism', which invite qualification and contextualization, it is increasingly common to find statements of a seamless association between the two. This is a good example of what Richard Jackson has called a culturally embedded 'hard' discourse, since so many other assumptions compound and reinforce it.[57] One example is Melanie Phillips's statement that, 'after the Rushdie affair, Islam in Britain became fused with an agenda of murder'.[58] This characterization conceives the violence that is committed by Muslims as 'something inherent in the religion, rendering any Muslim a potential terrorist'.[59] While some scholars have gone to great lengths to argue that most Muslims consider violence and terrorism to be an egregious violation of their religion,[60] at the level of public discourse, attempts to decouple the two are sometimes dismissed as oversensitive.[61] And it is worth remembering that, in Field's analysis, 56 per cent of survey respondents believed that a strongly held Muslim identity could lead to violence.[62] It is therefore surprising to learn the following from our broadcast journalist about their organization's internal debates over terminology:

> In the end we've used a number of terms and you have to appreciate this is always tricky because in journalism you have to find more than one way of saying everything, otherwise it becomes boring. So we talk a lot about al-Qā'ida-inspired terrorism; the word 'Islamist' has become reasonably accepted as a way of describing a certain type of person who takes a view ... but all these terms are tricky because there are people who might well describe themselves as an 'Islamist' but who would never dream of wanting to blow people up. ... I've certainly been in meetings with ... Muslims who have challenged the [broadcaster]... I suppose that's what I mean by 'we've come a long way', we have been forced quite rightly to think about all these issues and I think we still wrestle with it, but I think we are better.

57 Richard Jackson, 'Constructing enemies: "Islamic terrorism" in political and academic discourse', *Government and Opposition*, vol. 42, no. 3, 2007, 394–426.
58 Melanie Phillips, 'After the Rushdie affair, Islam in Britain became fused with an agenda of murder', *Observer*, 28 May 2006.
59 Elizabeth Poole, *Reporting Islam: Media Representations of Muslims* (London and New York: I. B. Tauris 2002), 4.
60 See Fred Halliday, *Islam and the Myth of Confrontation: Religion and Politics in the Middle East* (London and New York: I. B. Tauris 2003), 107.
61 See Melanie Phillips, *Londonistan: How Britain Is Creating a Terror State Within* (London: Gibson Square 2006); Michael Gove, *Celsius 7/7* (London: Weidenfeld and Nicolson 2006); Nick Cohen, *What's Left? How Liberals Lost Their Way* (London: HarperPerennial 2007); and Andrew Anthony, *The Fallout: How a Guilty Liberal Lost His Innocence* (London: Jonathan Cape 2007).
62 Field, 'Islamophobia in contemporary Britain', 457.

This is an instructive account because it suggests not only that broadcasters with a public remit in particular can be lobbied to take greater account of compelling sensitivities, but also that they have undergone an internal learning process that leads them to continue to 'wrestle' with the issues. The respondent balances their statement, however, with another in which they reiterate that the 'real dangers for us and for all journalists in shying away from some of the real challenges that al-Qā'ida-inspired philosophy presents for British society as a whole and indeed for all Muslims within British society'. On this issue, even our respondent from a centre-left national broadsheet shares a similar concern elaborated in the following extract:

> I went to see Musharaf [the former president of Pakistan, on a visit to London] earlier this week and he got quite belligerent about this, and he was saying 'don't you point the finger at Pakistan, most of your home-grown people [terrorist suspects] are home-grown, that means they were born, they were bred, they were educated here ...' Of course, he's got a point; he's got a very good point!

It is arguable that these attitudes give rise to the perception of the Muslim minority as a threat rather than in terms of measures designed to eliminate discrimination. This may of course stem from the ways in which some find it difficult to sympathize with a minority that is perceived to be disloyal or associated with terrorism.

Summary

This article has explored why there may be little sympathy for the notion that Muslim minorities are subject to racism by virtue of their real or perceived 'Muslimness' (in the way it is rightly accepted that Jewish minorities are sometimes the object of racism by virtue of their real or perceived 'Jewishness'). It finds that the reasons are four-fold. First, there is a conceptualization of racism that assumes that the protections afforded to racial minorities conventionally conceived as involuntarily constituted should not be extended to Muslims because theirs is a religious identity that is voluntarily chosen. One salient, discursive, trope germane to this view chides Muslim minorities for the adoption of a 'victim mentality'. Second, the way in which religion *per se* is frowned upon by the contemporary intelligentsia invites the conclusion that the ridiculing of Muslims is a sign of the health of intellectual debate and not, therefore, a matter of discrimination. Third, while ethnic identities are welcomed in the public space, there is much more unease about religious minorities. This means that some commentators, who may otherwise sympathize with Muslim communities, argue that it is difficult to view Muslims as victims when they may themselves be potential oppressors. Finally, some find it difficult to sympathize with a minority that is perceived to be disloyal or associated with terrorism, a view that leads to a perception of Muslims as a threat rather than as a disadvantaged minority subject to increasingly pernicious discourses of racialization. Each of these findings invites further study and underscores the need for a more profound analysis of anti-Muslim discourse.

'Get shot of the lot of them': election reporting of Muslims in British newspapers

JOHN E. RICHARDSON

ABSTRACT   Journalism provides us with a window on the ways that social, ethnic and religious sameness/diversity is viewed. Hence, an examination of the ideas and arguments in the journalistic media provides us with insights into social ideas and attitudes, specifically into the understandings of who 'we' are and who 'they' are that are circulating at any one time. Richardson examines the ways that British Muslims were represented in British national newspapers, both broadsheet and tabloid, during the general elections of 1997, 2001 and 2005. Two weeks of press reporting immediately prior to each election day were sampled, with any journalistic text referring to 'Islam', 'Muslim' or 'Moslem' in the context of the United Kingdom recorded for analysis. Quantitative analysis, focusing on lexical collocation, was used initially to assess the frequency of key ideational frames in the newspaper reporting of British Muslims over the three elections. The analysis of the sample was enriched, through qualitative critical discourse analysis, to determine *how* British Muslims were depicted in these journalistic texts. The findings demonstrate a quantitative expansion of reports, and a qualitative shift in the texts' arguments towards a constellation of negative representations. Richardson argues that the changes in reporting British Muslims are entirely a response to the so-called 'war on terror' in general, the invasion of Iraq in particular, and how these events were thought to be playing out in the national political sphere.

Most modern democratic societies 'espouse the virtues of social stability alongside notions of equality and human/citizenship rights'.[1] Too frequently, however, at some point the (perceived) values or (alleged) practices of some social group become viewed as being so different that they threaten social stability: the group's (supposed) difference comes to be perceived as a threat. Currently Muslims constitute the group whose difference is thought to be most threatening, and it is hardly an exaggeration to claim that the political and ideological significance of Islam and Muslims

---

1 Peter Ratcliffe, *Race, Ethnicity and Difference: Imagining the Inclusive Society* (Maidenhead: Open University Press 2004), ix.

has never been higher.[2] However, as Kerry Moore, Paul Mason and Justin Lewis point out, 'the representation of Islam in the West as a dangerous cultural "other" and as a potential "enemy within"' is not a post-9/11 development.[3] The exact form of the negative depiction of Muslims has shifted from one era to the next, though a common thread throughout has been the presence and use of 'essentialising caricatures' that impoverish 'the rich diversity of Islam'.[4] The construction of a single Orient is one of the more significant accomplishments of Orientalist representations. Amir Saeed argues: 'Orientalism does not allow for diversity; contradictions and semiotic tensions are ignored as the homogenising ethnocentric template of otherness assumes that there is only one interpretation of Islam.'[5] The depiction of a single 'Orient', or a single 'Muslim community' that can be studied as a discrete and cohesive whole works to produce the image of an essentialized, archetypal (and usually male) 'Oriental', unchanging in 'his' primitive, culturally specific beliefs and practices. More specifically,

> orientalism provides accounts of Islam (and the Orient) which are organised around four main themes: first, there is an 'absolute and systematic difference'

2 See, for instance, Malcolm D. Brown, 'Conceptualising racism and Islamophobia', in Jessika ter Wal and Maykel Verkuyten (eds), *Comparative Perspectives on Racism* (Aldershot: Ashgate 2000), 73–90; Peter Manning, 'Arabic and Muslim people in Sydney's daily newspapers, before and after September 11', *Media International Australia*, no. 109, November 2003, 50–70; Kerry Moore, Paul Mason and Justin Lewis, *Images of Islam in the UK: The Representation of British Muslims in the National Print News Media 2000–2008* (Cardiff: Cardiff School of Journalism, Media and Cultural Studies 2008); Elizabeth Poole, *Reporting Islam: Media Representations of British Muslims* (London: I. B. Tauris 2002); Elizabeth Poole and John E. Richardson (eds), *Muslims and the News Media* (London: I. B. Tauris 2006); John E. Richardson, *(Mis)Representing Islam: The Racism and Rhetoric of British Broadsheet Newspapers* (Amsterdam: John Benjamins 2004); John E. Richardson, 'British Muslims in the broadsheet press: a challenge to cultural hegemony?', *Journalism Studies*, vol. 2, no. 2, 2001, 221–42; John E. Richardson, '"Now is the time to put an end to all this": argumentative discourse theory and "letters to the editor"', *Discourse and Society*, vol. 12, no. 2, 2001, 143–68; John E. Richardson, 'On delineating "reasonable" and "unreasonable" criticisms of Muslims', *Fifth-Estate-Online: International Journal of Radical Mass Media Criticism*, August 2006, at www.fifth-estate-online.co.uk/criticsm/ondelineatingreasonableandunreasonable.html (viewed 27 May 2009); and Amir Saeed, 'Media, racism and Islamophobia: the representation of Islam and Muslims in the media', *Sociology Compass*, vol. 1, no. 2, 2007, 443–62.
3 Moore, Mason and Lewis, *Images of Islam in the UK*, 6. See also Fred Halliday, *Islam and the Myth of Confrontation: Religion and Politics in the Middle East* (London: I. B. Tauris 1996); Jochen Hippler and Andrea Lueg (eds), *The Next Threat: Western Perceptions of Islam*, trans. from the German by Laila Friese (London: Pluto Press 1995); and Edward W. Said, *Covering Islam: How the Media and the Experts Determine How We See the Rest of the World*, revd edn (London: Vintage 1997).
4 Bobby S. Sayyid, *A Fundamental Fear: Eurocentrism and the Emergence of Islamism* (London: Zed Books 1997), 32.
5 Saeed, 'Media, racism and Islamophobia', 457.

between the West and the Orient. Secondly, the representations of the Orient are based on textual exegesis rather than 'modern Oriental realities'. Thirdly, the Orient is unchanging, uniform and incapable of describing itself. Fourthly, the Orient is to be feared or to be mastered. ... All these narratives rest upon the assumption that Islam is ontologically distinct from the West.[6]

Developing such arguments, Ziauddin Sardar suggests that

The history of Orientalism shows that it is not an outward gaze of the West toward a fixed, definite object that is to the east, the Orient. Orientalism is a form of inward reflection, preoccupied with the intellectual concerns, problems, fears and desires of the West that are visited on a fabulated, constructed object by convention called the Orient.[7]

It is for this reason—that Orientalism is a form of inward reflection constructed via the Other—that the exact form of 'Islamic Otherness' shifts over time.[8] In contemporary western scholarship, grand narratives of 'civilizations', Ours and Theirs, are frequently undercut by presumed western superiority, emphasized in preference to a frame of reference that foregrounds the lived perspectives of ordinary people. Several recent studies of 'political Islam' adopt such an Orientalist approach. For instance, the influential neo-Orientalist Daniel Pipes has claimed that 'Muslim countries host the most terrorists and the fewest democracies in the world', and related such startling generalizations to the *Muslim-ness* of these nations above all other explanations.[9] According to Beverley Milton-Edwards, such neo-Orientalism 'associates Islamic politics exclusively with violence, authoritarianism, terrorism, fundamentalism, clerical domination and hostility to modern, "western", secular democratic government, a constellation of negatives that the "radical" in "radical Islam" then signifies and invokes'.[10] From this perspective, 'Muslim extremists' are repositioned as simply 'extremely Muslim'.

The way that sameness/diversity is represented and understood has a crucial influence on social stability and social conflict. Journalism provides us with a window on the ways that social, ethnic and religious sameness/diversity is viewed. Print journalism, in particular, 'serves as a forum for communication between political and other elites in ways which potentially

6 Sayyid, *A Fundamental Fear*, 32.
7 Ziauddin Sardar, *Orientalism* (Buckingham: Open University Press 1999), 13.
8 See Norman A. Daniel, *Islam and the West: The Making of an Image* (Edinburgh: Edinburgh University Press 1960).
9 Daniel Pipes, 'The Muslims are coming! The Muslims are coming!', *National Review*, 19 November 1990.
10 Quoted in Hastings Donnan and Martin Stokes, 'Interpreting interpretations of Islam', in Hastings Donnan (ed.), *Interpreting Islam* (London: Sage 2002), 1–19 (9).

influence the political and policy agenda'.[11] Hence, an examination of the ideas and arguments in the journalistic media provides us with insights into social ideas and attitudes, specifically into the understandings of who 'we' are and who 'they' are that are circulating at any one time.

The data for this article were collected as part of a research project, conducted for the Commission for Racial Equality (CRE), on the ways that 'Britishness' and 'being British' are reported in British newspapers.[12] Specifically, this article examines the ways that Muslims were represented in national newspapers, both broadsheet and tabloid, during the past three British general elections, in May 1997, June 2001 and, most recently, in May 2005. The sample of newspaper articles was limited to the two weeks prior to each election, but the findings are nevertheless revealing of the role that Muslims are perceived—by both press and politicians—to play in the nation, and the ways that this has shifted since 1997. Quantitative analysis, focusing on lexical collocation, was used initially to assess the frequency of key ideational frames in the newspaper reporting of Muslims over the three elections. A more qualitative approach, drawing on critical discourse analysis, was then adopted to examine how Muslims were depicted in the most recent election. I argue that the rise in articles reporting British Muslims is a response to the so-called 'war on terror' in general, the invasion of Iraq in particular, and how these events are thought to be playing out in the national (that is, domestic) political sphere.

The corpus

Issues relating to immigration, asylum, and cultural, religious and 'racial' difference are currently prominent in British domestic politics to a degree not seen for over twenty years. The wider CRE study, from which this article in drawn, demonstrates that, during the 1997 election, immigration and racial or cultural difference barely featured as reporting themes: mentioned in only 1 per cent of coded election news reports, these issues ranked fourteenth, significantly behind more 'bread and butter' issues.[13] Since then, they have steadily crept up the league table of supposedly salient electoral issues: twelfth in the 2001 general election, above employment and defence, and up to the *fourth* most frequently reported issue during the 2005 election. During that (most recent) election, these campaign themes were more prominent in newspaper reports than crime, the National Health Service and even education.

11 Moore, Mason and Lewis, *Images of Islam in the UK*, 7.
12 Michael Billig, John Downey, John Richardson, David Deacon and Peter Golding, *'Britishness' in the Last Three General Elections: From Ethnic to Civic Nationalism* (London: Commission for Racial Equality 2006).
13 Ibid.

The corpus analysed in this article included all election-related articles that referred to 'Islam' or 'Muslim(s)'—or the outdated colonial spelling 'Moslem(s)'—published in British national newspapers, including broadsheets and tabloids, during the two weeks prior to each general election.[14] The frequencies of relevant articles for each campaign are as follows:

Table 1   Frequency of articles mentioning 'Muslims' in the past three general elections

Newspaper	Frequency		
	1997	*2001*	*2005*
Daily Express	0	0	4
Daily Mail	1	0	13
Daily Mirror	0	0	8
Daily Star	0	0	16
The Sun	0	2	7
Morning Star	0	0	3
Financial Times	0	0	13
Guardian	1	5	24
Independent	6	5	13
Telegraph	3	3	7
The Times	0	3	13
The People	0	0	0
News of the World	0	0	0
Mail on Sunday	0	0	6
Sunday Express	0	0	2
Sunday Mirror	0	0	1
Independent on Sunday	0	0	1
Observer	0	1	3
Sunday Telegraph	0	0	2
Sunday Times	2	0	5
Total	**13**	**19**	**141**

In 1997 there were very few election stories that mentioned Islam or Muslims ($n = 13$) with only a modest increase in 2001 ($n = 19$). However, following the terrorist attacks on the United States in 2001 and the subsequent military invasions of Afghanistan and Iraq, the 2005 election brought a massive proliferation of references to Islam and Muslims, increasing from an average of one per day in 1997 to 10 per day for the sampled two weeks of 2005. This finding supports the recent research of Moore, Mason and Lewis, who also connect the significant increase in the reporting of Muslims since 2000 to the 'war on terror'.[15] As Table 1 demonstrates, 2005 saw an increase in both breadth and depth of coverage, that is, an increase in both the number of newspapers reporting Muslims and the number of articles in each newspaper. With the exception of the Sunday newspapers, *The People* and *News of*

14 'Moslem' was used by the *Financial Times* until around 1999, and by the *Daily Mail* until around 2003.
15 Moore, Mason and Lewis, *Images of Islam in the UK*.

the World, which did not include any articles referring to Islam or Muslims at all during these two election weeks 2005, all national newspapers presented Islam and/or Muslims as a newsworthy election issue.

Quantitative analysis: collocation

The words or phrases with which 'Islam' and 'Muslim' were collocated in the corpus act as a broad but illuminating quantitative measure of the ideational contents of the sampled texts. Collocations are patterns or consistencies in language use that create an expectancy that a word or phrase will be accompanied by other specific words. According to the frequently cited maxim of the British linguist J. R. Firth, 'you shall know a word by the company it keeps'. That is, the meaning of a word (including any positive or negative connotations) may be fixed from a range of possibilities by the words that surround it, enabling an insight into one way in which language and ideology are bound together.[16] Traditionally, collocations are studied rather rigidly: a researcher counts the words appearing immediately before and after a particular word. Such an approach tends to return high incidences of articles (such as 'a' and 'the'), possessives ('my') and conjunctions ('and'), which are not overly interesting for my purposes. Here, the method is a little more interpretive: in examining the collocates for 'Muslim' and 'Islam', I recorded not merely immediately adjacent words, but also coded words linked as '*attributes* (in the form of adjectives, appositions, prepositional phrases, relative clauses, conjunctional clauses, infinitive clauses and participial clauses or groups), [and] by *predicates* or *predicative nouns/adjectives/pronouns*'.[17] That is, I attended not just to the lexical collocates for Islam/Muslim, but also their *ideational* collocates, or the kinds of ideas and representations that are linked to Muslims. In presenting frequencies, these collocates have been grouped under headings in order to better reflect their grammatical and ideational functions. Tables 2, 3 and 4 present only the most numerically significant groupings of collocates for each election. The categories listed in the tables differ slightly, reflecting changes in the way that Muslims were reported across the three elections. The categories include:

- 'collectivizations', which amass Muslims into a singular, usually homogeneous group;
- 'individualizations', which refer to single Muslims;

16 Ramesh Krishnamurthy, 'Ethnic, racial and tribal: the language of racism?', in Carmen Rosa Caldas-Coulthard and Malcolm Coulthard (eds), *Texts and Practices: Readings in Critical Discourse Analysis* (London: Routledge 1996), 129–49.
17 Martin Reisigl and Ruth Wodak, *Discourse and Discrimination: Rhetorics of Racism and Antisemitism* (London: Routledge 2001), 54.

- 'institutionalizations', which refer to a single institution to which some Muslims belong;
- 'negativizations', which assign a negative quality to Muslim individuals and/or institutions, usually by referring to attributes (in the form of adjectives, appositions, prepositional phrases and so on), by use of predicates or comparisons, or by representing Muslims as the agent of negatively sanctioned actions;
- 'ordinals', or the placement of individuals in a sequence (the 1997 'ordinal' occurrences all refer to Mohammed Sarwar, 'the first Muslim MP');
- and 'quantifications', which count or measure the number of Muslims in an absolute, relative, exact or fractional way.[18]

Table 2   Collocates for 'Islam/Muslim/Moslem' in the 1997 general election

Collocate	Sum	Rate (out of 13 articles)
Collectivization	11	0.85
Individualization	8	0.62
Institutionalization	6	0.46
Ordinal	6	0.46

Table 3   Collocates for 'Islam/Muslim/Moslem' in the 2001 general election

Collocate	Sum	Rate (out of 19 articles)
Collectivization	25	1.32
Quantification	6	0.32
Negativization	5	0.26
'The Muslim vote'	3	0.16

Working with such small numbers of articles, we need to be careful when commenting on significant patterns. It would be wrong to claim a categorical conclusion about Muslim collocates on the basis of a sample of this size. However, across these two elections, the collocates for 'Muslim' do appear to be clustered around certain ideational categories.

First, *collectivizations* were the most frequently used collocates, and these included terms such as 'conservative Muslims of the world' , 'the Muslim community' and 'the international Islamic community'. For the 1997 general election, there was a rate of 0.85 collectivizations per article (or, if such collocates were evenly spread across the sample, they would have been present in 85 per cent of the articles). In the 2001 campaign, this rose substantially to a rate of 1.32 collectivizations per article. While such

18 Examples of each are provided in the discussion that follows the tables.

collective terms may be used to refer to actual Muslims, in these cases they were used in a far more abstract manner, indexing the more mercurial idea of 'Muslim opinion' or what 'the community' (as a singular) was experiencing, thinking and/or doing. *Institutionalized* collocates provide us with examples of concrete Muslim organizations and groups, but they appeared far less regularly than collectivizations and not at all in the case of the 2001 election. These collocates included terms such as 'the Oxford Centre for Islamic Studies', 'an Islamic Trust' and 'The Muslim League'.

What was observable during the 2001 election was an increased use of quantifications, and three explicit references to 'Muslim voters' and 'the Muslim vote'. While the idea of Muslim political participation was present during the 1997 election, it was only indexed through references to the political views of individuals, such as 'a Muslim accountant', named Muslim candidates and a single reference to 'Putney's Muslim vote'.[19] *Quantifications* included terms such as 'all Asian, all Muslim', 'some Muslims of Pakistani origin' and 'most of Bradford West's Asians are Muslims'. Such quantifications were completely absent in the reporting of the 1997 election. The 2001 election also saw the rise of *negative* ideational frames of reference that were absent from the 1997 collocates. These included 'militant Islam', 'one religion which is now flexing its muscles is Islam' and, in one of the few openly racialized references to the disturbances in Oldham, 'young disaffected Muslims attacking white people'.

In sum, the collocations show that, between 1997 and 2001, the ideational frame of reference for 'Islam' and 'Muslim' had started to change in two discernible ways: first, newspaper reports shifted away from conceptualizing Muslims in either individualized or abstract homogeneous terms and towards a more concrete voting public; and, second, these newspaper reports intimated a growing unease with the (negative) influence that Muslims may have on 'us', discernible in the increasing presence of the 'numbers game' of quantification and the use of negative adjectives and predicates. These patterns developed further in the 2005 election:

Table 4   Collocates for 'Islam/Muslim/Moslem' in the 2005 general election

Collocate	Sum	Rate (out of 141 articles)
Quantification	98	0.70
'The Muslim vote'	64	0.45
Negativization	62	0.44
Collectivization	44	0.31

As Table 4 shows, a key feature of the 2005 election reporting was the quantification of Muslims, and such collocates took one of several forms:

19 'Jemima steals the political show and father's thunder', *Daily Telegraph*, 26 April 1997.

- *exact* quantification of Muslims: 'the one million strong British Muslim community', '1.2 million Muslims', 'the 1.6 million Muslims in Britain';
- *relative* quantification of Muslims: 'lots of Muslims', 'a large Muslim population', 'significant Muslim populations';
- and *fractional* quantification: '39 percent of the population is Muslim', 'nearly half Muslim' and 'more than 50% of voters are Muslim'.

It should again be emphasized that quantification was wholly absent from the representation of Muslims during the 1997 election and was relatively marginal in 2001. During the 2005 general election, we recorded a rate of 0.70 quantifying collocates per article, more than double that observed in the 2001 election. In 2005 such numbers talk was a rhetorical move ubiquitously used in the reporting of Muslims, leading to a dramatic *de*crease in the kind of abstract collectivization (e.g. 'Muslim groups', 'Muslim youth') prominent during the 2001 election.

It should be clear from the wide variance of exact quantifiers—are there 1 million, 1.2 million or 1.6 million British Muslims?—that the actual numbers cited were relatively unimportant, not least because numbers do not, in themselves, carry either positive or negative connotations. Rather, the importance of quantification needs to be viewed alongside the other two leading clusters of collocations in 2005: 'the Muslim voter' and the use of negative and stereotypical terminology. In line with the numbers talk referred to above, references to 'Muslim votes' took one of three forms: exact quantification of the number of Muslim voters; fractional quantification of the proportion of the electorate that was Muslim in a particular constituency; and more abstract reference to 'the Muslim vote' across the country. Negative collocates for Islam and Muslim (0.44 collocates per article) were far more diverse although, in keeping with past studies of the negative representation of minority ethnic communities, they tended to revolve around notions of deviance, violence and mental illness/imbalance.[20] They included 'aggressive Islamic fundamentalists', 'vociferous and belligerent Islam', 'brainwashed young British Muslims', 'fundamentalist Muslims', 'homegrown Islamic extremists', 'Islam loonies', 'Islamic extremists', 'Islamic militants', 'Islamist fundamentalists', 'militant anti-Semitic Muslim groups', 'Muslim extremists', 'Muslim fanatics', 'Muslim maniacs', 'the Muslim lunatic fringe' and many others. Such over-wording, or over-lexicalization,[21] should be taken to indicate an intense ideological preoccupation with the views and actions of the purported 'Muslim threat'.[22]

20 Teun A. van Dijk, *Racism and the Press* (London: Routledge 1991).
21 Roger Fowler, Robert Hodge, Gunther Kress and Tony Trew, *Language and Control* (London: Routledge and Kegan Paul 1979).
22 Moore, Mason and Lewis also identify such an ideological preoccupation, arguing: 'Decontextualizations, misinformation and a preferred discourse of threat, fear and danger . . . were strong forces in the reporting of British Muslims in the UK national press' during this period (*Images of Islam in the UK*, 4).

Both negativizing collocates and references to 'the Muslim vote' were present, proportionally, in a little less than half of the sampled 141 articles, though they were not evenly distributed across the studied newspapers. Stories about and references to 'the Muslim vote'—the definite article 'the' presupposing that such a thing exists—were concentrated in the broadsheet newspapers; in contrast, stories about and references to 'Muslim fanatics', 'Islamic extremists' and so on tended to be concentrated in the tabloid newspapers. The common thread that linked the stories in both types of papers was the spectre of 'Muslim power'. That is, the idea that Muslims were having a greater influence on the public sphere and in the political arena. For the broadsheets this power was being expressed principally through the ballot box. While the participation of this political voice was legitimate, this did not stop the broadsheets from fixating on the issue, compulsively discussing 'what it means for the/our country', thereby marking it out as discursively aberrant. For the tabloids, Muslim power was being expressed through the violent threat that 'Muslim fanatics' posed to 'our lives' and the lives of 'our children', and as such was illegitimate. The function that these collocates played in relation to their more general articles will now be examined in greater detail.

The Muslim vote

Quantification was primarily used to press home the decisive influence that the broadsheet newspapers presumed Muslims were going to play in deciding the results of the election. For instance, on the day of the election, a column in the *Guardian* stated:

> Today up to 1.2 million Muslims, most of them in Labour-held inner-city constituencies, will vote. In over 30 seats the number of Muslim voters exceeds the current majority, and in many more the population is significant enough to assist a wider swing against the incumbent.[23]

No other faith or ethnic group was singled out in such a prominent and recurring way during the election. Nowhere did newspapers examine the voting behaviour of Britain's Catholics, nor were such people ever written about as 'the Catholic community'. In contrast, every newspaper was preoccupied with Britain's Muslim electorate, arguing that their vote would be dictated by their opposition to Britain's role in the invasion of Iraq. Time and again, newspapers argued that this single issue was driving Muslims away from voting Labour, thus disrupting the 'natural' voting behaviour of minority ethnic communities. For instance:

23 Faisal Bodi, 'Ties that no longer bind: a new generation of Muslims is breaking with Labour', *Guardian*, 5 May 2005.

> Whitechapel, with a large Bengali and Muslim immigrant community, *should be* a
> *natural* Labour heartland—*but* our meeting with Friday worshippers at the east
> London mosque showed that the 'war on terror' and the *perception* that Muslims
> and Islam are *being stigmatised* have started a backlash, much of it directed
> personally at Tony Blair.[24]

Here, the use of the strong modal claim 'should be' and the qualifying 'but'
stress the disparity between the usual political behaviour of Muslims and
their current views of the Labour government. The relationship between the
Muslim Whitechapel electorate and voting Labour is labelled 'natural', a
term that attempts to objectivize the claim: that is, it is simply *accepted* that
areas with comparatively large Muslim communities are Labour heartlands,
it is not the view of the journalist. In contrast, the reason behind such
'unnatural' voting behaviour is partly subjectivized into a '*perception* that
Muslims and Islam are being *stigmatised*' by the actions of the Labour
government. This transitive choice presents the reported activity as a mental
process, as a perception sensed by someone; further, stigmatization entails
symbolic devaluation rather than material disadvantage or discrimination.
The implication, therefore, is that the 'problem' of Muslims deserting Labour
could be solved by a battle for hearts and minds, a campaign of messages, to
alter Muslims' *perception* that the party considers them to be unimportant or
without value.

This explanation as to why some British Muslims were apparently turning
away from Labour was not always phrased in such a mitigated way. For
example, in a different column, Tariq Modood (Professor of Sociology at
Bristol University) argued: 'Riots in some northern towns in that year [2001]
and, above all, the "war on terrorism" *have made* Muslims the *principal
victims* of the UK's draconian security policies.'[25] The difference between
these two explanations for the apparent change in Muslims' voting
behaviour is significant: in the first, Muslims perceive stigmatization; in
the second, Muslims *are* the victims of draconian policing. Here the process
is relational rather than mental; that is, victimization via 'draconian security
policies' has taken place. Thus, according to Modood, a more significant
reversal at the level of policy and practice is what is required to stem the tide
of Muslim dissatisfaction with Labour.

The invasion of Iraq, as the most significant foreign policy decision of the
'war on terror', was often presented as an election issue that divided Muslim
and non-Muslim Britons. Occasionally such a comparison was explicit:

24 Andy McSmith, 'The hidden election', *Independent on Sunday*, 24 April 2005 (emphases
    added).
25 Tariq Modood, 'Disaffected Muslims will make their votes count', *Financial Times*, 28
    April 2005 (emphases added).

The political fall-out from the Iraq war has done enormous damage to Prime Minister Tony Blair's trust ratings. But in stark contrast to last year's elections in the US and Spain, the war itself does not seem to be an issue for most British voters. The exception is places such as Bethnal Green and Bow in London's East End. Framed by the skyscrapers of London's financial district, the deprived inner-city constituency has long been home to the capital's poorest immigrant communities and it has one of the biggest concentrations of Muslim voters.[26]

Here, the newspaper claimed that, 'in stark contrast' to its importance in recent US and Spanish elections, the invasion of Iraq was only a prominent issue in British constituencies with 'concentrations of Muslim voters'. Faced with such a realization, and assuming that it was accurate, the newspaper could have explored this in one of two ways. First, it could have asked what it was about the majority of *non-Muslims* in the United Kingdom that made them so *uninterested* in an invasion of dubious legality, spearheaded by their own country, that had resulted in the deaths of (by that date) more than 100,000 Iraqi civilians. Second, the paper could have asked what it was about the majority of British *Muslims* that made them so *interested* in an invasion of dubious legality, spearheaded by their own country, that had resulted in the deaths of more than 100,000 Iraqi civilians. In this article, the *Financial Times* chose the second of these options. This meant that they, like the rest of the broadsheets, emphasized the assumed peculiarity, abnormality and, in some cases, sectarianism of 'the Muslim vote'.

More often, the comparison of issues of concern to Muslim and non-Muslim Britons was made implicitly via the terms of reference employed. For instance, alongside Andy McSmith's article 'The Hidden Election', the journalist grouped together under a series of headings what different voters identified as the 'real issues' of the election:

AT THE EAST LONDON MOSQUE

The real issues for Muslims, young and old, are living conditions at home and the war in Iraq . . .

AT THE ISLINGTON DINNER PARTY

Trust is the real issue for former Blairites at Frederick's restaurant in New Labour's spiritual heartland . . .

AT THE SUSSEX NATURE RESERVE

The real issue for people enjoying the countryside at Woods Mill is the environment, hardly mentioned in the campaign so far . . .

AT THE SCHOOL GATES

Labour says the votes of 'school-gate mums' will be decisive. At Duncombe primary in London, some say the real issue 'as ever' is money . . . [27]

26 Frederick Studemann, 'Muslim voters turn their backs on Blair because of the war', *Financial Times*, 21 April 2005.
27 McSmith, 'The hidden election'.

The organization of these *vox populi* illustrates the simplistic way that voting behaviour is conventionally approached by both journalists and mainstream political parties. Voters are grouped together in semi-arbitrary ways according to lifestyle, consumption or in response to prevailing political anxieties. So, while Muslims were almost wholly ignored as a target audience in 1997, their concerns were acknowledged in 2005 due to wider geopolitical events. Similarly, while 'Mondeo-man' was thought to be decisive to New Labour's political marketing in the 1997 election campaign, in 2005 this shifted to 'school-gate mums'.

The problem with using such terms is not only that they are blunt devices for predicting political behaviour, but also that they imply a crude, mono-dimensional notion of identity. Is the mosque the only place where one could ask Muslims to identify the 'real issues' of the election? Don't Muslims also go to dinner parties, nature reserves or drop their children off at school gates? While such editorial decisions may have been made with the best of intentions—for instance, to report the views of sections of the population often ignored by mainstream journalism—the choice inevitably distances the Muslim electorate from non-Muslims. It implies that British Muslims' voting preferences are driven by a set of concerns that are different to those of 'the rest of us', that Muslims are different to 'the rest of us'. In the case of the 2005 election, newspapers implied that Muslims were more preoccupied by the state of Iraq than by the state of Britain, and more concerned with the troubles of foreigners than their fellow countrymen. More recently, and more stridently, Richard Littlejohn took up this theme in his *Daily Mail* column, writing: 'Young Muslims ... are encouraged to put loyalty to their faith above personal responsibility to the country of their birth. They are brainwashed into treating any misfortune which befalls any Muslim anywhere in the world as a personal insult.'[28] As Amir Saeed argues, such claims place British Muslims outside, and in conflict with, the imagined community of the British nation.[29]

Assumed throughout this presentation of the potential power of 'the Muslim vote' were two questions that were only acknowledged in a *single* column: 'First, is a "Muslim vote" emerging—in other words, will Muslims vote together or at least on the basis of a distinctive set of concerns? Second, will this vote "punish" Labour for the Iraq war?'[30] According to the vast majority of broadsheet reports, the guaranteed answers to these questions were 'yes' and 'almost certainly'. The 'Muslimness' of British Muslims was assumed to be so powerful that there was never any question that their affiliation, or perhaps allegiance, to Iraqi Muslims would trump all other policy issues.

28 Richard Littlejohn, 'If they hate us so much, why don't they leave?', *Daily Mail*, 8 August 2006.
29 Saeed, 'Media, racism and Islamophobia', 458.
30 Modood, 'Disaffected Muslims will make their votes count'.

Despite this certainty, evidence in fact existed to contradict both assumptions, evidence that was often cited but passed over in these same columns and reports:

> ... There is not much evidence of Asians losing faith with Labour. Shaheda Rashid, 32, says: 'Most of the community are voting Labour. Labour has always helped ethnic minorities.' Shamsooddin and Fatema Patel, young parents, agree. 'Labour do more for the community. We've got a SureStart nursery now.' And Mohammed Bilal, a shop assistant, says: 'Like Robin Cook said, Tony lied, but you should still vote Labour because they've done a lot of good work.'[31]

Here, there is a striking incongruence between the gist of the report—reflected in the article's headline—and the views of the British Muslims quoted in the body of the report. Of course it is *possible* that the 'legacy of Iraq war *could* undo Straw', but what are the chances that it *will*? The body of this article, encapsulated in the opinions of the four Muslims quoted above, suggests the chances were very slim indeed. In fact, in keeping with the rest of the British voting public, Blackburn's Muslims appeared far more inclined to cast their vote in response to a *variety* of factors, national and international, giving priority to their quality of life and that of their families.

In short, news reports that claimed that British Muslims vote on the basis of a set of concerns different to non-Muslim Britons (that is, their opposition to the invasion of Iraq or the 'war on terror' more generally) were repeatedly undermined by the quoted views of British Muslims themselves. But the strong commonalities shared between Muslim and non-Muslim Britons were repeatedly overlooked due to a seemingly unshakeable belief that 'they' were different from 'us'. In these cases, the structuring influence of prejudicial ideas of 'us' and 'them' were such that difference was proclaimed even while staring sameness in the face. This is a rhetorical *division* that, while not racist, nevertheless provides the framework on to which a racist rhetoric of religious *rejection* can be projected.

The limits of tolerance

A key underlying assumption of the majority of newspaper reports analysed as part of this study was that British people—and British newspapers—tolerate difference. However, as Ghassan Hage has argued, we do well to remember that 'when those who are intolerant are asked to be tolerant, their power to be intolerant is not taken away from them. It is, in fact, reasserted by

31 Mary Ann Sieghart, 'Legacy of Iraq war could undo Straw in battle for Blackburn's Muslims', *The Times*, 28 April 2005.

the very fact of the request not to exercise it.'[32] Wendy Brown has also critically examined the notion of tolerance and its discourses, arguing that it is

> a mode of late modern governmentality that iterates the normalcy of the powerful and the deviance of the marginal, responds to, links and tames both unruly domestic identities or affinities and non-liberal transnational forces that tacitly or explicitly challenge the universal standing of liberal precepts.[33]

She elaborates:

> In every lexicon, tolerance signifies the limits on what foreign, erroneous, objectionable or dangerous element can be allowed to cohabit with the host without destroying the host ... The very invocation of tolerance in each domain indicates that something contaminating or dangerous is at hand, or something foreign is at issue, and the limits of tolerance are determined by how much of this toxicity can be accommodated.[34]

Following Hage, I argue that these discursive enactments and others like them, are best conceived 'as nationalist practices: practices which assume, first, an image of a national space; secondly, an image of the nationalist himself or herself as master of this national space and, thirdly, an image of the "ethnic/racial other" as a mere object within this space'.[35] In essence, they are based on a 'white fantasy' regarding the rights and abilities of mainstream 'white' society to regulate the parameters of British society, to tolerate or proscribe, to include or exclude, both physically and verbally. British newspapers, particularly the right-wing tabloids, are only 'tolerant' of Muslims up to a point. After this point—which may be crossed when there are 'too many of them' or when 'those that are here' are apparently doing things that 'we' disapprove of—then it presumably becomes acceptable for tolerant newspapers to become intolerant. Jan Blommaert and Jef Verschueren call this the 'threshold of tolerance', satirically arguing that the tolerant European does not become intolerant 'until this threshold has been crossed. Just let him or her step back over the same threshold, i.e. just reduce the number of foreigners again, and the good old tolerance will return.'[36] Of course, the exact point of this threshold is kept utterly vague: 'How many foreigners may present themselves, or what aspects of belief or behaviour they should display before the "threshold" is crossed, remains an *ad hoc*

32 Ghassan Hage, *White Nation: Fantasies of White Supremacy in a Multicultural Society* (Annandale, NSW: Pluto Press 1998), 85.

33 Wendy Brown, *Regulating Aversion: Tolerance in the Age of Identity and Power* (Princeton, NJ: Princeton University Press 2006), 8.

34 Ibid., 27.

35 Hage, *White Nation*, 28.

36 Jan Blommaert and Jef Verschueren, *Debating Diversity: Analysing the Discourse of Tolerance* (London: Routledge 1998), 78.

decision' for these self-appointed ethnic managers of the national space.[37] In short, tolerance is always an uneasy social condition, as the 'tolerators' can withdraw their toleration when they feel it has reached its limit. Those defined as 'foreign' are therefore always on their toes, never quite sure when some group, party or individual will feel that the line has been crossed and will once again shout 'that's enough'. This threshold of tolerance was most clearly visible during the 2005 general election in the reporting in the tabloid newspaper the *Daily Star*.

The *Daily Star* is, arguably, an easy target when it comes to examining anti-Muslim prejudice, given how little deconstruction their reporting requires. However, the paper's reporting is also symptomatic of the sudden, convulsive press interest in Muslims: it showed the highest increase in reports of Muslims of the sampled newspapers, going from zero articles in both the 1997 and 2001 elections to 16 during the 2005 election. These articles amounted to over 11 per cent of the total for 2005. For this reason alone, their reporting warrants a closer look.

Across the two weeks sampled, the *Daily Star* ran a high-profile and strident campaign against what it called 'Muslim loonies' and the threat that they posed to Britain. The front-page story on 21 April 2005 accurately demonstrates the negativity of the campaign.

37 Ibid., 80.

In a single headline, this report condensed many of the key ideological terms of reference for the paper: these Muslim are 'loonies', they hijack (an especially resonant verb to describe Muslim actions) and they're compulsive funda-mentalists aiming to make Britain an Islamic state. All that was missing was the term 'jihad'. The magnitude of the *Daily Star*'s reaction was hardly warranted by the reported events. Without wanting to underplay the seriousness of the death threats referred to in the article (around thirty young men calling themselves the 'Saviour Sect' burst into an election meeting and shouted threats at George Galloway MP), to claim that the very small group of men involved were poised to 'wreck the election' is simply hyperbole.

The article that continued on the next page, under the headline 'Muslim Maniacs Want to Make Us an Islamic State', stepped up the rhetoric still further, elevating a single criminal act and the website of a tiny fringe party into a violent campaign intent on world domination:

> Islamic extremists want Muslims to boycott the General Election ... and help turn Britain into an Islamic state. A group of religious militants has already stormed political rallies and issued death threats to politicians standing for Parliament on May 5. And global Islamic political party Hizb ut-Tahrir's British website states that they won't stop until they get world power.

It is interesting to note that the inside report followed an identical argumentative structure as the front-page story: Muslim extremists want to make Britain ('Us' in the second headline) an Islamic state; they plan to do this by disrupting the election, as evidenced by the violent actions of one group and the website of another. However, this second article extends the argument beyond Britain to suggest that these activities are part of a *global* campaign to seize 'world power'. Although this shifts the frame of the story, suggesting that the 'bloodthirsty radicals' organizing the campaign may be foreign, the article subsequently foregrounds a quote from 'Hizb's *British* leader' (emphasis added). While this modifier implies that Hizb ut-Tahrir also has non-British leaders, and hence activities in countries other than Britain, the focus of the article remains the threat posed by British 'Islamic extremists' rather than by foreign invasion. This fits with a wider pattern in the representation of Muslim extremism since 2001. Examining the centrality of 'extremism' for representations of Muslims in the press, Elizabeth Poole argued that, prior to 11 September 2001,

> British Muslims were not attributed so blatantly with this label. Rather it was Muslims in Britain, exiles, who were categorised as extremists ... [and] physical threat remained at a distance. There has now been a significant shift in the definition of British Muslims as terrorists.[38]

38 Elizabeth Poole, 'The effects of September 11 and the war in Iraq on British newspaper coverage', in Poole and Richardson (eds), *Muslims and the News Media*, 89–102 (95–6).

The following day the *Daily Star* dedicated an editorial and a further two articles to the problem posed by 'Islamic extremists'. The longest of these reports focused on the reaction of the Muslim Council of Britain (MCB) to the violent provocation of the Saviour Sect:[39]

> British Muslim leaders have branded homegrown Islamic extremists as 'hooligans who are NOT real Muslims'. The damning verdict was issued by the Muslim Council of Britain yesterday. ... Inayat Bunglawala, spokesman for the Muslim Council of Britain, said: 'We condemn these people who we believe are a new party called The Saviour Sect.' ... He called on Muslims in Britain to ignore the fanatics who he says are filled with hate of Western culture. They should use their vote and embrace mainstream society.[40]

This article consolidated the idea that *British* Muslims should now be considered a threat to 'our' security and, since they had clearly crossed the threshold of tolerance, it was now perfectly acceptable to demand, as the headline did, that they be 'booted out' of the country. The Britishness of these individuals was illustrated in the first line of the report, which went on to use two referential strategies to represent them: the first, that they were 'homegrown Islamic extremists', was assumed, while the other, the MCB's view that they were 'hooligans who are NOT real Muslims', was new (or asserted). Clearly the two strategies offered significantly different ways of describing the men. The MCB did not describe them as Islamic anything; indeed, as the quote illustrates, they explicitly argued that the men were not 'real' Muslims. Later in the article, Bunglawala was directly quoted saying as much: 'We would even question whether they are Muslims at all. We certainly don't regard them as Muslims.'[41] Instead, he referred to 'hooligans' and people who 'have a hooligan outlook', referential strategies that clearly framed the men as thugs or yobs, and their crimes as public order offences rather than political or religious extremism. Despite this, the paper persisted in using the term 'Islamic' and co-opted the MCB into their own framing of the reported event: namely, the danger that certain 'Muslim loonies', 'filled with hate of Western culture', represented to Britain. In using the comments of the MCB in such a prominent way, the article made use of a familiar binary system for representing 'the ethnic Other': as loyal subjects or as fifth columnists. The newspaper shut down the debate, in effect denying that

39 It is interesting to note that the views of the MCB, as well as all other 'mainstream' Muslims, were conspicuously absent from the reports of the previous and later days.

40 'Boot 'em out: Muslim leaders turn against the extremist thugs', *Daily Star*, 22 April 2005.

41 Ibid. Bunglawala's quoted explanation for the charge was a weak one: 'In Islam, if there are two groups of people and one says that the other is a non-believer that is a very serious thing. These people have done that again and again. When that happens one of the groups must not be Muslim. So either these people are not Muslims—or every other Muslim in Britain is not.'

there was any space between these polarized positions. Accordingly, the only choice open to British Muslims was to 'embrace mainstream society' or prepare to be 'booted out'.

It is hard to gauge the effect that this demand for Muslim assimilation had on the readers of the newspaper, though the reactions printed in the paper's Forum page on different days are instructive. The bulk of Forum was taken up by mobile phone text messages (a feature called 'Text Maniacs') and, to a much lesser extent, letters and jokes written by readers. Over the three editions following the front-page splash on 21 April ('Muslim Loonies Hijack Election'), a debate on 'what we should do about Muslims' raged on the Forum page. Some of the text messages are reproduced here, complete with text spellings:

[22 April 2005]

FUNDAMENTALISTS WONT STOP UNTIL UK IS AN ISLAMIC STATE. SHOW THEM WHY WERE PROUD TO B BRITSH. R OUR GOVERNMENT SPINELESS? GET SHOT OF THE LOT OF THEM. PHIL FROM WORKINGTON

let what hapend in Bethnal green b a lesson. islam is a sleeping tiger and when it is fully awake beware! James

The time for action has come. We british cant let the muslims win. Or uk will be like iraq! Dave from Barking

Britain an Islamic State? Not in my lifetime if I can help it! We should stand up and ban islam now! Adz

I reckon we shud al vote 4 whoever is goin t get rid of th muslim extremists who wan t make us muslim state. Blair is too soft. donna

[23 April 2005]
Wonder what brave men who died in the Battle of Britain would have made of Muslim fanatics trying to wreck our general election. Steve, London

Go live in another country, u live by their rules. Should happen ere 2. Wise up people. Kick out the parasites! Buzz, Banbury

AS A BRITISH ASIAN PLEASE DNT MAKE COUNTRY AN ISLAMIC STATE. I AM A SIKH – SUM PEOPLE CNT TELL DIFF BTWN SIKHS N MUSLIMS. I DNT WNT TRUBLE IN FUTURE. VPEEDOFF

[25 April 2005]
Easy 2 tell Sikhs + muslims apart. Sikhs got turbans and fought + died alongside us many wars. Muslims just hate us all. MAC

before judging muslims mabe u should look at r so-called war criminal leaders
bush + blair. adnan

Newspapers frequently use letters' pages to include but rhetorically distance
themselves from racist or controversial comment.[42] Although the arguments
of letters and texts are authored by (or ascribed to) readers, by choosing to
print them, the paper ratifies their content. They are selected by the
newspaper and, by virtue of their inclusion, they are presented as 'reasonable comment'.[43] The vitriol of these texts is so extreme, it is astonishing they
were printed. Most would be better placed on the website of racist parties
such as the British National Party or the National Front; some arguably
contravene laws against incitement to racial hatred. Though their manifest
hatred hardly requires further analysis, certain points are apposite.
Throughout, the terms of reference are 'us British' versus 'them Muslims',
a contrast that at least implicitly suggests that Muslims are presumed to be
foreign. Muslims are represented as a problem that 'we patriots' need to
solve. For most of these readers, the solution to the 'problem' of Islam
involves the removal of Muslims from Britain: it is 'time for action', we
should 'GET SHOT OF THE LOT OF THEM' and 'ban islam'. This solution is
apparently required because, as 'MAC' asserts in the penultimate text (and
the only one to respond explicitly to a prior text), 'Muslims just hate us all'.
In others (such as the text from 'donna'), the solution appears to involve the
removal of Muslim extremists, though, as ever, no criteria are offered to
distinguish between the 'extremists' and 'the rest'. The sense one gains from
these texts is that, like naughty children, Muslims have 'gone too far'
because we and our political leaders have been 'too soft' on them. The
solution, it seems, is to be stricter and less sparing in our discipline. The final
text from 'adnan' is presumably included to provide some sense of 'balance'
to the 'debate', though it in no way counters the other nine. Indeed, given the
dominance of assimilationist rhetoric in this paper, this final text, ascribed to
a texter with a Muslim name, may in the eyes of some readers confirm the
idea that Muslims are anti-western: 'they hate *our* leaders'.

The failure to report the lives and activities of Muslims adequately has
significantly 'negative implications for all Muslims because it implies that
the problem resides in the religion and in the people who follow it, rather
than in alternative factors'.[44] These implications are spelled out in both the
racist reaction of the readers of the *Daily Star* to the story—a reaction that
the newspaper then ratified by publishing—and, in a less direct way, in the

42 See Albert Atkin and John E. Richardson, 'Arguing about Muslims: (un)reasonable
   argumentation in letters to the editor', *Text and Talk*, vol. 27, no. 1, 2007, 1–26; John E.
   Richardson and Bob Franklin, '"Dear editor": race, readers' letters and the local
   press', *Political Quarterly*, vol. 74, no. 2, 2003, 184–92.
43 Richardson, 'Now is the time to put an end to all this', 148.
44 Poole, *Reporting Islam*, 9.

significant increase in racist harassment, vandalism and other violence that British Muslims have suffered since the election.[45]

Windows on sameness/diversity

In this article I have examined how Islam and Muslims were represented in newspaper reporting of the past three UK general elections. Taking comprehensive samples of British newspapers over the two weeks prior to election day, I was able to demonstrate a marked quantitative increase in press reports referring to Islam and Muslims, from an average of 1 report per day in 1997 to slightly over 10 per day in 2005. This increase was accompanied by shifts in the ideational framing of Muslims, reflected in changing patterns of collocation from individuals and abstract collectives to specific quantifications, reminiscent of immigration 'numbers talk', and/or negativized predicates. The variety and strength of these negative modifiers speak to an intense and growing ideological preoccupation with the presence and political activities of Muslims.

Journalism provides us with a window on the way that sameness/ diversity is viewed. Alternate research methodologies would provide other ways to examine journalists' engagements with sameness/diversity and its significance to their reporting practices. Production surveys and ethnographic research (as difficult as these are to initiate given journalists' reluctance to open their doors to critical analysis) are unquestionably important in examining the discursive processes underlying the actual putting together of the news, the values and principles of journalism as a profession and how those aims are actualized, reinforced and challenged on a daily basis in both the routines and outputs of journalists.[46] Indeed, I have argued as much elsewhere.[47] Nonetheless, like Elfriede Fürsich, I suggest that 'media texts present a distinctive discursive moment between encoding and decoding that justifies special scholarly engagement'.[48]

45 Liz Fekete, 'Protecting ethnic minorities', *European Race Bulletin* (Institute of Race Relations), no. 53, 2005, 15–30 (21–6).
46 See John E. Richardson and Leon Barkho, 'Reporting Israel/Palestine: ethnographic insights into the verbal and visual rhetoric of BBC journalism', *Journalism Studies*, 'early look' published online 13 February 2009 at www.informaworld.com/smpp/ content ∼ db = all ∼ content = a908690878?words = richardson&hash = 843258562 (viewed 27 May 2009); Leon Barkho and John E. Richardson, 'The impact of BBC production strategies on news discourse', *Journal of Pragmatics*, forthcoming.
47 John E. Richardson, 'Language and journalism: an expanding research agenda', *Journalism Studies*, vol. 9, no. 2, 2008, 152–61; Geert Jacobs, Tom Van Hout, Ellen Van Praet, Daniel Perrin, John E. Richardson and Felicitas Macgilchrist (NewsTalk&Text Research Group), 'Towards a linguistics of news production', *Journal of Pragmatics*, forthcoming special issue on NewsTalk&Text.
48 Elfriede Fürsich, 'In defense of textual analysis: restoring a challenged method for journalism and media studies', *Journalism Studies*, vol. 10, no. 2, 2009, 238–52 (238).

A key consideration for such analysis ought to be the (ideological) ideational contents of such discourse, and the potential detrimental effects these may have, particularly on minority and/or racialized communities.

The examination of these newspaper reports indicates the extent to which Muslims and Islam have become significant issues in party politics and general elections and, arguably, British political discourse as a whole. It should be stressed that, while my findings are derived from comparatively small periods of time prior to successive election days, they nevertheless reflect wider changes in the ways that Islam and Muslims are represented in journalistic discourse since 1997. Whether focusing on the presupposed particularity of 'the Muslim vote' or amplifying the threat of 'Muslim loonies', prevailing journalistic discourses increasingly 'imply that Muslims are alien to indigenous culture',[49] while leaving what, exactly, is meant by 'the British way of life' conspicuously undefined: 'the racial-cultural identity of "true nationals" remains invisible, but can be inferred (and is ensured) *a contrario* by the alleged, quasi-hallucinatory visibility of the "false nationals": the Jews, "wogs", immigrants, "Pakis", natives and blacks.'[50] Hence: *they* vote according to the troubles of foreigners (while *we* think of our country-men); *they* are dangerous radicals (while *we* are law-abiding democrats); *they* are intolerant (while *we* are tolerant, for it is *their in*tolerance that transgresses *our* threshold of tolerance).

The qualitative analysis of the reporting, in particular, suggests that the rise of press interest in Islam and Muslims has been accompanied by the rise of a hostile and stereotyping discourse that emphasizes the putative threat that Muslims pose to '*our* way of life'. The reports in the *Daily Star* were preoccupied by, and hence magnified, the idea of a Muslim 'threat within'. Although one or two of its articles did acknowledge the fact that the majority of British Muslims abhor criminal violence and the kind of views associated with the individuals and groups the paper so repeatedly criticized, there was zero interest in reporting the views and activities of Britain's Muslim communities outside of this violent and divisive frame of reference. In particular, the *Daily Star* repeatedly failed to make an adequate distinction between Islam and Islamist, or between violent extremism and Islamist political campaigning.

Such journalistic discourse should be viewed pragmatically, as serving the very practical function of removing British Muslims from empowered positions in and affecting the public sphere by demanding either their cultural and political assimilation or expulsion. It should be viewed as an example of a 'discourse of spatial management', founded on the 'white fantasy' of the journalists and readers,[51] according to which they have the

49 Saeed, 'Media, racism and Islamophobia', 459.
50 Etienne Balibar and Immanuel Wallerstein, *Race, Nation, Class: Ambiguous Identities* (London: Verso 1991), 60.
51 Hage, *White Nation*.

right and ability to regulate the ethnic and religious parameters of British society.

Where do Muslims stand on ethno-racial hierarchies in Britain and France? Evidence from public opinion surveys, 1988–2008

ERIK BLEICH

ABSTRACT   Bleich assesses levels of anti-Muslim prejudice in two important European countries—Britain and France—to begin a process of systematically evaluating the status of Muslims on national ethno-racial hierarchies. He reviews major scholarly and institutional public opinion polls from 1988 through 2008 to discern attitudes towards Muslims over time and in comparison to other religious and ethnic groups. The findings support the following conclusions: negative attitudes towards Muslims have risen over the past twenty years in Britain and France; when compared to other *religious* groups, Muslims are viewed with tremendous suspicion by British and French respondents; and, in spite of the events of recent years, Muslims have not sunk to the bottom of the *ethno-racial* hierarchy, most measures suggesting that other groups remain more distant ethno-racial outsiders than Muslims in both Britain and France.

Until recently, Europe's Muslims were rarely the subject of sustained academic enquiry or political scrutiny. Throughout most of the post-war era, these individuals were defined not primarily by their religion but rather by their citizenship status, economic function, race, ethnicity or nationality. 'Muslim' was thus a far less meaningful category than 'immigrant', 'asylum-seeker', 'refugee', 'foreigner', 'guestworker', 'Black', 'Arab', 'Kurd', 'Pakistani', 'Algerian' or 'Turk'. Over the past two decades, however, European Muslims have increasingly come to be understood *qua* Muslims, with this aspect of their identity viewed as trumping others, and with 'Muslim' frequently racialized as an essential category of identity, difference and inferiority.

Yet the extent to which Muslims have been constructed as ethno-racial outsiders remains unclear. Much of the recent work on Islamophobia suggests that Muslims are currently in an extremely low position on the

For helpful comments on this essay, I thank Christopher Bail, Joel Fetzer, Clive D. Field and the editors and anonymous reviewers of *Patterns of Prejudice*. I also thank Colette van der Ven and especially Alexander Ferrell Hall for superior research assistance.

ethno-racial hierarchy. The 1997 Runnymede Trust report *Islamophobia: A Challenge for Us All*, for example, defined 'Islamophobia' as comprising eight types of 'closed' views about Islam and justified the use of this neologism on the grounds that 'anti-Muslim prejudice has grown so considerably and rapidly in recent years that a new item in the vocabulary is needed'.[1] The term was firmly inserted into the French debate with the 2003 publication of Vincent Geisser's *La Nouvelle Islamophobie*, which suggested that 'ordinary racism' had found a new hook: 'the Muslim religion as an irreducible identity marker between "us" and "them".'[2]

Discussions about the spread of Islamophobia extend well beyond these two seminal publications. For example, Fred Halliday uses the term 'anti-Muslimism' to argue that 'the attack now is not against Islam as a faith, but against Muslims as a people',[3] while Jocelyne Cesari claims that there is an overarching conflation between 'an Islam perceived as an international political threat and the individual Muslim living in Western societies' that has translated into a sense of Muslims as 'The Enemy'.[4] More concretely, Clive Field's overview of British public opinion towards Muslims concludes that 'mutual suspicion and fear are fueling a worsening Islamophobia'.[5] Yet a 2003 French Commission nationale consultative des droits de l'homme (CNCDH) report on the extent and meaning of Islamophobia in the French context found that Islamophobia was difficult to define and that there was no obvious surge in such a sentiment at that time.[6]

Just where do Muslims stand on European ethno-racial hierarchies? Is their status similar or different across countries? Is Islamophobia rampant, is the term a red herring, or is the situation more complicated than that? This essay seeks to assess the levels of anti-Muslim sentiment in two important European countries—Britain and France—to begin a process of systematically evaluating the status of Muslims on national ethno-racial hierarchies. Thus far, there have been strikingly few attempts to develop concrete measures for estimating the position of Muslims as ethno-racial outsiders and for evaluating their rank relative to other groups. Any definitive assessment of this issue would entail interpreting and aggregating multiple types of data, such as those on political and media portrayals of different

1 Commission on British Muslims and Islamophobia, *Islamophobia: A Challenge For Us All* (London: Runnymede Trust 1997), 4.

2 Vincent Geisser, *La Nouvelle Islamophobie* (Paris: La Découverte 2003), 10. All translations from the French are by the author unless otherwise stated.

3 Fred Halliday, *Two Hours That Shook the World. September 11, 2001: Causes and Consequences* (London: Saqi Books 2002), 128–30.

4 Jocelyne Cesari, *When Islam and Democracy Meet: Muslims in Europe and in the United States* (Basingstoke and New York: Palgrave Macmillan 2004), 21–2, 35–7.

5 Clive D. Field, 'Islamophobia in contemporary Britain: the evidence of the opinion polls, 1988–2006', *Islam and Christian–Muslim Relations*, vol. 18, no. 4, 2007, 447–77 (469).

6 CNCDH, *2003. La Lutte contre le racisme et la xénophobie* (Paris: La Documentation Française 2004), 179–230.

groups, incidents of hate crimes and acts of discrimination, social interactions between groups, state policies and public opinion. While this enormous task is not possible within the confines of a single essay, this contribution hopes to make progress towards that goal by examining the critical variable of public attitudes towards Muslims. Public opinion polls are a particularly important tool for this purpose as they provide direct information about majority attitudes towards Muslims across time and in comparison to other ethno-racial groups.[7]

Britain and France were selected for this study because they are large European countries with sizeable Muslim citizen populations. Although the precise number of Muslim citizens is difficult to assess, Britain's 2001 Census revealed 1.6 million Muslims in the country and more recent estimates place the figure closer to 2 million.[8] In France, where there is no census data on religion, credible estimates revolve around 4–5 million Muslims in the overall population. Because of the relatively inclusive citizenship and naturalization policies in these countries, a majority of these Muslims are now or will one day become citizens. The public's assessment of Muslims is thus less influenced by the notion that Muslims are foreigners, as might be the case in countries like Germany or Switzerland that have more restrictive naturalization laws and an extremely high percentage of non-citizen Muslims.[9]

Public opinion polls can offer important insights into the relative standing of Muslims on the ethno-racial hierarchy, yet it is important to identify their limitations. As Field states in his comprehensive overview of British polls between 1988 and 2006, the bulk of surveys about Muslims were conducted for media outlets in the immediate aftermath of a contentious event; these surveys thus catch respondents at moments when they are least favourably disposed to populations perceived to be problematic.[10] To compensate for this effect, this essay utilizes only surveys undertaken by scholarly or research institutions that have not based the timing of their polls on media-driven events. Naturally, by chance, some of these polls were conducted during crisis moments. But they were carefully planned, and did not pose sensational questions.[11] Furthermore, they have often asked similar questions over time,

---

7   This essay focuses on how majority populations view Muslims, based on the logic that majorities hold most of the power to determine national ethno-racial hierarchies. It therefore excludes questions from surveys such as the Gallup series on 'Muslims in Europe' that, while extremely interesting, focus primarily on Muslim attitudes towards their host societies.

8   According to a 2008 estimate by the Home Office: see Alan Travis, 'Officials think UK's Muslim population has risen to 2m', *Guardian*, 8 April 2008.

9   Although Germany relaxed its naturalization laws in 2000, there remain many fewer Muslim citizens in Germany than in either Britain or France.

10 Field, 'Islamophobia in contemporary Britain', 449–50.

11 Space constraints make it impossible to include the wording of the questions asked in each survey. Please contact the author directly for this information.

and will continue to ask similar questions in coming years, making it possible in the future to build on the findings presented here. Another challenge inherent in survey research is that individuals may find it difficult to disentangle their sentiments about Muslims from those about ethnic groups that are predominantly Muslim (such as Asians, Pakistanis or Bangladeshis in Britain, or Arabs, Maghrebis or Beurs in France), or from those about immigrants in general, who in turn remain conflated with other ethno-racial categories.[12] To address this problem, this essay has focused as often as possible on surveys that directly compare sentiments towards these entangled groups in order to understand if negative sentiments vary consistently across the ethnic and religious components of identity. While these are not perfect solutions to the problems of entanglement—and while more sophisticated solutions may emerge in future research—they offer a useful starting-point for assessing the place of Muslims on national ethno-racial hierarchies.

The findings support the following conclusions: negative attitudes towards Muslims have risen over the past twenty years in Britain and France; when compared to other *religious* groups, Muslims are viewed with tremendous suspicion by British and French respondents; and, in spite of the events of recent years, Muslims have not sunk to the bottom of *ethno-racial* hierarchies in either country, most measures suggesting that other groups remain more distant ethno-racial outsiders than Muslims in both Britain and France. The following section sets the stage for this analysis by defining an ethno-racial hierarchy and by contextualizing the place of Muslims on British and French national hierarchies over the longer term. Subsequent sections draw on surveys from the past two decades to present the concrete evidence that leads to each of the three conclusions. The final section outlines additional implications of the findings.

Ethno-racial hierarchies and Muslims in Britain and France

A national ethno-racial hierarchy is determined by the relative status of different groups within a society. The concept draws on longstanding work in social psychology on social comparison, which demonstrates that respondents across cultures are able to rank different categories of people on status and competence measures.[13] Most parallel research in ethnic and

---

12 For an extended discussion of this problem, see CNCDH, 2003. *La Lutte contre le racisme et la xénophobie*, 179–230; and Miranda Lewis, *Asylum: Understanding Public Attitudes* (London: Institute for Public Policy Research 2005), 36–45.

13 For a general overview of the field, see Serge Guimond (ed.), *Social Comparison and Social Psychology: Understanding Cognition, Intergroup Relations, and Culture* (Cambridge: Cambridge University Press 2006). For specific work on intergroup ranking, see Susan T. Fiske and Amy J. C. Cuddy, 'Stereotype content across cultures as a function of group status', in Guimond (ed.), *Social Comparison and Social Psychology*, 249–63.

racial studies has focused on identifying ethno-racial outsiders. According to Richard Alba, for example, the boundaries between high-status groups and ethno-racial outsiders are 'bright' not 'blurry', with 'unambiguous' distinctions between them.[14] For Aristide Zolberg and Long Litt Woon, outsiders share 'an essentialized negative identity as dangerous strangers'.[15] Louk Hagendoorn has applied the concept of hierarchies most directly to the study of race and ethnicity, arguing that 'outgroups are rank-ordered in ethnic hierarchies'.[16]

Developing status measures is the only way to understand the number of ethno-racial outsider groups in a society, and the relative intensity with which that outsider status is experienced. Given the assertions about the extent of Islamophobia in Europe (and challenges to its value as a concept[17]), it is important to assess the place Muslims occupy on national ethno-racial hierarchies to assess the degree of the problem. Whether Islamophobia is rampant or a chimera can only be known in light of multiple sources of evidence, of which public opinion polls are one important type. This information can also help us determine the steps that need to be taken to address the challenges facing Muslims as well as other ethno-racial outsider groups.[18]

As a prelude to analysing the public opinion polls of the past two decades, it is helpful to examine the status of Muslims in Britain and France over the longer term. Because this is a comparative study, it is also important to ask whether we expect attitudes towards Muslims to be similar or different across the two countries. There are significant parallels in how British and French publics have viewed Muslims over time, just as there are meaningful national dissimilarities that could generate divergence in how people rank Muslims on their country's contemporary ethno-racial hierarchy.

14 Richard Alba, 'Bright vs. blurred boundaries: second-generation assimilation and exclusion in France, Germany, and the United States', *Ethnic and Racial Studies*, vol. 28, no. 1, 2005, 20–49.

15 Aristide R. Zolberg and Long Litt Woon, 'Why Islam is like Spanish: cultural incorporation in Europe and the United States', *Politics and Society*, vol. 27, no. 1, 1999, 5–38 (6).

16 Louk Hagendoorn, 'Ethnic categorization and outgroup exclusion: cultural values and social stereotypes in the construction of ethnic hierarchies', *Ethnic and Racial Studies*, vol. 16, no. 1, 1993, 26–51 (27). See also Milton Kleg and Kaoru Yamamoto, 'As the world turns: ethno-racial distances after 70 years', *Social Science Journal*, vol. 35, no. 2, 1998, 183–90. A similar research agenda on ethnic hierarchies is pursued by Robert Ford in his paper, 'Not all immigrants are equal: the ethnic hierarchy in British immigration preferences', *Manchester–Harvard Summer School on Immigration*, 2008.

17 Christian Joppke, 'Limits of integration policy: Britain and her Muslims', *Journal of Ethnic and Migration Studies*, vol. 35, no. 3, 2009, 453–72.

18 Specifying the ethno-racial hierarchy in a given society, however, does carry the *political* risk of generating a competition over victimhood; if some groups argue they are more disadvantaged than others, it may weaken potential coalitions of ethno-racial outsiders.

Some of the most important differences that might affect British and French attitudes towards Muslims stem from longstanding national church–state arrangements, from the experiences of colonialism and decolonization, and from overarching policy approaches towards immigrant integration. Britain has an established church, whereas France has a much vaunted tradition of church–state separation known as *laïcité*.[19] The French colonial experience was deeply marked by its decolonization war with predominantly Muslim Algeria in the 1950s and 1960s, traces of which still colour much of French public discourse and political attitudes.[20] By contrast, British colonial history involved tensions in South Asia that involved both Muslims and Hindus, although the history of Britain's relations with Catholic Ireland can be seen as equally if not more powerfully formative.[21] Furthermore, whereas Britain has affirmed its commitment to a multicultural approach to immigrant integration since the 1960s (with notable variations and rhetorical caveats), France has tended towards an assimilationist philosophy based on equal national citizenship.[22] Together, these factors suggest that the British public would be much more favourable towards Muslims than French respondents, and may even call into question the wisdom of comparing these two countries.

Yet there have been multiple studies of Muslims in Europe based on the premise that all of these differences amount to less than the sum of their parts. Prominent authors such as David Theo Goldberg, Nancy Foner and Richard Alba, and Aristide Zolberg and Litt Woon Long have started from the assumption that there are more commonalities in how European countries view Muslims than there are differences.[23] For Goldberg, anti-Muslim attitudes have deep roots in many countries, with 'the Muslim' portrayed as 'inevitably hostile, aggressive, engaged for religious purpose in

19 For an extended discussion of the implications of different church–state relations on policies towards Muslims, see Joel S. Fetzer and J. Christopher Soper, *Muslims and the State in Britain, France, and Germany* (Cambridge: Cambridge University Press 2005).

20 See Benjamin Stora, *La Gangrène et l'oubli: la mémoire de la guerre d'Algérie* (Paris: La Découverte 1991); Leo Lucassen, *The Immigrant Threat: The Integration of Old and New Migrants in Western Europe since 1850* (Urbana: University of Illinois Press 2005).

21 See Ian S. Lustick, *Unsettled States, Disputed Lands: Britain and Ireland, France and Algeria, Israel and the West Bank–Gaza* (Ithaca: Cornell University Press 1993); Lucassen, *The Immigrant Threat*.

22 Adrian Favell, *Philosophies of Integration: Immigration and the Idea of Citizenship in France and Britain* (Basingstoke: Macmillan 1998).

23 This is true in scholarship that both pre-dates and post-dates the events of 9/11. See Joseph H. Carens and Melissa S. Williams, 'Muslim minorities in liberal democracies: the politics of misrecognition', in Rainer Bauböck, Agnes Heller and Aristide Zolberg (eds), *The Challenge of Diversity: Integration and Pluralism in Societies of Immigration* (Aldersot: Avebury 1996), 157–86; and Jytte Klausen, *The Islamic Challenge: Politics and Religion in Western Europe* (Oxford: Oxford University Press 2005).

constant jihad against Europe and Christianity'.[24] Foner and Alba, and Zolberg and Long each contrast European and American attitudes towards religion, finding broad similarities across the European continent. Foner and Alba argue that in Western Europe 'religion is at the top of the scholarly agenda, with the extensive literature overwhelmingly concerned with the Islamic presence'.[25]

Zolberg and Long assert that the comparative approach to Muslims in Europe is justified by several sets of common experiences. All Western European countries share a Christian heritage and a broadly secular outlook that set practising Muslims at odds with the dominant modes of identity within their new countries.[26] Moreover, Europeans have all been exposed to domestic tensions surrounding 'areas of religious stress', such as the hijab, religiously slaughtered meat and the observance of rituals in the work-place.[27] International crises have also generated common experiences for European publics, which have witnessed, in addition to more recent events, the murder of Israeli athletes by the Palestinian group Black September at the 1972 Munich Olympics and the rise of Islamist radicalism heralded by the 1979 Iranian Revolution. For Zolberg and Long:

> These developments transformed the image of Islam in the West from a passive to an aggressive civilization, while lending support to established Orientalist beliefs, especially the idea that Islam is inherently incompatible with liberal democracy and that individual Muslims function as docile instruments of ruthless secular leaders and equally ruthless ayatollahs.[28]

Which of these views is correct? Are there dramatic differences in public attitudes across countries based on longstanding divergences in church–state relations, colonial histories and integration philosophies? Or do the common European experiences trump national distinctions to create broadly similar attitudes across these two countries? Our findings below do show a few notable differences in public attitudes on either side of the English Channel. Most significantly, according to many surveys, French respondents tend to have less favourable attitudes towards Muslims than their British counterparts. On the whole, however, the ranking of ethno-racial groups and the relative magnitude of estimated prejudice are much more similar in the

---

24 David Theo Goldberg, 'Racial Europeanization', *Ethnic and Racial Studies*, vol. 29, no. 2, 2006, 331–64 (344).
25 Nancy Foner and Richard Alba, 'Immigrant religion in the U.S. and Western Europe: bridge or barrier to inclusion?', *International Migration Review*, vol. 42, no. 2, 2008, 360–92 (360).
26 Zolberg and Long, 'Why Islam is like Spanish', 18–20. The authors do note some national variation, but overall they emphasize cross-national similarities over differences.
27 Ibid., 18.
28 Ibid., 17.

two countries than they are different. While it is vital not to overlook distinctions between the states, given the scholarly purpose at hand, this essay focuses primarily on the similarities in British and French public attitudes when analysing ethno-racial hierarchies in the two countries.

The status of Muslims: comparisons over time

Because Muslims were not deemed a problematic group within Europe until recent years, there are relatively few surveys about Muslims prior to 1990. It was not until the 'Rushdie affair' in Britain and the 'headscarf affair' in France—both of which erupted in 1989—that Muslims in each country were crystallized into an identity group worthy of extensive investigation and intense concern. Only in the wake of these 'affairs' did opinion polls systematically begin posing questions about Muslims and religious minorities.[29]

Happily, however, the European Union (then the European Community) conducted one survey that pre-dated this fundamental turning-point, and that therefore provides a useful benchmark of attitudes prior to the politicization of Muslim identity in 1989. In late 1988 its Eurobarometer survey asked respondents to identify whether they thought there were too many people of certain groups in their country, and whether they were personally disturbed by the presence of people of other identifiable groups. The results demonstrate that religious difference was not the main axis of concern in either country. Over 40 per cent of respondents in both countries identified people of another race and nationality as having too strong a presence in the country, more than twice as many as identified those of another religion (Figure 1). Moreover, a greater number of respondents in both countries were personally disturbed by people of another race, nationality and even class than by people of another religion (Figure 2). Although these data do not reveal precise attitudes towards Muslims, they

29 A note on methodology. Most surveys discussed in this essay had sample sizes of approximately 1,000 for each question in each country. For the British Citizenship Survey questions, the *n* was at least 5,000. The sample sizes for the 2005 national survey, *Equality, Diversity and Prejudice in Britain* (see note 43), were at least 2,500, except for the question about experiences of discrimination, for which the sample size for Asians was 184 and for Muslims 128. The Pew sample size for all questions was at least 500, except for the July 2005 survey question about which religion was most violent where for Britain *n* was 352 and for France *n* was 345. With regard to weighting, all Eurobarometer, Citizenship Survey and World Values Survey data are weighted to produce representative national samples, with British Eurobarometer data excluding Northern Ireland. The Citizenship Survey data analysed here contain both Core and Minority Ethnic Boost samples weighted using the combined sample individual weight variable included in the data sets.

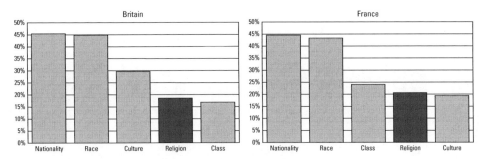

Figure 1 I feel there are too many people in this country of another…
Source: Eurobarometer 30, October–November 1988

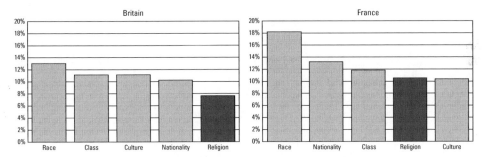

Figure 2 I personally find disturbing the presence of people of another…
Source: Eurobarometer 30, October–November 1988

strongly suggest that Muslims were not the overriding concern in either country in late 1988.[30]

Subsequent Eurobarometer surveys between 1992 and 2000 also periodically asked respondents if they were personally disturbed by the presence of people of another race, nationality or religion (Figure 3). On the whole, more respondents answered in the affirmative in each country in 2000 than in 1988 with respect to all groups, and notably more with respect to religious groups. But responses followed an S-shaped curve with a rise in the early 1990s, a dip in the mid-1990s and another rise in the late 1990s. The overall findings of rising discomfort with religious Others are somewhat off-set in both countries, however, by the opinions given in the World Values Surveys from 1990 and 1999 in which respondents were asked to state which types of people they would not like to have as neighbours.[31] In 1990, 17 per cent of British and 18 per cent of French

30 When asked which groups they thought of under the category 'other religion', a majority of French respondents and a plurality of British respondents replied 'Muslim'. In Britain, however, 'Catholics' were just behind Muslims, and 'Hindus' were not far behind 'Catholics'.
31 Surveys designed and executed by the European Values Study Group and World Values Survey Association.

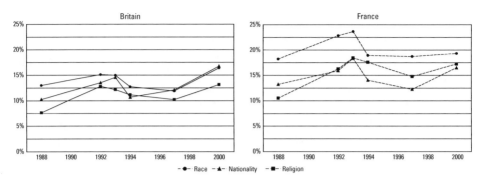

Figure 3 I personally find disturbing the presence of people of another...
Source: Eurobarometer 30, October–November 1988; Eurobarometer 37.0, March–April 1992; Eurobarometer 39.0, March–April 1993; Eurobarometer 42, November–December 1994; Eurobarometer 48.0, October–November 1997; Eurobarometer 53, April–May 2000

participants, respectively, listed 'Muslims', whereas, in the 1999 survey, the numbers had declined to 14 per cent and 16 per cent.[32]

While there are very few specific surveys about attitudes towards Muslims in the 1990s, the French government conducted polls as part of its annual report on domestic racism and xenophobia that included one especially relevant question.[33] From 1990 through 1998 it asked respondents if they thought there were too many people of a particular group in the country. The results (Figure 4) show that, by early 1990, in the wake of the 'headscarf affair' that emerged in late 1989, respondents had elevated Muslims well above Blacks—that is, religion was elevated above at least one type of race—as the group they thought was too numerous in the country. As animosity towards all groups declined through the 1990s, however, it is important to note that in every year marginally more respondents replied that there were too many Arabs than that there were too many Muslims. In other words, and as will be discussed in more depth in the following section, when forced to separate out their attitudes towards the ethnic category and the religious category, ethnicity trumped religion in each survey.[34]

32 It is possible that the 1989 'affairs' in each country and the first Gulf war elevated the 1990 responses. It is likely that this question will be asked again in the forthcoming World Values Survey, which will offer the opportunity to see trends over a longer period of time and in the context of the post-9/11 and 7/7 worlds.

33 These annual reports by the CNCDH, usually entitled *La Lutte contre le racisme, l'antisémitisme et la xénophobie*, are published each year on 21 March (the UN's International Day for the Elimination of Racial Discrimination) and recent ones are available online on the CNCDH website at www.cncdh.fr/rubrique.php3? id_rubrique = 27 (viewed 21 April 2009).

34 Not having access to the detailed data from each year, it is not possible to conduct systematic tests to determine if the difference is statistically significant.

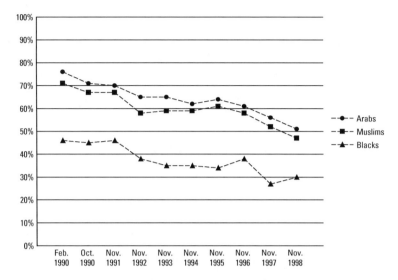

Figure 4 Would you say that in France there are too many...
Source: CNCDH, *1998. La Lutte contre le racisme et la xénophobie* (Paris: La Documentation Française 1999), 337

As with responses in the wake of the 'headscarf affair', the impact of events can also be seen in French responses to a question posed from 2002 to 2007 that asked whether French Muslims were French like everyone else. While fully 25 per cent of those surveyed in December 2002 thought they were not, the number declined to 20 per cent in December 2004 before spiking to 31 per cent in the heat of the November 2005 riots and then tapering off to approximately 26 per cent two years later. These levels of raw suspicion of Muslims' Frenchness are significant, and are 12 to 18 percentage points higher than the equivalent responses *vis-à-vis* Jews in the same surveys.[35]

The first British surveys with consistent questions about Muslims are the massive British Citizenship Surveys of 2003, 2005 and 2007.[36] These surveys asked respondents which group they felt was the target of more racial prejudice compared to five years earlier (Figure 5).[37] Although it may seem obvious that Muslims would be at the top of the list following the events of 9/11, this was not the case in 2003, when only 16 per cent of non-Muslim respondents named 'Muslims'. As the surveys progressed, however, the number of responses climbed significantly, to 37 per cent in 2005 and to

35 CNCDH, *La Lutte contre le racisme, l'antisémitisme et la xénophobie: année 2007* (Paris: La Documentation Française 2008), 311.
36 The bienniel Citizenship Survey was formerly under the auspices of the Home Office, and is now overseen by the Department of Communities and Local Government.
37 It first asked respondents whether they felt there was more racial prejudice than five years earlier; if they answered affirmatively, it then asked them to identify the groups that were the target of such prejudice. The data presented here represent the answers of non-Muslim respondents.

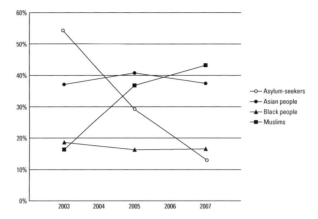

Figure 5   Groups against whom there is more racial prejudice today than five years ago
Source: Home Office Citizenship Survey 2003, SN 5087 (2005); Home Office Citizenship Survey 2005, SN 5367 (2006); Citizenship Survey 2007, SN 5739 (2008)

43 per cent in 2007, at which point Muslims were judged by non-Muslims to be the primary group against whom there was more racial prejudice than there was five years earlier, exceeding for the first time the more standard ethno-racial formulation of 'Asians'. This indicates both the perceived racialization of Muslims as a group within Britain as well as a sense that they were moving quickly down the ethno-racial hierarchy.

The finding that there was greater disadvantage associated with being a Muslim than in the past was echoed in the 2006 and 2008 Eurobarometer surveys, which asked which types of discrimination were greater now than five years earlier (Figure 6). In both Britain and France, religion and beliefs ranked very high. They were roughly on a par with ethnic origin in the two countries, and well ahead of the next most frequent answer, age. These data suggest that the stigma associated with religion and beliefs—which for many respondents in 2006 and 2008 was extremely likely to reflect feelings about Muslims—was growing and was being noted by large numbers of British and French citizens.

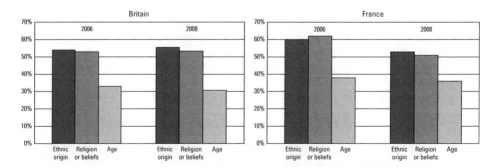

Figure 6   Discrimination is more common today than five years ago based on...
Source: Eurobarometer 65.4, June–July 2006; Eurobarometer 69.1, February–March 2008

Viewed in another light, however, what might be most striking about these data is the fact that respondents judged discrimination based on ethnic origin to be growing as rapidly as that based on religion and beliefs.[38] After all, both countries have decades of experience dealing with ethnic differences, and many of the ethnic differences within these countries do not correlate with citizenship or religious differences. It is thus important to investigate more closely attitudes towards Muslims in comparison with those towards other ethno-racial groups to understand not only trends over time, but also the relative standing of Muslims on the ethno-racial hierarchies of each country.

The status of Muslims: comparisons across religious groups

There is overwhelming evidence that Muslims are the most disliked group in both Britain and France when compared to other religions. When viewed from the long-term perspective of religious persecution and discrimination against Catholics and dissenters in Britain, and the longstanding traditions of separation of church and state in France, it is striking that Muslims have become the primary religious outsiders by a wide margin in both countries. Not all religions in Britain and France are constructed in ethno-racial terms today, but it is particularly revealing that attitudes towards Muslims are significantly more negative than those towards Jews, who were very low on national hierarchies throughout the twentieth century.

As noted above, the French surveys from 2002–7 demonstrated higher numbers of people stating that Muslims were not French like everyone else, compared to those that said the same about Jews.[39] The 2005 and 2007 British Citizenship Survey respondents who believed there was more religious prejudice than five years previously overwhelmingly believed that this prejudice was directed towards Muslims. Just over 90 per cent in 2005 and just under 90 per cent in 2007 identified Muslims as the target of such prejudice, with fewer than 12 per cent in each year selecting Christians, Sikhs, Hindus or Jews as the victims of increased prejudice.

Dislike and suspicion of Muslims have also been revealed by the Pew Global Attitudes surveys from 2004, 2005 and 2006. These surveys asked respondents to name the religious groups about which they had unfavourable opinions (Figure 7). Significantly higher numbers had unfavourable opinions

38 The difference in the response rate between the two categories was not statistically significant in either country in 2006 or in 2008.

39 Interestingly, however, when the question was only posed about Jews—i.e. with no comparison to Muslims—the negative responses were substantially higher for Jews. The 23 per cent in 2000 and 20 per cent in 2001 were in the same range as responses about Muslims in 2002–4, which declined from 25 to 20 per cent over those years. For all data, see CNCDH, *La Lutte contre le racisme, l'antisémitisme et la xénophobie: année 2007*, 311.

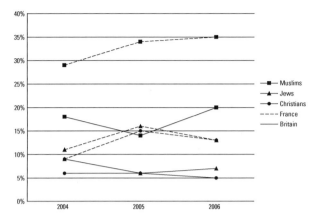

Figure 7   Respondents have an unfavourable opinion of…
Source: Pew Global Attitudes Project, 22 June 2006

of Muslims than of Jews or Christians in both countries, with an especially strong differential in France. In addition, just under half of all Pew respondents in 2005 thought that certain religions were prone to violence and, of those who did, clear majorities in each country pinpointed Islam as the most violent religion, with this number being particularly elevated in France (Figure 8). Moreover, in the Pew surveys from 2005 and 2006, between 63 and 70 per cent of respondents in Britain and France believed that Muslim identity was growing; and of those that thought it was growing, between 56 and 59 per cent of Britons and between 87 and 89 per cent of French respondents viewed this as a 'bad thing' (Figure 9).[40] What emerges is a picture of Islam and

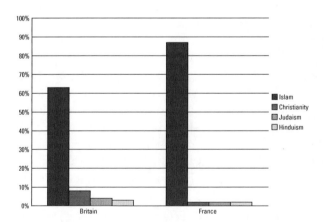

Figure 8   Which one religion is most violent?
Source: Pew Global Attitudes Project, 14 July 2005

40 In these same surveys, between 76 and 82 per cent of British and French respondents stated that Muslim identity in their country was 'strong', irrespective of whether they viewed it as growing.

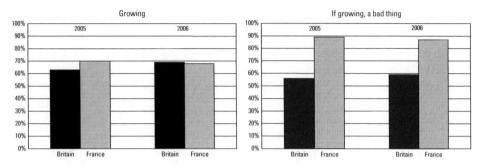

Figure 9 Muslim identity in our country is…
Source: Pew Global Attitudes Project, 6 July 2006

Muslims within each country (particularly in France) as objects of fear and aversion, when compared with other religions.

The status of Muslims: comparison across ethno-racial groups

While these surveys emphasize the presence of a good deal of anti-Muslim prejudice in Britain and France and the fact that Muslims have displaced *religious* outgroups of previous eras, they do not address Muslims' status on domestic *ethno-racial* hierarchies. It may appear self-evident that Muslims would have become the ultimate ethno-racial outsiders in Europe in the wake of 9/11, the Madrid train bombings, the assassination of Theo van Gogh, and the London transportation system bombings of 2005. But have they become more stigmatized than Blacks, Jews, immigrants, Roma and other ethnic minorities in Britain and France? Most of the polling evidence suggests that they have not, or at least not yet.

This argument may seem to contradict some evidence presented in Figures 5 and 6, which identified the perceived targets of increased prejudice and discrimination compared to five years earlier. In 2007 a thin plurality of British Citizenship Survey respondents identified Muslims as the group experiencing more prejudice at that time, and a thinner plurality of French respondents in the 2006 Eurobarometer survey thought that religion and belief were the most important elements generating increased discrimination.[41] However, the wording of these questions—comparing the present day to the recent past—did not require respondents to evaluate the relative position of these groups on the national ethno-racial hierarchy, but rather to assess which groups they felt were sinking most quickly on that hierarchy.

41 In the 2006 and 2008 Eurobarometer surveys, a thin plurality of British respondents tipped towards ethnic origin over religion and belief, as did a thin plurality of French respondents in 2008, suggesting—when combined with the British Citizenship Survey results—that ethnicity and religion were perceived as essentially equal vectors of increasing prejudice and discrimination.

These survey results support the claim that there is more anti-Muslim prejudice now than in the past in both countries, but they do not provide direct information about Muslims' current status compared to other groups.

The bulk of the direct evidence suggests that Muslims are perceived as lower on status hierarchies than other important ethno-racial groups, but that they are almost never the lowest-ranking group. For example, Britain's 2005 national survey, *Equality, Diversity and Prejudice*,[42] shows that 10 per cent of respondents had negative feelings about black people, whereas 19 per cent admitted to negative feelings about Muslims.[43] Yet 38 per cent of those responding to a similar question had negative feelings about asylum-seekers, placing them lower on the hierarchy than Muslims.[44] Moreover, majorities of Muslim and Asian respondents—two overlapping but not identical categories of people—said they had personally suffered discrimination based on ethnicity, whereas only minorities of those groups claimed to have suffered it based on religion.[45] Of course, many survey respondents have difficulty distinguishing clearly between categories such as asylum-seeker, Asian and Muslim,[46] but to the extent that both majorities and minorities do so, the evidence suggests that ethnicity is a more important vector of real-world discrimination than religion.

In a similar vein, greater numbers of respondents in the 1990 and 1999 World Values Surveys identified Muslims as opposed to someone of a 'different race' as the group they would not like to have as neighbours. Yet, between 1988 and 2000, every Eurobarometer survey showed more respondents disturbed by people of another race than by another religion (see Figure 3).[47] Moreover, even the 1999 World Values Survey showed that British respondents had a slightly greater aversion to immigrants than to Muslims, and that respondents in both countries had a much stronger aversion to 'Gypsies' as neighbours than to any other ethno-racial group (Figure 10).[48]

Another way to gauge the ranking of different groups on the status hierarchy is to ask people to assess their fellow citizens' views of justifiable

---

42 Dominic Abrams and Diane M. Houston, *Equality, Diversity and Prejudice in Britain: Results from the 2005 National Survey* (Canterbury: University of Kent Centre for the Study of Group Processes 2006).

43 There was no direct comparison to the ethnic group 'Asians' in this question.

44 Abrams and Houston, *Equality, Diversity and Prejudice in Britain*, 34.

45 Ibid., 42–3.

46 See CNCDH, *2003. La Lutte contre le racisme et la xénophobie*, 179–230; and Lewis, *Asylum*, 36–45.

47 These differences were statistically significant at the .05 level in four of the six years in each country, and at the .10 level in five of the six years in each country.

48 The 2008 Eurobarometer survey reinforced these findings, with 22 per cent and 15 per cent of British and French respondents, respectively, saying they would be uncomfortable having a 'Gypsy' as a neighbour, 4 per cent and 3 per cent uncomfortable with a neighbour of a different ethnic origin, and only 1 per cent and 2 per cent claiming discomfort with someone of a different religion.

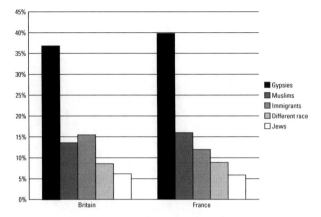

Figure 10 Which groups would you not like to have as a neighbour?
Source: European and World Values Surveys Integrated Data File (1999 survey)

types of discrimination. These questions reveal the extent to which people believe certain groups are seen as legitimate targets of discrimination. The 2002 Eurobarometer data showed that ethnic origin was perceived in both countries to be a more legitimate basis for discrimination than religion, suggesting that ethnicity remained a more salient marker of ethno-racial outsider status (Figure 11).[49]

In addition, the 2006 and 2008 Eurobarometer surveys included a direct question about the grounds on which discrimination was considered widespread in the country. Discrimination on the basis of religion or belief was seen to be widespread in both Britain and France, but appreciably more respondents saw discrimination on the basis of ethnic origin as widespread in both countries (Figure 12).

Moreover, according to the 2006 Eurobarometer survey, belonging to a minority religious group was considered significantly less of a disadvantage than belonging to several other categories, most notably, for the purposes of this essay, those of ethnic minority origin or Roma (Figure 13). Reinforcing this point, when asked annually between 2002 and 2007 which groups were the principal victims of racism or discrimination in France, more respondents spontaneously named 'Arabs', 'Maghrebis', 'foreigners' and 'Blacks' than 'Muslims' in every survey, typically by at least a two to one margin.[50]

49 These differences are statistically significant at the .01 level in both countries. One potential qualification is illuminated in European Social Survey data from 2002–3, in which ethnic/racial/religious majority respondents in both Britain and France thought it marginally more important that a hypothetical immigrant to their country came from a Christian background than be white: see Christopher Bail, 'The configuration of symbolic boundaries against immigrants in Europe', *American Sociological Review*, vol. 73, no. 1, 2008, 37–59, although Bail also raises the question of whether the tempered responses on race understated respondents' true aversion to racial difference (because of a social desirability effect common in survey research).
50 CNCDH, *La Lutte contre le racisme, l'antisémitisme et la xénophobie: année 2007*, 296–99.

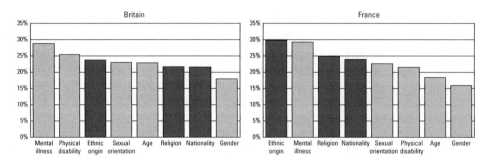

Figure 11   Generally, people believe discrimination is always, usually or sometimes right based on...
Source: Eurobarometer 57.0, February–April 2002

Finally, it is not the case that the increasing stigma associated in the public's mind with being a Muslim has had a dramatic effect on attitudes about immigration from predominantly Muslim countries. Pew research data from 2002, 2005 and 2006 demonstrate that respondents in both Britain and France had identical and generally positive attitudes towards immigrants from the Middle East or North Africa as compared to attitudes towards migrants from Eastern Europe, who were presumably white and Christian (Figure 14). This suggests that there is a limit to the intensity of

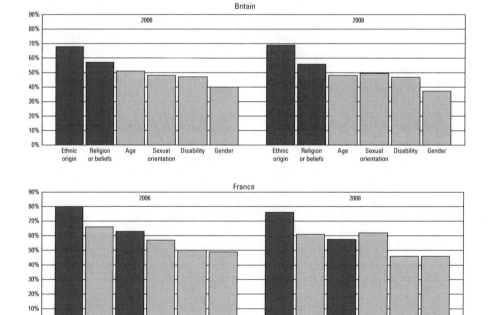

Figure 12   Discrimination in your country is considered widespread on the basis of...
Source: Eurobarometer 65.4, June–July 2006; Eurobarometer 69.1, February–March 2008

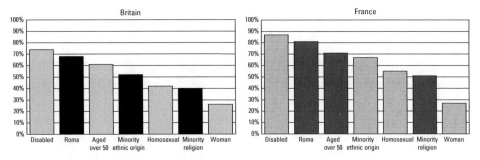

Figure 13 Belonging to the following group is generally a disadvantage.
Source: Eurobarometer 65.4, June–July 2006

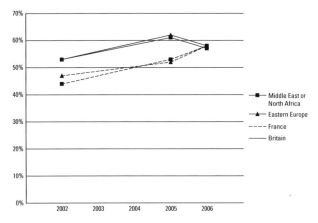

Figure 14 It is a good thing that people come to work and live in this country from...
Source: Pew Global Attitudes Project, 6 July 2006

Muslim ethno-racial identities and outsiderness as constructed by majority populations in both countries, at least in certain respects.

Muslims and ethno-racial hierarchies: implications of the findings

If, as Karl Deutsch has observed, truth lies at the confluence of independent streams of evidence, the surveys reviewed here provide sufficient evidence to support three central propositions with respect to public attitudes towards Muslims in Britain and France: anti-Muslim sentiment is higher today than in the late 1980s; Muslims are clear and distant outsiders compared to other religious groups; and Muslims are not the lowest group on national ethno-racial hierarchies. Islamophobia is thus a concrete, measurable phenomenon, but it is also one that evidence suggests is not more severe than other longstanding forms of stigmatization based on ethnic or racial prejudices.

As convincing as the bulk of survey data may be, it is important to emphasize that this essay offers a preliminary analysis that has to be supplemented by further research. For example, it relies on straightforward frequencies of responses, without analysing subgroups to identify better the categories of people (old versus young, educated versus uneducated, women versus men etc.) most likely to hold anti-Muslim sentiments. More work needs to be done to disaggregate the effects of anti-Muslim prejudice from anti-Arab or anti-Asian prejudice, since these categories overlap quite a bit in practice. And a close examination of survey responses by Muslims is necessary to understand how prejudice is experienced by the victims themselves.[51] Moreover, while the study of public opinion polls is extremely revealing, a full understanding of ethno-racial hierarchies requires research into other arenas, such as political and media representations of different groups, incidence of hate crimes and acts of discrimination, social interactions between groups, the extent and valence of state policies towards different ethno-racial groups, and ethnographic work on minorities' perspectives on societal prejudice. Together, these constitute multiple streams of evidence that can be aggregated to form a richer portrait of national ethno-racial hierarchies. It is also worth examining whether the forces that drive considerable similarities in the status of Muslims in Britain and France apply in other Western European states, just as it is important to note and to explore important dimensions of cross-national divergence. Outlining the limitations of the current study—whether in the methodology and types of polls analysed, in the comparison of polling versus other data, or in its spatial scope and approach—reveals that more can be done to evaluate Muslims' place on ethno-racial hierarchies. It also suggests a specific and robust research agenda for future efforts.

There are further implications of the data presented here that merit closer attention. To some, it may appear logical and unavoidable that attitudes towards Muslims have become more negative over the past two decades given the rising salience of Muslim identity in this time period. Yet, examining the long-term patterns (to the extent that this is possible given the limited time-series data available) demonstrates that this trend has not been linear. Figures 3 and 4 reveal a dip in anti-religious minority and anti-Muslim sentiment in the mid-1990s. What can account for this dip? One obvious hypothesis is that anti-Muslim sentiment surges following high-profile events, such as the 1989 Rushdie and headscarf affairs in Britain and

51 Some of this next level of analysis can be derived from existing surveys, especially the large British ones. In France, authors Sylvain Brouard and Vincent Tiberj have carried out and analysed a number of surveys that allow a deeper comparison of Muslim and non-Muslim public opinion. See, for example, Sylvain Brouard and Vincent Tiberj, 'The challenge to integration in France', in Ariane Chebel d'Appollonia and Simon Reich (eds), *Immigration, Integration, and Security: America and Europe in Comparative Perspective* (Pittsburgh: University of Pittsburgh Press 2008), 283–99.

France (Figure 3), the 9/11 bombings,[52] the 7/7 London Transport attacks (Figures 5 and 7), and the 2005 riots in France.[53] It follows then that these high levels taper off after the initially hostile reactions subside. In certain cases, strong anti-Muslim opinion appears to recede in the year or so following an event (Figure 4).[54] If this pattern holds up under further scrutiny, it implies that the passage of time and a lack of incidents may be the most significant factors explaining diminishing anti-Muslim sentiment. However, Figure 3 also indicates an increase in negative attitudes between 1997 and 2000 in both countries that is not easily explained by a domestic or international event. Because the interactions between events and anti-Muslim prejudice are not entirely clear, it is critical to study the relationship more closely, perhaps focusing in particular on the mid- to late 1990s as an era when anti-Muslim sentiment fluctuated without obvious explanation. Doing so may also provide insights into whether government integration policies and civil society actions—as opposed to time and a lack of violence—significantly affect group status on national hierarchies.

Finally, it is worth reflecting on the relative importance of a group's absolute status versus the pace of its movement up or down the ethno-racial hierarchy over time. Contrary to what may seem obvious or at least plausible, Muslims are *not* the most distant ethno-racial outsiders in Britain and France. Being a Muslim appears to be less of a disadvantage than being Asian, Arab or Roma, even if some surveys suggest that it may be a greater disadvantage than being black. This implies that, if societies wish to concentrate attention and resources on fighting stigmatization, discrimination and prejudice against the worst-off groups, they should not necessarily prioritize Muslims over those who may be even more vulnerable; at a minimum, it implies that they need to be aware of the multiple and overlapping reasons for Muslims' ethno-racial outsiderness, among which outward appearance, country of origin and migration status may be just as important as religion.

On the other hand, there is a compelling argument for worrying most about a group if it is sinking fast on a national hierarchy. Some measures imply that Muslims are slipping quickly both in Britain and in France. This is particularly visible in data comparing prejudice today against attitudes from five years ago. If this trend is confirmed by additional research, it may provide the best justification for deploying the concept of 'Islamophobia' to

---

52 This finding is partially confirmed by Fetzer and Soper's pre- and post-9/11 surveys of public attitudes towards Muslim practices in Britain, France and Germany: see Fetzer and Soper, *Muslims and the State in Britain, France, and Germany*, 143–4. Unfortunately, the major surveys under review do not have systematic cross-time data covering the pre- and post-9/11 eras.

53 CNCDH, *La Lutte contre le racisme, l'antisémitisme et la xénophobie: année 2007*, 311.

54 Ibid.

mobilize states and civil society actors to combat anti-Muslim prejudice in Britain, France and beyond.

Confronting Islamophobia in the United States: framing civil rights activism among Middle Eastern Americans

ERIK LOVE

ABSTRACT   In recent years, significant research on Islamophobia has created an important literature about anti-Islamic and anti-Muslim discourses in the United States. However, the term 'Islamophobia' has come to refer to racialized bigotry, discrimination, policies and practices directed towards a range of groups, Muslim and otherwise. Love establishes racial formation as a conceptual framework for understanding Islamophobia in the United States, beginning with an examination of the linked and racialized history of American communities with ancestry in North Africa and southwestern Asia, that is, Middle Eastern Americans. He then explores the roots of Islamophobic discourses in the United States in terms of popular culture stereotypes, discriminatory state actions and bigotry, including hate crimes. This leads to a discussion of anti-Islamophobia civil rights activism situated within the historical context of organizational responses to racialized discrimination in the United States. The analysis shows that it remains unclear whether diverse and historically divergent Middle Eastern American communities will remain divided along national-origin, religious, cultural and class lines. Taking historical models of advocacy into account, Love suggests three likely avenues for advocacy organizations that confront Islamophobia in the United States.

> *I urge everyone to join in and not leave the field of values, definitions, and cultures uncontested. They are certainly not the property of a few Washington officials, any more than they are the responsibility of a few Middle Eastern rulers. There is a common field of human undertaking being created and recreated, and no amount of imperial bluster can ever conceal or negate that fact.*
>
> —Edward Said[1]

I am grateful to the Richard Flacks Democracy Fund and the National Science Foundation for supporting this research. I wish to thank Lisa Hajjar, Kathleen Moore and Howard Winant for advice on earlier drafts and related analyses. The author accepts sole responsibility for the final version.

1 Edward Said, 'The imperial bluster of Tom Delay', *Counterpunch*, 20 August 2003, available at www.counterpunch.org/said08202003.html (viewed 12 May 2009).

'Islamophobia' is a problematic neologism, and the one that is currently the most common term used to refer to bigotry, discrimination, policies and practices directed towards Islam and a racialized group of people that includes Muslims. In the context of the United States, the chief problem with this terminology is that Muslims constitute only one of the range of groups directly affected by Islamophobia. One of the most troubling incidents to be called 'Islamophobia' occurred in Arizona on 16 September 2001, when Balbir Singh Sodhi was shot and killed by a man who shouted 'I stand for America all the way' as he was arrested.[2] Sodhi wore a turban in accordance with his Sikh faith, and he was killed in a deliberate hate crime explained only by his supposedly 'Muslim-like' appearance. Unfortunately, this incident has not been unique. The complex, racialized phenomenon now known as 'Islamophobia' has affected the lives of many people across the United States with a 'Muslim-like' appearance.

This article offers an analytic approach that places Islamophobia in the context of race in the United States. Efforts to distort the teachings of Islam, to discredit and defame Islamic organizations and to marginalize and impugn the religion itself are widespread in contemporary American society. The approach proposed here posits that Islamophobia both results from and contributes to the racial ideology of the United States, an ideology based on socially constructed categories of phenotypical characteristics, on how individuals physically appear. In other words, wearing a hijab or a turban, having certain skin tones or speaking with certain accents are all physical markers that are enough to create a vulnerability to Islamophobia in the United States. As a result of this racialized process, Islamophobia affects Christians, Muslims and Sikhs from all backgrounds and, in particular, people who have ancestry in North Africa as well as in western and southern Asia. Islamophobia, in short, affects a racialized group of people— Middle Eastern Americans[3]—that, like any racialized group, is in fact comprised of an irreducibly diverse collection of individuals who identify with many different ethnicities, nationalities and religions.

Unfortunately, contemporary scholarship about Islamophobia often fails to examine critically the racialized nature of this particular bigotry. In many recent studies, the groups affected by Islamophobia are described simply as 'Muslims' or 'Muslims and Arabs'. In actuality, most Muslim Americans are

---

2 Michael Ellison, 'Sikh shot dead in US "retaliation" attack', *Guardian*, 17 September 2001, 10.
3 Despite the term's offensive colonialist origins, for want of a better alternative, for brevity's sake and in part because it reflects the contemporary mainstream American definition, the term 'Middle East' will be used in this article to refer to Northern Africa and Southwestern Asia, and 'Middle Eastern Americans' can be defined as members of the diverse groups of immigrants and their descendants who identify with or trace their heritage to those regions.

not Arab, just as most Arab Americans do not identify as Muslim.[4] Furthermore, neither Arab Americans nor Muslim Americans are monolithic groups. Still, in contemporary mainstream American discourses, these two identity categories have been largely conflated. Scholarship that frames Islamophobia as an issue affecting only Muslims reinforces this racialized confusion while neglecting the obvious fact that because physical character-istics are often crude shortcuts used to characterize groups of people—because of *race*—a wide range of groups are impacted by Islamophobia.

Gaining a clearer understanding of American Islamophobia requires looking at cultural discourses that shape racial ideology in the United States, but that is just the first part of the story. It is crucial also to examine the efforts to confront Islamophobia made by individuals and groups affected by it. After showing how migrants from the Middle East have never had a clearly defined place in the American racial order, this article argues that they have been as affected by racial ideologies as all other groups of immigrants to the United States. It then describes how what is now called 'Islamophobia' has historically been directed against a range of collectively racialized ethnic groups in the United States. Finally, it evaluates how Middle Eastern Americans might work to confront Islamophobia through advocacy organiza-tions and the building of political coalitions across the lines of ethnicity, religion and other markers of difference. This article thus contributes to a wider project of collecting and re-examining the linked histories of the range of ethnic and religious communities affected by American Islamophobia.

Islamophobia and American racial ideology

Approaching Islamophobia as a product of racial dynamics in the United States brings certain analytical advantages. First, this approach draws on a wealth of knowledge about race and ethnicity to explain how Islamophobia does not always target Islam and Muslims *per se*, but instead takes on the familiar pattern of racial scapegoating: fear and hatred, prejudice and discrimination directed towards groups crudely demarcated primarily by

---

4 Although surveys provide conflicting numbers, it appears that South Asians constitute the largest subgroup among Muslim Americans. Most studies indicate that the majority of Arab Americans are non-Muslims, but this may have changed over the past decade. See Yasmeen Shaheen-McConnell, 'Arab Americans: demographics', 2003, available on the Arab American Institute website at www.aaiusa.org/arab-americans/22/demographics (viewed 12 May 2009); Pew Research Center, *Muslim Americans: Middle Class and Mostly Mainstream* (Washington, D.C.: Pew Research Center 2007), 15, available on the Pew website at www.pewresearch.org/pubs/483/muslim-americans (viewed 12 May 2009); and Philippa Strum, 'Executive summary', in Philippa Strum and Danielle Tarantolo (eds), *Muslims in the United States: Demography, Beliefs, Institutions* (Washington, D.C.: Woodrow Wilson International Center for Scholars 2003), 1–4.

physical appearance.[5] Race clearly plays a role when Sikh American and African American Muslim children are harassed in similar ways in class-rooms, when Syrian Americans along with Pakistani Americans have to present themselves to immigration authorities for 'special registration', when Lebanese American and Iranian American workers lose their jobs for the same discriminatory reasons, and when Chaldean churches and Sunni mosques alike are vandalized and receive the same kinds of hate mail. These kinds of incidents, which impact on a large range of communities in spite of their diversity, occur primarily as a result of the racial lens through which Americans understand the world.

The ideology of race is understood as a flexible social construct, subject to modification through the work of actors who target the state as they seek recognition and redress.[6] The process of racialization profoundly affects all individuals in the United States, because each person is perceived to belong to socially constructed racial categories. The categories themselves change over time, as do the criteria for membership in any particular category; people recognized as belonging to the Irish race, for example, later became 'white' due to changes in the predominant racial ideology. These identity categories take on meaning and have material consequences via state policy and resource provision, through representa-tions in cultural space and through the organization of institutions in civil society. The prevailing 'racial order' at any point in history indicates the schema or hierarchy of recognized racial identity categories, created through a 'compromise between racial movements and the state'.[7] From the latter part of the twentieth century to the present day (the so-called 'post-civil rights era'), the 'racial pentagon' of black, white, Latino, Asian and Native American has been described as the prevailing list of recognized racial identity categories in the United States.[8] Where do individuals and groups affected by racialized Islamophobia 'fit'?

According to the United States Census, people from the broadly defined Middle Eastern region legally count as racially white. This creates a paradox, as described by John Tehranian:

---

5 Racial scapegoating in the United States, as a method of producing white American solidarity and nationalism, dates back to the founding days of the nation. See Anthony Marx, *Making Race and Nation: A Comparison of the United States, South Africa, and Brazil* (Cambridge: Cambridge University Press 1998).
6 Michael Omi and Howard Winant, *Racial Formation in the United States: From the 1960s to the 1990s*, 2nd edn (New York: Routledge 1994).
7 Ibid., 78–89.
8 David Hollinger, *Postethnic America: Beyond Multiculturalism* (New York: Basic Books 1995); Yen Le Espiritu and Michael Omi, '"Who are you calling Asian?" Shifting identity claims, racial classifications, and the Census', in Paul M. Ong (ed.), *Transforming Race Relations: A Public Policy Report* (Los Angeles: LEAP Asian Pacific American Public Policy Institute and UCLA Asian American Studies Center 2000).

On one hand, [Middle Eastern Americans] suffer from the types of discrimination that face minority groups. On the other hand, formally speaking, Middle Easterners are deemed white by law. This dualistic and contested ontology of the Middle Eastern racial condition creates an unusual paradox. Reified as the other, Americans of Middle Eastern descent do not enjoy the benefits of white privilege. Yet, as white under the law, they are denied the fruits of remedial action.[9]

The unclear position caused by this racial paradox—in terms of citizenship, rights and identity—of migrants and their descendants who came to the United States from North Africa and western and southern Asia, a large region now vaguely defined as the Middle East, dates back to the eighteenth century if not earlier. The groups under the Middle Eastern racial umbrella often have little in common with one another except that, in the United States, Islamophobia lumps them together and makes them targets of discrimination and racism. In other words, 'Islamophobia' is the latest term for a centuries-long history of American state policy, cultural discourses and discriminatory practices that enforce racial boundaries around Middle Easterners in America.

Islamophobia and migration to the United States

From the founding of the United States to the present, US immigration policy has had a history of collectivizing people from North Africa, and western and southern Asia. The racialized linkages, in both state actions and in cultural discourses, between these diverse ethnic, national-origin and religious communities have continued into the present despite the era of multiculturalism being swept into place by the civil rights movements of the 1950s and 1960s, reforms that were meant to usher in a 'post-racial' America.[10] To describe the linkages between these groups first requires outlining their migration histories. The earliest recorded appearance of Middle Easterners in the Americas dates to the slave trade,[11] but there is consensus among historians that the most significant migration of these groups to the United States began near the end of the nineteenth

---

9   John Tehranian, 'Selective racialization: Middle-Eastern American identity and the Faustian pact with whiteness', *Connecticut Law Review*, vol. 40, no. 4, 2008, 1–33 (2).

10 I raise this issue here only tangentially to counter briefly the frequent claim that an era of 'colour-blindness' has begun in which race no longer matters. For a more thorough discussion, see Junaid Rana, 'The story of Islamophobia', *Souls*, vol. 9, no. 2, 2007, 148–61.

11 Sylviane Diouf, *Servants of Allah: African Muslims Enslaved in the Americas* (New York: New York University Press 1998); Aminah Beverly McCloud, 'Islam in America: the mosaic', in Yvonne Yazbeck Haddad, Jane I. Smith and John L. Esposito (eds), *Religion and Immigration: Christian, Jewish, and Muslim Experiences in the United States* (Walnut Creek, CA: AltaMira Press 2003), 159–74 (160).

century.[12] This first 'wave' of Middle Eastern immigration took place despite explicitly racist immigration controls in the United States. Prior to reforms enacted in the 1950s and 1960s, only 'free white' persons (and, to a certain extent, former slaves and some Native Americans) were able to become naturalized citizens of the United States.

In her thorough survey *Al-Mughtaribun*, Kathleen Moore describes the struggles of Middle Eastern immigrants to define their identities and gain basic civil rights.[13] In addition to the 1790 Naturalization Act (which specified that only white people could become citizens), further require-ments for entry and naturalization affecting Middle Easterners included the creation of 'barred zones' in the Immigration Act of 1917. This law specifically prohibited 'immigrants from India, Siam, Arabia, Indo-China, the Malay Peninsula, Afghanistan, New Guinea, Borneo, Java, Ceylon, Sumatra, Celebes, and parts of Russian Turkestan and Siberia'.[14] This provides a clear example of the state lumping these groups together on account of perceived non-white racial origins, and then using that classification to withhold benefits. This led to confusion over racial classification as many immigrants fought to obtain 'officially white' status in the courts. Case histories show mixed results as some judges denied citizenship to persons of Middle Eastern origin while others *were* simulta-neously granted white status and citizenship.[15] Outside the courtroom, individuals from these communities faced rampant racism, discrimination, including voter intimidation and, in some extreme cases, lynching.[16]

Immigration to the United States increased rapidly after policy underwent significant changes in the mid-twentieth century. By 1965 most explicitly racist limits on immigration were removed. Thereafter, a new immigration framework meant that highly educated migrants were most likely to receive visas. The result was a 'brain drain' from around the world towards the United States, whereby professionals from developing nations were often allowed easier entry than working-class migrants. This was particularly

---

12 Karen Leonard, *The South Asian Americans* (Westport, CT: Greenwood Press 1997), 39–84; Amir Marvasti and Karyn McKinney, *Middle Eastern Lives in America* (Lanham, MD and Oxford: Rowman and Littlefield 2004), 3–40; Mohammad T. Mehdi, 'Arabs and Muslims in American society', in Wilbur C. Rich (ed.), *The Politics of Minority Coalitions: Race, Ethnicity, and Shared Uncertainties* (Westport, CT: Praeger 1996), 249–56 (249).

13 Kathleen Moore, *Al-Mughtaribun: American Law and the Transformation of Muslim Life in the United States* (Albany: State University of New York Press 1995), 47–67.

14 Ibid., 29.

15 There is extensive scholarship on the 'racial pre-requisite cases' involving Middle Eastern immigrants. See Sarah Gualtieri, 'Strange fruit? Syrian immigrants, extralegal violence and racial formation in the Jim Crow South', *Arab Studies Quarterly*, vol. 26, no. 3, 2004, 63–85; John Tehranian, 'Compulsory whiteness: towards a Middle-Eastern legal scholarship', *Indiana Law Journal*, vol. 82, no. 1, 2007, 11–17.

16 Gualtieri, 'Strange fruit?', 1; Moore, *Al-Mughtaribun*, 47.

the case with migrants from the Middle East.[17] This generation of Middle Eastern immigrants entered a post-civil rights movement America where assimilation was no longer the only acceptable option (as it had been for earlier immigrants). Multiculturalism meant that these immigrants worked to maintain their cultural heritage by forming many more associations and organizations than did previous immigrants. The post-1965 generation built more churches, gurdwaras, mosques and other places of worship, and generally (but not always) found that the United States in the latter half of the twentieth century was accepting of their efforts to maintain the cultural traditions they brought from their homelands. These post-1965 Middle Eastern immigrants, and their descendants, have borne the brunt of American Islamophobia in recent decades.[18]

Before examining details of Islamophobic discourse in the United States, a sketch of current Middle Eastern American demographics will be useful. However, even without taking into consideration important issues of gender, sexuality and hybrid identities, there is great diversity across Middle Eastern American communities, and space constraints do not permit a full discussion of the contemporary demographics of these groups.

Groups in the United States who trace their heritage to southern Asia—a region usually defined to include Afghanistan, Bangladesh, Bhutan, India, Pakistan, Nepal and Sri Lanka—are quite diverse and difficult to describe in general terms. Aside from the many national-origin groups elided under the pan-ethnic label 'South Asian', there are several ethnic groups from this region that are well represented in the United States, including Bengali, Pashtun and Punjabi Americans. In terms of religion, immigrants from this region belong to many denominations of Islam and Christianity, and there are Sikh, Hindu, Parsi and other religious identifications as well.[19] Socio-economically, South Asian Americans have one of the highest levels of education and income of any demographic group, but the most recent (since 1990) immigrants from this region are more often working-class and relatively less well off financially.[20]

The category 'Arab' similarly defies easy definition. There is considerable disagreement among people who trace their heritage to the Arab world about whether everyone from an Arab country should identify as Arab, or whether Arab ethnicity is purely voluntary. In terms of demographics, Arab Americans today include families who moved to the United States as many as five or six generations ago, and there are also a significant number of

17 Marvasti and McKinney, *Middle Eastern Lives in America*, 19–21.
18 Islamophobia also affects non-immigrant Muslim Americans; the work of these groups to confront Islamophobia will be discussed below.
19 Prema Kurien, 'Religion, ethnicity and politics: Hindu and Muslim Indian immigrants in the United States', *Ethnic and Racial Studies*, vol. 24, no. 2, 2001, 263–93; Karen Leonard, 'South Asian religions in the United States: new contexts and configurations', in Gita Rajan and Shailja Sharma (eds), *New Cosmopolitanisms: South Asians in the US* (Stanford, CA: Stanford University Press 2006), 91–114.
20 Leonard, *The South Asian Americans*, 77, 82.

recent (post-1970) immigrants from the more than twenty nations in the Arab world.[21] In terms of religion, Arab Americans belong to many different religious communities, including several denominations of Christianity and Islam, along with Judaism and other faiths. The largest nationality groups among Arab Americans include Lebanese, Syrians, Palestinians, Egyptians, Iraqis and people from Gulf states like Yemen and the United Arab Emirates. Socio-economically, Arab Americans have similar characteristics to South Asian Americans. Arab Americans who immigrated earlier in the twentieth century tend to have higher educational attainment and income levels than the average American family, while the most recent immigrants tend to have a range of socio-economic class backgrounds.[22]

Further complicating the demographic picture are the many Americans who trace their heritage to parts of the Middle East (including parts of the Arab world) and do not identify as Arab American. These include Iranians, Turks, Assyrians, Chaldeans, Druze, Kurds, Copts and people who identify with many other ethnicities, religions and nationalities. The demographics of these communities in the United States are often the inverse of that found in their nations of origin, as minority populations in the Middle East, particularly in terms of religious identification, tend to emigrate in higher numbers.[23] Detailed demographic information on these communities is particularly difficult to find, since most surveys overlook them or simply count them as 'Arabs'.[24] In terms of religion, these Middle Easterners belong to several denominations of Islam as well as Christianity, Judaism, Zoroastrianism and other religions as well.

Neither can Muslim Americans be easily categorized: there are Muslim Americans in every demographic group, and they follow several different Islamic traditions (or denominations) while holding a wide range of personal religious beliefs within those traditions. Rendering a coherent description of Muslim American communities is particularly difficult because surveys about religious identity are notoriously inaccurate and contradictory. Still, there is considerable recent literature describing Muslim American demography in terms of ethnicity and nationality, socio-economic class, geographic concentration and political tendencies.[25] There have been substantial

21 Shaheen-McConnell, 'Arab Americans: demographics'; Michael Suleiman, 'Introduction: the Arab immigrant experience', in Michael Suleiman (ed.), *Arabs in America: Building a New Future* (Philadelphia: Temple University Press 1999), 1–24.
22 Randa A. Kayyali, *The Arab Americans* (Westport, CT: Greenwood Press 2006), 33–4.
23 Sally Howell and Andrew Shryock, 'Cracking down on diaspora: Arab Detroit and America's "war on terror"', *Anthropological Quarterly*, vol. 76, no. 3, 2003, 443–62 (446).
24 Marvasti and McKinney, *Middle Eastern Lives in America*, 3–8.
25 See Yvonne Yazbeck Haddad, *Not Quite American? The Shaping of Arab and Muslim Identity in the United States* (Waco, TX: Baylor University Press 2004); Kathleen M. Moore, 'Muslims in the United States: pluralism under exceptional circumstances', *Annals of the American Academy of Political and Social Science*, vol. 612, no. 1, 2007, 116–32; and Karen Leonard, *Muslims in the United States: The State of Research* (New York: Russell Sage Foundation 2003).

changes in Muslim American demographics in a short period of time. One widely cited recent survey from the Pew Research Center reports that some two-thirds of immigrant Muslim Americans are first-generation immigrants, with more than a third of those arriving after 1990. In terms of numbers, the survey reports that the largest ethnic group of Muslim Americans are from South Asia and Iran, followed by families from the Arab world. The survey also reports that many Muslims migrated from Europe, and there are also many Muslim converts representing all heritages and backgrounds.[26] Prior to the most recent migration of Muslims to the United States after 1990, the largest subgroup under the Muslim American umbrella were those Muslims who also identified as African Americans, a group sometimes referred to as 'indigenous Muslims'.[27] There are significant differences between immigrant and indigenous Muslim Americans, in terms of theology, socio-economic status and political involvement.

In short, there is vast diversity among Middle Eastern Americans. But in spite of the diversity across all these groups, the ideology of race means that any of these groups is a potential target of American Islamophobia.

Islamophobia in American discourse

Islamophobic discourses that specifically disparage the Islamic faith have appeared especially frequently in the past decade, and these anti-Islam discourses have been carefully examined elsewhere.[28] Here, the focus is on longstanding racialized discrimination against Middle Eastern Americans, regardless of ethnicity and religious beliefs. This section will examine Islamophobia expressed in mainstream cultural discourses, in discriminatory state policies and in hate crimes.

Edward Said's treatise *Orientalism* brought into focus western cultural, academic and imperial projects that have created a dehumanizing representation of an exotic and barbarous Orient existing in opposition to the enlightened Occident.[29] Said (and others) note that, since at least the period of European colonialism in the seventeenth century, the Orient has been seen as Other, mostly through projecting depraved characteristics on to people from the region, invalidating non-Christian religions (especially Judaism and Islam) and asserting that the Orient is irrational, backwards and in need

26 Pew Research Center, *Muslim Americans*, 1.
27 Sherman A. Jackson, *Islam and the Blackamerican: Looking Toward the Third Resurrection* (Oxford and New York: Oxford University Press 2005), 23.
28 See Fachrizal Halim, 'Pluralism of American Muslims and the challenge of assimilation', *Journal of Muslim Minority Affairs*, vol. 26, no. 2, 2006, 235–44; Moore, 'Muslims in the United States'; Rana, 'The story of Islamophobia'.
29 Edward W. Said, *Orientalism* (New York: Vintage Books 1979).

of salvation.[30] In the 1700s the Orientalist tradition crossed the ocean from Europe to the United States. As Douglas Little argued in his analysis of American policy towards the Middle East: 'A quick look at eighteenth- and nineteenth-century popular culture shows that Muslims, Jews, and most other peoples of the Middle East were "orientalised" and depicted as backward, decadent, and untrustworthy.'[31] And these representations have been part of American culture and politics ever since. While elements of the 'exotic' and 'backward' Orient remain in mainstream representations of the Middle East and South Asia today, in the course of the previous century, representations shifted away from 'exotic' and towards 'dangerous'.

In the United States of the twentieth century, the frame of the dangerous Middle East (a contemporary term for the Orient) appeared frequently in popular culture, as Melani McAlister notes in her comprehensive study.[32] Tracing cultural representations from 1945, McAlister identifies the 1967 war between the state of Israel and several Arab nations as a crucial turning-point.[33] This war, in which Arab nations lost spectacularly to the West's ally Israel, had the effect of codifying the image of a fanatical and dangerous Middle East in the American mind. This led to three decades, between the war in 1967 and the turn of the century, of rapid devolution in the already racialized American discourses concerning Middle Easterners.

Beginning with the oil crisis of the 1970s, the racialized image of a villainous Middle Eastern 'oil sheik' supplemented the 'dangerous' stereotype of mainstream representations. The 'oil sheik' served as a scapegoat for Americans upset by economic recession and high petrol prices. Repetitively similar (and highly racialized) images depicting swarthy and duplicitous 'oil sheiks' appeared in countless editorial cartoons and films in the 1970s and early 1980s.[34] The 'oil sheik' representation was so ubiquitous that the Federal Bureau of Investigation set up a sting operation to catch corrupt members of Congress by assigning covert Italian American agents, with ostensibly convincing Middle Eastern appearances, to pose as wealthy oil executives from Lebanon and other Arab countries.[35] (That Lebanon has no oil reserves did not seem to occur to either the FBI or the members of Congress.)

30 Norman Daniel, *Islam and the West: The Making of an Image* (Edinburgh: Edinburgh University Press 1960); John Victor Tolan, *Saracens: Islam in the Medieval European Imagination* (New York: Columbia University Press 2002).

31 Douglas Little, *American Orientalism: The United States and the Middle East since 1945* (Chapel Hill: University of North Carolina Press 2002), 3.

32 Melani McAlister, *Epic Encounters: Culture, Media, and U.S. Interests in the Middle East, 1945–2000* (Berkeley: University of California Press 2001), 112–25.

33 Ibid., 82–3.

34 Peter Gottschalk and Gabriel Greenberg, *Islamophobia: Making Muslims the Enemy* (Lanham, MD: Rowman and Littlefield 2007), 118–25.

35 Jack G. Shaheen, *Abscam: Arabiaphobia in America*, ADC Issues (Washington, D.C.: American-Arab Anti Discrimination Committee 1980).

After the American embassy in Tehran was seized, and televised gun-toting revolutionaries held American citizens hostage there for months, the 'oil sheik' stereotype began to give way to the 'terrorist' stereotype. The word 'terrorist' would become fully synonymous with Middle Easterners by the 1980s. As thoroughly documented by Jack Shaheen, the racialized image of maniacal, inhuman terrorists was reinforced again and again in popular culture caricatures seen in big-budget Hollywood films like *Iron Eagle*, *True Lies* and *The Siege*, along with many others in the 1980s and 1990s.[36]

It is important to emphasize that, by the 1980s, the stereotypical image of the 'terrorist' was not applied specifically to Muslim groups; but there was an association that included many Middle Eastern communities, especially Arab Americans and Sikh Americans. In 1984 the Indian government carried out a military crackdown against Sikh militants and, later that year, in reaction to the heavy loss of life in the crackdown, Prime Minister Indira Gandhi was assassinated by two of her Sikh bodyguards. As discussed by Brian Keith Axel and Tony Ballantyne, racialized notions of South Asian Americans, particularly Sikhs, became associated in American discourses to a violent Middle East.[37] The Indian government later apologized for the violent crackdown on the Sikh minority but, at the time, Sikhs were explicitly labelled as 'terrorists' by officials in the Indian government in an attempt to rally international support for their efforts.[38] While this is just a single discursive moment, the incident illustrates how the differences between Arabs, Pakistanis and Indians, and especially between people of the Sikh and Muslim faiths, have experienced a racialized erasure in mainstream American discourses for at least two decades.

By the middle of the 1990s, the racialized stereotype that held that all terrorists must be Middle Eastern became so pervasive that, when the Murrah Federal Building in Oklahoma City was destroyed in a 1995 terror attack, many professional analysts, investigators and journalists immediately assumed that the attacks were carried out by 'Arabs'.[39] Similar reactions were seen after an accidental explosion caused the destruction of TWA flight 800 in 1998. In that case, before any evidence was available, CIA investigators conducted their work with the presumption that Middle Eastern terrorism was involved, and the assertion expressed repeatedly by experts on television news programmes was that 'Arab terrorists' were the

36 Jack G. Shaheen, 'Reel bad Arabs: how Hollywood vilifies a people', *Annals of the American Academy of Political and Social Science*, vol. 588, no. 1, 2003, 171–93.

37 Brian Keith Axel, *The Nation's Tortured Body: Violence, Representation, and the Formation of a Sikh 'Diaspora'* (Durham, NC: Duke University Press 2001); Tony Ballantyne, *Between Colonialism and Diaspora: Sikh Cultural Formations in an Imperial World* (Durham, NC: Duke University Press 2006).

38 Axel, *The Nation's Tortured Body*, 79–120.

39 Lou Michel and Dan Herbeck, *American Terrorist: Timothy McVeigh & the Oklahoma City Bombing* (New York: ReganBooks 2001), 249.

most likely cause of the explosion.[40] A few scholars and cultural critics working around this time observed that the only prejudice openly tolerated in American culture was racism against ethnic groups perceived to be synonymous with terrorists.[41] Thus, by the turn of the century, the popular American conception of terrorism was closely linked with the racialized image of Middle Easterners.

When the events of 9/11 occurred, the framework was in place for a popular culture backlash against Muslims, Middle Easterners and South Asians. Intriguingly, however, although the reaction in terms of hate crimes and state policy was severe, by and large the kind of popular culture stereotyping seen in the 1980s and 1990s disappeared in the first decade of the twenty-first century.[42] In part due to the framework of multiculturalism that had become predominate in the post-civil rights movement era, in part because of the work of advocacy organizations and perhaps in part because of revulsion to highly publicized violent hate crimes, after 9/11 it was suddenly no longer considered acceptable to blatantly portray Muslims, Middle Easterners and South Asians stereotypically as terrorists in mainstream American television and film. With a few exceptions, much Hollywood-produced popular culture shed what had been a ubiquitous trope rather quickly. But, outside television and film, new political discourses about uniquely dangerous Muslims and Middle Easterners, some subtle and some quite overt, emerged frequently in the first decade of the 2000s.

After 2001 a racialized political rhetoric became dominant, with many mainstream American political leaders, from President Bush to New York City Mayor Rudolph Giuliani and many others, warning about the dangers (at home and abroad) presented by 'Islamo-facism', 'Islamists' and 'sleeper cells'. The discourse was used most often by politicians on the right wing, but some left-leaning commentators and political leaders used the spectre of 'Middle Eastern' oil as a particular threat that required more careful environmental policies so as to reduce American partnerships with the uniquely dangerous Middle East. The fearmongering of these political leaders persisted despite the lack of evidence of a unique threat from the Middle East. Indeed, the most deadly terrorists in American history have arguably been American-born radical Christians, such as the perpetrators of the bombing of the Murrah building in Oklahoma City or the Ku Klux Klan and similar Christian white supremacist organizations that remained active throughout the twentieth century. But these American-born, Christian

---

40 Kevin Fedarko, 'Who wishes us ill?', *Time Magazine*, 29 July 1996.
41 Nabeel Abraham, 'Anti-Arab racism and violence in the United States', in Ernest McCarus (ed.), *The Development of Arab-American Identity* (Ann Arbor: University of Michigan Press 1994), 159; Nadine C. Naber, 'Ambiguous insiders: an investigation of Arab American invisibility', *Ethnic and Racial Studies*, vol. 23, no. 1, 2000, 37–61 (42–3).
42 Hussein Ibish, 'Islamophobia', manuscript (publication forthcoming by the Muslim Public Affairs Council).

terrorists have never constituted a racialized threat for American politicians and their supporters among the commentariat. The stereotypical image of the Middle Eastern terrorist does, and American politicians seized on the image after 2001. The invented term 'Islamo-facism' and related discourses became so frequently trotted out that Juan Cole rightly predicted a backlash against that discourse in the 2008 US elections, when the Republican party's rather obvious 'Islamophobia as a campaign strategy' largely failed at the polls.[43]

Still, the political rhetoric that incorporated Islamophobia has gone beyond simply pandering to voters in electoral campaigns. The racialized caricature of 'Islamo-fascism' and related discourses has served as a fresh coat of paint for justifications that excuse discriminatory state policies and practices. Many of these state actions (such as the use of secret evidence in terrorism trials) do not necessarily have a discriminatory intent, but in practice they clearly do discriminate against Middle Eastern Americans.

Islamophobia in American policy

The rise of Islamophobia in the United States is linked with several events in the Middle East, and it is also a reaction to the civil rights movements of the 1960s. In particular, American policy towards so-called 'rogue states' like Iraq, Iran and Syria, and its simultaneous support for the state of Israel in its conflict with Palestinians, has relied upon a racialized narrative about Middle Easterners, Arabs and Muslims. The connection between domestic policy and foreign policy is perhaps strongest within the influential neo-conservative project, which has been developing since the end of the Second World War. The policy proscriptions of neo-conservatism have partly used the reaction to the disruptions of the civil rights movement to justify a robust internal (or 'homeland') security apparatus, as well as an expansionist foreign policy. Since the 1970s, and accelerating in the last decade of the twentieth century, Islamophobia has thus often been utilized to construct a bridge between many of the domestic and foreign policies of the United States.

Neo-conservatism has at its core the philosophies of Leo Strauss and his academic progeny, the 'Straussians'. Anne Norton, a student of the Straussians at the University of Chicago, critiques the behaviour, thought and politics of this group, noting that many of its adherents see themselves as 'the salvation of modernity'.[44] She reveals the racialized origins of Straussian and neo-conservative designs on the Middle East:

43 Juan Cole, 'Blowback from the GOP's holy war', *Salon.com* (online), 1 February 2008, at www.salon.com/opinion/feature/2008/02/01/islamophobia/index.html (viewed 13 May 2009).
44 Anne Norton, *Leo Strauss and the Politics of American Empire* (New Haven, CT: Yale University Press 2004), 114.

204 Anti-Muslim Prejudice

> From the time I first came to Chicago to the present day, I have seen Arabs and
> Muslims made the targets of unrestrained persecution, especially among the
> Straussians. At school, Straussian students told me that Arabs were dirty, they
> were animals, they were vermin. Now I read in Straussian books and articles, in
> editorials and postings on websites, that Arabs are violent, they are barbarous,
> they are the enemies of civilization, they are Nazis.[45]

The neo-conservative portrayal of Arabs as the specific 'enemies of
civilization' has mirrored the increasing tensions of the Israeli–Palestinian
conflict, including the growing divide among Palestinians between the
secular movement for Palestinian self-determination and the Islamic
Hamas party. The neo-conservative reaction to the growth and electoral
success of the latter was predictable: the enemy of civilization became not
just Arab, but Islamic as well.

Tracing this shift from anti-Arab to anti-Muslim narratives within the
neo-conservative movement since the 1960s, Norton quotes Straussians
David Frum and Richard Perle, who wrote of the need to 'police' Muslims,
'including Muslim minorities in the West'.[46] Norton describes how several
figures involved in the American neo-conservative project (including key
architects of the 1991 Gulf war and the 2003 Iraq war) eschewed traditional
small-state conservatism in favour of advocating a strong and intrusive
internal security programme, closely allied with corporations and religious
groups. Simultaneously, Straussians supported a belligerent American
foreign policy that included warfare against those they considered the
greatest global threat: Muslim-majority nations unfriendly to the United
States or its allies. In the view of the Straussians, the benefits to American
society of war against Islam would serve to 'restore the public spirit'.[47] Led
by William Kristol and others at the Project for a New American Century
think tank, in recent decades neo-conservative policymakers have used the
image of a war with Islam to underpin American policy both domestically
and internationally. Norton quotes Paul Wolfowitz and other neo-con-
servatives in the Bush administration who justified the 2003 invasion of
Iraq along these lines. The same political ideology connects the so-called
'war on terror' in American foreign policy with domestic policy ostensibly
designed to combat terrorism, and the results have been a set of laws that
target Middle Eastern Americans as the supposed primary source of
terrorism.

In 1996 the Anti-Terrorism and Effective Death Penalty Act was signed
into law. This policy gave the federal government the power to designate
any entity a 'terrorist' organization, and it allowed the use of secret

45 Ibid., 210–11.
46 David Frum and Richard Perle, *An End to Evil: How to Win the War on Terror* (New
   York: Random House 2003), 35.
47 Norton, *Leo Strauss and the Politics of American Empire*, 178–9.

evidence in detention hearings and trials. The vast majority of cases in which this law has been used have been against Middle Eastern organizations or against Middle Eastern American individuals.[48] Then, in 2001, the FBI ordered local police forces around the United States to conduct 'voluntary interviews' with Middle Eastern Americans and immigrants, and immigrants from Middle Eastern countries (and North Korea) had to submit to 'special registration' and exceedingly long waiting periods in order to qualify for a visa.[49] Later, the Transportation Security Administration was created, with the authority to create 'no-fly' lists, lists that included Middle Easterners almost exclusively.[50] The 2001 Patriot Act and associated legislation gave the state sweeping new powers, including those of indefinite detention and surveillance. Even when the Patriot Act explicitly limited government power, the government ignored those provisions. Beginning in 2002, the FBI and Department of Energy conducted the secret and possibly extralegal monitoring of American Muslim sites, including mosques and private homes.[51] Simultaneously, a clandestine National Security Agency effort, with no judicial oversight, monitored the emails and telephone conversations of American citizens and others in what was known as the 'President's Program'.[52]

Apart from federal policy, across the country, at airports and in public places, profiling based on appearance led to discriminatory conduct on the part of local law enforcement and security personnel towards Middle Eastern Americans. For example, in 2005, security agents detained several people (with various religious and ethnic backgrounds) at two separate professional sporting events at Giants Stadium outside New York City. In one of the incidents, two suspects were held because 'they had been taking pictures of the [football] field' and, in the other, five men were detained because they were observed praying near 'a food-preparation area and the

48 Aladdin Elaasar, *Silent Victims: The Plight of Arab & Muslim Americans in Post 9/11 America* (Bloomington, IN: AuthorHouse 2004), 80; Mohamed Nimer, 'Muslims in American public life', in Yvonne Yazbeck Haddad (ed.), *Muslims in the West: From Sojourners to Citizens* (Oxford and New York: Oxford University Press 2002), 169–86 (178).

49 Sunaina Maira, 'Youth culture, citizenship and globalization: South Asian Muslim youth in the United States after September 11th', *Comparative Studies of South Asia, Africa and the Middle East*, vol. 24, no. 1, 2004, 221–35.

50 Anny Bakalian and Mehdi Bozorgmehr, 'Government initiatives after the September 11th attack on America', in Pyong Gap Min (ed.), *Encyclopedia of Racism in the United States* (Westport, CT: Greenwood Press 2005). For more on how the 'no-fly' lists were created, see Anny Bakalian and Mehdi Bozorgmehr, *Backlash 9/11: Middle Eastern and Muslim Americans Respond* (Berkeley: University of California Press 2009), 182–4.

51 David E. Kaplan, 'Nuclear monitoring of Muslims done without search warrants', *USNews.com* (online), 22 December 2005, at www.usnews.com/usnews/news/articles/nest/051222nest.htm (viewed 14 May 2009).

52 James Risen and Eric Lichtblau, 'Bush lets U.S. spy on callers without courts', *New York Times*, 16 December 2005, A1.

stadium's main air duct'. Some of those detained by security felt that the main reason they aroused suspicion was the colour of their skin.[53] These anecdotes are part of a widely reported pattern of racial profiling experienced by Middle Eastern Americans across the United States.[54]

Workplaces are another area where discrimination against Middle Eastern Americans has been widespread. Advocacy organizations have been asked to provide legal counsel in thousands of discrimination cases across the country, after employers unlawfully fired, refused to hire or failed to accommodate employees properly with regard to their religious or ethnic background. This sort of discrimination affected Americans from many backgrounds, but reports of racialized discrimination against Middle Eastern Americans increased to such an extent following 9/11 that the U.S. Equal Employment Opportunity Commission published a document specifically about 'individuals who are or are perceived to be Muslim, Arab, South Asian, or Sikh'. According to this document, complaints of discrimination by members of the groups on this list—a list explained only by race—saw 'a significant increase'.[55]

Hate crimes—from threatening telephone calls to vandalism, assault and murder—targeting these racialized groups also dramatically increased in frequency immediately after the September 11th attacks. After a few months, such hate crimes seemed to decrease in frequency, at least according to FBI statistics.[56] Whether the number of attacks has actually dropped to pre-2001 levels is unclear since good statistics are simply not available. First of all, only hate crimes reported to a law enforcement organization appear in FBI statistics. Second, FBI statistics are categorized according to the official 'racial pentagon', which means that anti-Middle Eastern American hate crimes might end up categorized as 'anti-white' or as 'other'. Hate crimes against religious groups are also reported, categorized as 'anti-Catholic', 'anti-Jewish', 'anti-Protestant', 'anti-Islamic', 'anti-Other religion' or 'anti-multiple religions/group'. This means that there are no FBI categories that fit anti-Middle Eastern American hate crimes, or anti-Arab or anti-Sikh crimes. 'Anti-Islamic crimes' is the best available category for Islamophobic

53 Makeba Hunter Scott, 'Non-Muslim men allege profiling at Giants game', *The Record* (Bergen Country, NJ), 12 November 2005, A1.
54 See Amnesty International, *Threat and Humiliation: Racial Profiling, Domestic Security, and Human Rights in the United States* (New York: Amnesty International USA 2004), available on the Amnesty International website at www.amnestyusa.org/ racial_profiling/report/rp_report.pdf (viewed 14 May 2009).
55 The U.S. Equal Employment Opportunity Commission, 'Questions and answers about the workplace rights of Muslims, Arabs, South Asians, and Sikhs under the Equal Employment Opportunity laws', 14 May 2002, available on the EEOC website at www.eeoc.gov/facts/backlash-employee.html (viewed 14 May 2009).
56 Federal Bureau of Investigation, Uniform Crime Reports, *Hate Crimes Statistics, 2006* (2007), available on the FBI website at http://www.fbi.gov/ucr/hc2006/index.html (viewed 14 May 2009).

hate crimes, but whether attacks against non-Muslim Middle Eastern Americans appear there is unclear.[57] Rather than continue to describe in detail the Islamophobic policies, hate crimes and discriminatory practices that have been documented elsewhere,[58] the last section of this article will consider the advocacy work being done to confront Islamophobia in the United States.

Confronting Islamophobia

Despite the difficulties in recognizing Islamophobia as a significant social problem, several advocacy organizations have worked for decades to confront the problem at the national level in the United States. Some of the notable organizations are the American-Arab Anti-Discrimination Committee (ADC, founded in 1980), the Arab American Institute (1984), the Association of Arab-American University Graduates (1967), the Council on American-Islamic Relations (CAIR, 1994), the Islamic Society of North America (1982), the Muslim American Society (1992), the Sikh American Legal Defense and Education Fund (SALDEF, 1996) and South Asian Americans Leading Together (2000). In addition to these national organizations, hundreds of local and regional bodies work to confront Islamophobia across the country.[59] These groups engage in political lobbying and electoral activism; they provide legal assistance and publish research detailing trends in hate crimes and discrimination.

In recent years, Middle Eastern American advocacy organizations have enjoyed a number of successes, including policy changes and the institution of cultural awareness training for law enforcement officials. They have also begun to wield increasing political power through coalitions and a growing electoral base. In one recent case, the Sikh Coalition and Muslim American Society won reforms to Federal Transportation Security Administration guidelines concerning religious attire while working at an airport.[60] In another case, the Muslim Public Affairs Council and South Asian Americans Leading Together began a co-ordinated

---

57 Federal Bureau of Investigation, Uniform Crime Reports, *Hate Crimes Statistics*, 2001–6, available on the FBI website at http://www.fbi.gov/ucr/ucr.htm (14 May 2009).

58 See Hussein Ibish (ed.), *Report on Hate Crimes and Discrimination against Arab Americans: The Post-September 11 Backlash* (Washington, D.C.: American-Arab Anti Discrimination Committee Research Institute 2003); *The Status of Muslim Civil Rights in the United States*, annual report compiled (since 1996) by the Council on American-Islamic Relations, Washington, D.C., available on the CAIR website at www.cair.com/CivilRights/CivilRightsReports.aspx (viewed 14 May 2009).

59 Leonard, *Muslims in the United States*, esp. appendices.

60 Muslim American Society, 'TSA develops new procedure for screening religious headwear at US airports', 28 October 2007, available on the MAS website at www.masnet.org/takeaction.asp?id = 4464 (viewed 14 May 2009).

campaign to discover community concerns over immigration policy and hate crimes.[61] Nonetheless, these organizations have also faced serious setbacks. Extreme scrutiny of donations to Middle Eastern American advocacy organizations has had a chilling effect on fundraising. In the past, these organizations have been the target of violent bomb attacks (including one that killed Alex Odeh, an ADC executive in California).[62] They have also been subject to federal infiltration and eavesdropping.[63] Significant questions remain about the trajectory of advocacy groups that appeal to the state for redress in circumstances like these.

Given the persistence and prevalence of Islamophobia and other forms of racism, a great number of questions remain about how racialized ethnic and religious minority groups make space in the United States. The racial dynamics at play with regard to American Islamophobia point to important lessons about racism in the contemporary United States: it is flexible, reactive *vis-à-vis* perceived threats from within and from without, and it depends on a crude categorization of Others according to physical appearance. In the post-civil rights movement era, the processes by which minority groups gain acceptance and a sense of belonging is still not fully understood by sociologists or by advocates. There is a pressing need for general research along these lines and particularly for research into how Middle Eastern Americans have organized to confront Islamophobia. With the caveat that more research is clearly needed, there is room here for some speculation on how Islamophobia might be confronted.

Research on Middle Eastern American efforts to confront Islamophobia should consider how they have drawn on the experience of other racialized communities. Specifically, what is the role of ethnic identity in civil rights activism among Middle Eastern Americans? Is the situation similar to what happened during the Second World War when Chinese Americans posted signs in front of their homes declaring that they were not Japanese? Or is it more akin to the situation during the 1960s when dedicated activists constructed a pan-ethnic Asian American identity?

The situation facing Middle Eastern Americans today has much in common with that facing Asian Americans in the middle of the twentieth century. In both instances, international issues linked inextricably with domestic civil rights concerns. Middle Eastern Americans today contend with a political apparatus preoccupied with wars in Afghanistan and Iraq,

61 Muslim Public Affairs Council, 'MPAC signs onto D.C. area civic engagement program', 24 October 2007, available on the MPAC website at www.mpac.org/ article.php?id = 550 (viewed 14 May 2009).
62 Federal Bureau of Investigation, 'Seeking information: domestic bombing', available on the FBI website at fbi.gov/wanted/seekinfo/odeh.htm (viewed 14 May 2009).
63 Joe Stork and Rene Theberge, 'Any Arab or others of a suspicious nature . . .', *MERIP Reports*, no. 14, 1974, 3–6, 13.

and a conflict between Israelis and Palestinians, to say nothing of additional tensions with Iran, Syria, Pakistan and other places. The need for 'homeland security' in this environment has perhaps inevitably affected the civil rights of individuals and groups linked—with the perceived links often being predominantly (or exclusively) racialized—to the regions of the globe where these conflicts are raging. The ways that foreign and domestic policies intertwine with Islamophobia has few parallels in the civil rights histories of other American communities. The success of efforts to confront Islamophobia might require development of a new narrative that de-links international events and civil rights. Absent such a discourse, which recognizes the needs and rights of American communities regardless of racialized connections to international conflicts, the success of efforts to confront Islamophobia might hinge on transnational events beyond the control of activists and, indeed, beyond the control of the United States. Still, the forms of advocacy used by Asian Americans, African Americans, Latino/as and others have been the basis for activism since the 1960s, and in many ways they have formed the basis for confronting Islamophobia as well.

Taking historical and sociological models of civil rights advocacy into account, there are at least three possible avenues along which the struggle against Islamophobia is likely to proceed in the United States. The first model is based on the African American civil rights organizations of the 1950s and 1960s, characterized by civil disobedience and large-scale, visible protest actions. A second possibility is the model of Asian Americans, Latino/a Americans and other pan-ethnic identity-based coalitions that look to leverage racialized solidarity for co-ordinated political clout and access to specific remedies reserved for racial discrimination. The third possibility, the one that appears best to fit the available empirical data on the trajectory of anti-Islamophobia advocacy organizations, is the model of most interest groups of all sorts in the United States, characterized by legal activism, co-operation with law enforcement and legislative lobbying, without claiming access to racialized remedies.

While the first model of African American civil rights organizations from the mid-twentieth century remains influential for many activists, there are few organizations working in the contemporary period that use marches and civil disobedience to achieve political aims. While some groups (notably the Council on American Islamic Relations and the Muslim Student Association) might have the kind of grassroots capacity needed to launch a wider campaign of civil disruption, there has to date not been much direct action of this kind. There have been sporadic moments of protest and disruption, for example from student organizations on several American college campuses. Still, it is telling that no wide-scale protest movement of any kind (anti-Islamophobia, anti-war) emerged in the decade that saw the worst Islamophobic hate crimes, the rapid expansion of the state security apparatus and a massive increase in American military involvement in the Middle East.

Even a cursory comparison of some of the largest national organizations of Middle Eastern Americans (ADC, CAIR, SALDEF) with counterparts in the African American civil rights movement (Southern Christian Leadership Council (SCLC), Student Non-violent Coordinating Committee (SNCC), National Association for the Advancement of Colored People (NAACP)) suggests some commonalities but much greater differences. While the ADC and NAACP, for instance, both engage/d in legal and cultural campaigns, and both the CAIR and SCLC have/had their grassroots base in mosques and churches, respectively, they have/had completely different constituencies. The constituency of the NAACP, SCLC and SNCC faced legalized and racist discrimination on a scale never experienced by Middle Eastern Americans. Research shows that many Middle Eastern Americans, when asked, will say that discrimination is not a factor in their daily lives.[64] The sense of urgency for an immediate end to Islamophobic policies has clearly not reached the level of the Jim Crow era. That kind of urgency might not be necessary to spark a mass movement, but it seems safe to conclude that discriminatory conditions in the American political structure to date have not reached the level at which analysts would expect a widespread protest movement to emerge among those affected by Islamophobia. In any event, only a cursory analysis of the possibility of a wide-scale protest movement is presented here. A carefully researched comparison of the trajectories of the African American civil rights organizations and those of Middle Eastern Americans would provide useful insights for determining the future shape of anti-Islamophobia activism, even if there is little indication of substantial similarities between these groups.

The second paradigm for activism against Islamophobia is suggested by the pan-ethnic identity formation model of political advocacy as seen within the Asian American, Latino/a American and Native American communities. Ethnogenesis, when minority ethnic groups foster a sense of common identity through pan-ethnic political and social coalitions demanding redress for racialized discrimination, has a long history in the United States.[65] In the latter half of the twentieth century, organizations representing constituencies based on a collective racialized identity have come to be a principal vehicle for advocating civil and political rights. Such organizations often themselves work to establish identity categories, or they rely on socially constructed identity categories in order to generate sufficient

---

64 Marvasti and McKinney, *Middle Eastern Lives in America*, 111.
65 Yen Le Espiritu, *Asian American Panethnicity: Bridging Institutions and Identities* (Philadelphia: Temple University Press 1992); Aihwa Ong, 'Cultural citizenship as subject-making: immigrants negotiate racial and cultural boundaries in the United States', *Current Anthropology*, vol. 37, no. 5, 1996, 737–62; Felix M. Padilla, *Latino Ethnic Consciousness: The Case of Mexican Americans and Puerto Ricans in Chicago* (Notre Dame, IN: Notre Dame University Press 1985); Eugeen E. Roosens, *Creating Ethnicity: The Process of Ethnogenesis* (Newbury Park, CA: Sage Publications 1989).

resources and momentum. Following a pattern recognized by Michael Omi and Howard Winant, organizations that engage in racial projects to gain official and popular recognition as a collectively aggrieved minority group, when successful, have moved the state to remedy racial discrimination.[66] The results of this activism include the provision of resources to the communities through programmes ranging from tax incentives for minority business development, additional consideration in employment and education, and funding for special programnes for health and community services.

Despite the benefits that might come with a successful campaign to establish official recognition of 'Middle Eastern American' as an identity category, there are significant barriers that would seem to preclude any ethnogenesis among the communities affected by Islamophobia. Middle Eastern Americans have a wide range of socio-economic backgrounds, many different cultural traditions, ethnicities, nationalities and religious affiliations. Indeed, it is important to recognize the differences within these groups so as not to repeat bigoted assumptions that all Middle Easterners are alike. However, similar diversity among Asian American communities was not itself sufficient to preclude development of a race-based coalition. Yen Le Espiritu's seminal work on pan-ethnic political activism and identity formation shows that racist discrimination, when in combination with certain other conditions, can create an opportunity for bridging organizations that pull people together across ethnic lines.[67]

Whether the shared experience of racialized Islamophobia has led otherwise disparate groups to coalesce around a newly emergent pan-Middle Eastern identity has been a topic of debate for scholars and activists. Some scholars have suggested that such a Middle Eastern American ethnogenesis is, in fact, emergent.[68] Proponents of the ethnogenesis thesis point to the more than 20,000 individuals self-identifying as 'Middle Eastern' in the 2000 Census; while not in itself a staggering number, it is one that quadrupled since the 1990 Census.[69] In addition, at least two universities—the University

---

66 Omi and Winant, *Racial Formation in the United States*, 56.

67 Espiritu, *Asian American Panethnicity*, 3.

68 Importantly, the role of African American Muslims in anti-Islamophobia coalitions remains largely unexamined. Despite that frequent omission, there are some excellent analyses of Middle Eastern American identity formation: Anita Famili, 'What about Middle Eastern American ethnic studies', 17 May 1997, abstract available on the University of California, Irvine Undergraduate Research Opportunities Program website at www.urop.uci.edu/symposium/past_symposia/1997/ablist3.html (viewed 14 May 2009); Bruce B. Lawrence, *New Faiths, Old Fears: Muslims and Other Asian Immigrants in American Religious Life* (New York: Columbia University Press 2002); Marvasti and McKinney, *Middle Eastern Lives in America*; Tehranian, 'Selective racialization'; Leti Volpp, 'The citizen and the terrorist,' *UCLA Law Review*, vol. 49, 2002, 1575–99.

69 G. Patricia de la Cruz and Angela Brittingham, *The Arab Population: 2000: Census 2000 Brief* (Washington D.C.: U.S. Census Bureau 2003), available on the Census Bureau website at www.census.gov/prod/2003pubs/c2kbr-23.pdf (viewed 14 May 2009).

of California at Los Angeles and the City University of New York—have Middle Eastern American studies programmes.[70] In an interesting development, the state of Maryland has established a Governor's Commission on Middle Eastern American Affairs that, in 2009, was 'studying' the possibility of Middle Eastern American businesses qualifying for a state-sponsored minority business improvement programme.[71] Thus there are sporadic signs of a pan-ethnic 'Middle Eastern American' term gaining some currency as an identity category to which resources might be allocated.

However, even presuming the often disparate communities affected by Islamophobia were to somehow manage to achieve official recognition as a Middle Eastern American category, it remains unclear that this model would be successful in terms of actually wielding the political power necessary to challenge Islamophobia. Some scholars reject the idea of a new identity category as a solution to the problem. After detailing some results from a 2004 survey of Arab Americans in the Detroit area, where most respondents chose 'white' or 'other' (and not 'Middle Eastern' or even 'Arab') to describe their racial identity, Andrew Shryock explains the 'wariness' with which he approaches the 'racial identity politics' model.[72] He argues that such a framework would likely not bring any additional political clout when compared to the *status quo*. Shryock suggests that 'there are clear benefits—intellectual, moral, and political—to the taxonomic uncertainty that suspends Arab Americans between zones of whiteness, Otherness, and colour'.[73] He goes on to argue that Arab Americans in Detroit have been marginalized in virtually all aspects of American life: they are 'marginal even to the process of "racialization" which has failed to make them "white" or "non-white. ... "'[74] Shryock concludes that there are benefits to the *status quo*, to racial ambiguity, and perhaps those advantages serve to slow any impetus among Middle Eastern Americans towards embracing the American 'racial identity politics' model. John Tehranian also notes the advantages that come with the 'Faustian pact with whiteness', wherein some Middle Eastern American individuals can 'pass' as white to avoid racialized discrimination, and the community as a whole can aspire to a *de facto* white and mainstream identity, even if doing so causes the community to lose

---

70 For details, see UCLA and CUNY's joint database project, *Middle Eastern American Resources Online*, at www.mearo.org (viewed 14 May 2009).
71 For details, see the commission's webpage at www.middleeastern.maryland.gov (viewed 14 May 2009).
72 Andrew Shryock, 'The moral analogies of race: Arab American identity, color politics, and the limits of racialized citizenship', in Amaney Jamal and Nadine Naber (eds), *Race and Arab Americans before and after 9/11: From Invisible Citizens to Visible Subjects* (Syracuse, NY: Syracuse University Press 2008), 81–113.
73 Ibid., 111–12.
74 Ibid., 112.

access to group rights and racialized remedies for discrimination.[75] In short, it seems that many people affected by Islamophobia will find few incentives for recognizing and advocating a collective identity category. For these and other reasons, if present trends persist, the identity-based avenue followed by Asian Americans, Native Americans and other pan-ethnic American groups appears unlikely to be travelled by Middle Eastern Americans.

Finally, the third paradigm for anti-Islamophobia advocacy uses a race-neutral, less confrontational model. This approach would pursue a combination of co-operation with law enforcement, outreach through media and other cultural outlets, and legislative lobbying, following the pattern used by most interest groups of all sorts in the United States. It would not require much co-ordination among communities affected by Islamophobia, and it would favour a perspective that emphasizes different priorities for different groups (Arab Americans would not necessarily form coalitions or co-ordinate with Sikh Americans, for instance). There is some evidence to suggest that this model most closely fits the shape of anti-Islamophobia advocacy organizations since 2001. The move towards less confrontational methods of advocacy—without using race—may be, in part, a strategy that responds to the overall political climate in the United States in the present decade, when a 'post-racial' attitude is encouraged. Moreover, Middle Eastern American advocacy groups have been under increased scrutiny, which might further move organizational leaderships to steer away from confrontational approaches.

If the model developed by Debra Minkoff and other organizational scholars holds, then this approach to advocacy requires a shift among community organizations from a focus on education and culture towards one on political lobbying and judicial activism.[76] Just such a shift away from service and towards advocacy has been observed among anti-Islamophobia organizations. This began in the 1990s, and accelerated after 2001. The Sikh Mediawatch and Resource Task Force (SMART), founded in 1996, originally sought to look for and counter stereotypical images of Sikhs in American television and film. In 2004 SMART became the Sikh American Legal Defence and Education Fund (SALDEF), and dramatically expanded its scope to include lobbying and legal assistance.[77] The Muslim Public Affairs Council began in 1986 as an outreach division of a mosque in southern California, but by 2002 had become an independent organization with a

75 Tehranian, 'Selective racialization', 2.
76 Debra Minkoff, 'From service provision to institutional advocacy: the shifting legitimacy of organizational forms', *Social Forces*, vol. 72, no. 4, 1994, 943–69; Debra Minkoff, 'Bending with the wind: strategic change and adaptation by women's and racial minority organizations', *American Journal of Sociology*, vol. 104, no. 6, 1999, 1666–703.
77 More details on SALDEF's history are available on the organization's website at www.saldef.org (viewed 14 May 2009).

branch office in Washington, D.C.[78] Karamah, an organization started by a group of lawyers in 1992, originally focused on international issues affecting Muslim women but, after 2001, the organization expanded its work to include advocacy for American Muslims.[79] There are several other examples, but only additional research will clarify strategy decisions made within advocacy organizations to determine conclusively why and how shifts from service provision to political advocacy have occurred.

An important consideration for advocates will be the potential for success with a less confrontational model of advocacy. Minkoff's research shows that the shift from education and service towards advocacy often takes place in contradictory and uneven ways. As a result, while activists within organizations consider that they have appropriately responded to the political climate to achieve increased legitimacy, over time, those organizations that reject confrontational approaches increase their risk of failure.[80] The lack of confrontation with the state often leads to co-optation, or an obviation of the goals originally set by advocacy groups. The relationship between these advocacy organizations and the state is crucial, but very little research is available on this intersection.

As research on efforts to confront American Islamophobia moves forward, there are several urgent questions to consider. First, as discussed above, what is the role of identity? Second, what is the role of the state in post-civil rights movement America? The Department of Homeland Security has a civil rights division, as does the FBI and the Department of Justice. Does the work of these offices amount to co-opting resistance, or do they effectively safeguard civil rights? What does it mean that, at the same time that the government conducts extrajudicial surveillance on Middle Eastern American communities, it is also a primary agent bringing together civil rights organizations from different ethnic and religious communities for 'inter-agency meetings' to discuss new ways to fight discrimination and hate crimes? What does it mean that law enforcement actively seeks cultural sensitivity training in an effort to combat racism within police ranks? The interaction between advocacy organizations and the state is perhaps the area that most crucially needs the attention of scholars to determine the relative success of advocacy strategies that emphasize co-operation with law enforcement, ad hoc and non-racial legislative lobbying and legal claims, and other non-protest activities. Questions about the social dynamics of American Islamophobia will remain important as the second decade of the twenty-first century begins.

78   More details are available on the organization's website at www.mpac.org (viewed 14 May 2009). For additional information on MPAC's history, see Leonard, *Muslims in the United States*, 18.

79   More details are available on the organization's website at www.karamah.org (viewed 14 May 2009).

80   Minkoff, 'Bending with the wind', 1673.

In closing, it is important to note that the impact of Islamophobia in the United States extends beyond the local. Concern over the rise of non-state militant movements has been seen as an urgent justification for a powerful European and American military presence across the Middle East. At the core of the latest justifications for military intervention and tacit empire-building—the so-called 'war on terror'—is racialized Islamophobia. Middle Eastern Americans—the wide range of groups implied by that racialized term—have in many ways only just begun to find political power in the United States. A twenty-first-century America that is more responsive to the desires of Middle Eastern American communities will operate in very different ways than it did in the twentieth century.

Index

Page numbers in *Italics* represent tables.
Page numbers in **Bold** represent figures.

Attitudes Project 128, 181, **182**, **183**, 186, **187**; presence of people from another race 176-9, **177**, **178**, **179**; public opinion polls Britain and France 171, 173; racial prejudice 179, **180**; violent religion **182**; world values (1999) 184, **185**
Switzerland 64-5; anti-minaret campaign logos **117**; largest political party: Schweizerische Volkspartei (SVP) 104; minaret ban 104, 116

Taylor, C. 92, 93
terrorism 142
The Times 71, 159
Tocqueville, A. 53-5
Tozer, J.: Narain, J. 73
trade 10, 20
The True Nature of Imposture Fully Display'ed in the Life of Mahomet (Prideaux) 23
Turkey 36-7
Turks 13-14, 24, 35-6, 40

Uddin, B. 131
United States of America (USA) 59; 11 September (2001) 150, 202; activism against Islamophobia 210-11; Anti-Terrorism and Effective Death Penalty Act 204; census 194; equal employment opportunity commission 206; FBI 205-6; federal policy 205; Immigration Act (1917) 196; Middle Eastern migration 195-7; Murrah Federal Building in Oklahoma City 201;

Naturalization Act (1790) 196; Patriot Act (2001) 205; post-civil rights movement era 208; racial dynamics 208; Sikhs 192, 213; Supreme Court case *United States v. Thind* 106-7, *see also* America
universalism 84

Veneto-Ottoman war (1645-69) 34
Vlaams Belang 119
voting behaviour 158

war on terror 46, 146, 204
Ward, J. 15
west: Christian 2; Islam 1, 61-2, 109
western civilization 49
westernization 62
What Went Wrong? (Lewis) 15
Wilders, G. 111, 119-20, 123-4
Winant, H.: and Omi, M. 211
Windus, J. 23
Wolfowitz, P. 204
Wolter, J. 115
women: absence of consent 75; gender bias in the law 75; Muslim *see* Muslim women; oppression 68; prejudice 45; violence against women 74-5; westernized 68
writing: English 7; post-reformation apocalyptic 12

Yoshino 91, 93; covering 92
Yugoslav government 41

Ziegler, K.H. 51
Zolberg, A.R.: and Woon, L.L. 173, 175